Berlitz®

Russi

phrase book & dictionary

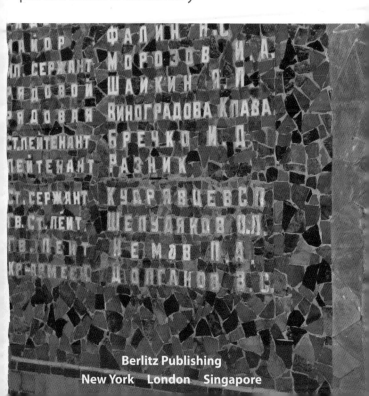

ФАЛИН
МОРОЗОВ И.А.
ШАЙКИН
ВИНОГРАДОВА КЛАВА
БРЕЧКО И. Д.
РАЗНИК
КУДРЯВЦЕВ С П
ШЕПУДЯКОВ О.Л.
НЕМОВ П.А.
ДОЛГАНОВ В.С.

Berlitz Publishing
New York   London   Singapore

Contacting the Editors
Every effort has been made to provide accurate information in this publication, but changes are inevitable. The publisher cannot be responsible for any resulting loss, inconvenience or injury. We would appreciate it if readers would call our attention to any errors or outdated information. We also welcome your suggestions; if you come across a relevant expression not in our phrase book, please contact us at: **comments@berlitzpublishing.com**

All Rights Reserved
© 2007 Berlitz Publishing/APA Publications (UK) Ltd.
Berlitz Trademark Reg. U.S. Patent Office and other countries. Marca Registrada. Used under license from Berlitz Investment Corporation.

Eleventh Printing: March 2012
Printed in China

Publishing Director: Mina Patria
Commissioning Editor: Kate Drynan
Editorial Assistant: Sophie Cooper
Translation: updated by Wordbank
Cover Design: Beverley Speight
Interior Design: Beverley Speight
Production Manager: Raj Trivedi
Picture Researcher: Steven Lawrence
Cover Photo: Cover images APA Richard Schofield and Istockphoto

Interior Photos: APA Richard Schofield 12, 39, 40, 58, 61, 65, 77, 91, 104, 118, 124, 130, 150, APA Abe Nowitz 45, 57, 81, 101,133, 141, APA Lucy Johnston 165, Istockphoto 70, 83, APA Greg Gladman 112, APA Britta Jaschinski 47

Contents

Food & Drink

People

Leisure Time

5

Special Requirements

In an Emergency

Dictionary

Pronunciation

This section is designed to make you familiar with the sounds of Russian using our simplified phonetic transcription. You'll find the pronunciation of the Cyrillic (Russian) letters explained below, together with their 'imitated' equivalents. To use this system, found throughout the phrase book, simply read the pronunciation as if it were English, noting any special rules below. Keep in mind that stress in Russian is irregular. In this phrase book, the stress is indicated with an underline.

Consonants

Letter	Approximate Pronunciation	Symbol	Example	Pronunciation
б*	like b in bit	b	был	bihl
в	like v in vivid	v	ваш	vahsh
г	like g in go	g	город	goh•raht
д	like d in do	d	да	dah
ж	like s in pleasure	zh	жаркий	zhahr•keey
з	like z in zoo	z	завтра	zahf•trah
к	like k in kitten	k	карта	kahr•tah
л	like l in lily	l	лампа	lahm•pah
м	likew m in my	m	масло	mahs•lah
н	like n in not	n	нет	nyet
п	like p in pot	p	парк	pahrk
р	trilled r	r	русский	roos•keey
с	like s in see	s	слово	sloh•vah
т	like t in tip	t	там	tahm
ф	like f in face	f	ферма	fyer•mah
х	like ch in Scottish loch	kh	хлеб	khlyep
ц	like ts in sits	ts	цена	tsih•nah

ч	like ch in chip	**ch**	**час**	_chahs_
ш	like sh in shut	**sh**	**ваша**	_vah•shah_
щ	like sh followed by ch	**shch**	**щи**	_shchee_

Capital **б** in writing appears as **Б**.

The pronunciation of Russian consonants can be either hard or soft. Consonants are soft when followed by the vowels **я, е, и, ё, ю** and the soft sign, **ь**. In the Russian phonetic transcription system, when a letter is soft it is generally followed by y + a vowel (as in **нет** _nyet_), or by an apostrophe (for example, **сколько** _skol'•kah_). The apostrophe, included in the phonetics, is commonly used to represent the soft sign when Russian is written in the Latin alphabet. When the letter **ъ**, known as the hard sign, is used, it precedes a vowel and is pronounced like the y in yet. It indicates that the preceding consonant is hard.

Vowels

Letter	Approximate Pronunciation	Symbol	Example	Pronunciation
а	between a in cat and u in cut	**ah**	**как**	_kahk_
е	like ye in yet	**ye/yeh**	**где**	_gdyeh_
ё*	like yo in yonder	**yo/yoh**	**мёд**	_myot_
и	like ee in see	**ee**	**синий**	_see•neey_
й	like y in boy	**y**	**бой**	_boy_
о	like o in hot	**o/oh**	**стол**	_stol_
у	like oo in boot	**oo**	**улица**	_oo•lee•tsah_
ы	like i in ill	**ih**	**вы**	_vih_
э	like e in met	**e/eh**	**эта**	_eh•tah_

| ю | like you in youth | **yoo** | **юг** | *yook* |
| я | like ya in yard | yah | **мясо** | *myah·sah* |

Capital **ё** in writing appears as **Ё**.

The vowels **o**, **e**, **a** and **я** are pronounced differently depending on whether or not they are stressed. This explains why a given vowel is not always represented the same way in phonetic transcription.

Vowel Combinations

Letter	Approximate Pronunciation	Symbol	Example	Pronunciation
ай	like y in my	**ie**	**май**	*mie*
яй	like y in my, preceded by y in yes	**yie**	**негодяй**	*nee·gah·dyie*
ой	like oy in boy	**oy**	**вой**	*voy*
ей	like ey in obey, preceded by y in yes	**yey**	**соловей**	*sah·lah·vyehy*
ий	like ee in see, followed by y in yes	**eey**	**ранний**	*rahn·neey*
ый	like i in ill, followed by y in yes	**iy**	**красивый**	*krah·see·viy*
уй	like oo in good, followed by y in yes	**ooy**	**дуй**	*dooy*
юй	as уй above, preceded by y in yes	**yooy**	**плюй**	*plyooy*

Like most of the languages of Eastern Europe, Russian is a Slavic language. It uses the Cyrillic alphabet.

How to use this Book

Sometimes you see two alternatives separated by a slash. Choose the one that's right for your situation.

ESSENTIAL

I'm here on vacation [holiday]/business.	**Я здесь в отпуске/по делу.** *yah zdyes' v ot·poos·kee/pah dyeh·loo*
I'm going to…	**Я еду в…** *yah yeh·doo v…*
I'm staying at the…Hotel.	**Я живу в гостинице…** *yah zhih·voo v gahs·tee·nee·tseh…*

Words you may see are shown in YOU MAY SEE boxes.

YOU MAY SEE…

ПРИБЫТИЕ *pree·bih·tee·yeh*	arrivals
ОТПРАВЛЕНИЕ *aht·prahv·lyeh·nee·yeh*	departures
ВЫДАЧА БАГАЖА *vih·dah·chah bah·gah·zhah*	baggage claim

Any of the words or phrases listed can be plugged into the sentence below.

Train

Where is/are…?	**Где…?** *gdyeh…*
the ticket office	**билетные кассы** *bee·lyet·nih·ee kah·sih*
the information desk	**справочное бюро** *sprah·vahch·nah·yeh byoo·roh*
the luggage lockers	**камеры хранения** *kah·mee·rih khrah·nyeh·nee·yah*

Russian phrases appear in purple.

Read the simplified pronunciation as if it were English. For more on pronunciation, see page 7.

Telephone Etiquette

Hello. This is...	**Алло. Это...** ah·*loh* eh·*tah*...
I'd like to speak to...	**Я хотел *m*/хотела *f* бы поговорить с...** *yah khah·tyel/khah·tyeh·lah bih pah·gah·vah·reet' s*...
Extension...	**Добавочный номер...** dah·*bah*·vahch·niy *noh*·meer...

For Numbers, see page 157.

Related phrases can be found by going to the page number indicated.

When different gender forms apply, the masculine form is followed by *m*; feminine by *f*.

Parking is usually unrestricted, except in central areas of Moscow and St. Petersburg, where parking meters and no-parking zones can be found. Illegally parked cars are subject to clamping and towing.

Information boxes contain relevant country, culture and language tips.

Expressions you may hear are shown in You May Hear boxes.

YOU MAY HEAR...

Ваш паспорт, пожалуйста.
vahsh *pahs*·pahrt pah·*zhahl*·stah

Your passport, please.

Color-coded side bars identify each section of the book.

Survival

ESSENTIAL

I'm here on vacation [holiday]/business.	**Я здесь в отпуске/по делам.** *yah zdyehs' v ot·poos·kee/pah dee·lahm*
I'm going to…	**Я еду в…** *yah yeh·doo v…*
I'm staying at the…Hotel	**Я живу в гостинице…** *yah zhih·voo v gahs·tee·nee·tseh…*

YOU MAY HEAR…

Ваш билет/паспорт, пожалуйста. *vahsh bee·lyet/pahs·pahrt pah·zhahl·stah*	Your ticket/ passport, please.
Цель Вашего визита? *tsel' vah·shee·vah vee·zee·tah*	What's the purpose of your visit?
Где вы остановились? *gdyeh vih ahs·tah·nah·vee·lees'*	Where are you staying?
Сколько вы пробудете здесь? *skol'·ka vih prah·boo·dee·tee zdyes'*	How long are you staying?
С кем вы приехали? *s kyem vih pree·yeh·khah·lee*	Who are you with?

Border Control

I'm just passing through.	**Я проездом.** *yah prah·yez·dahm*
I would like to declare…	**Я хочу предъявить…таможне.** *yah khah·choo pree·dyah·veet'…tah·mozh·nyeh*
I have nothing to declare.	**Мне нечего декларировать.** *mneh nyeh·chee·vah dee·klah·ree·rah·vaht'*

YOU MAY HEAR...

Есть ли у Вас вещи, подлежащие декларированию? *yest' lee oo vahs* *vyeh•shchee pahd•lee•zhah•shchee•yeh* *dee•klah•ree•rah•vah•nee•yoo*	Do you have anything to declare?
Вам надо оплатить пошлину. *vahm nah•dah ah•plah•teet' posh•lee•noo*	You must pay duty on this.
Откройте эту сумку. *aht•kroy•tee eh•too* *soom•koo*	Please open this bag.

YOU MAY SEE...

ТАМОЖНЯ *tah•mozh•nyah*	customs
ТОВАРЫ БЕЗ ПОШЛИНЫ *tah•vah•rih byez posh•lee•nih*	duty-free goods
ТАМОЖЕННЫЙ ДОСМОТР *tah•moh•zhih•niy dah•smotr*	goods to declare
СВОБОДНЫЙ КОРИДОР *svah•bod•niy kah•ree•dor*	nothing to declare
ПАСПОРТНЫЙ КОНТРОЛЬ *pahs•pahrt•niy kahnt•rol'*	passport control
МИЛИЦИЯ *mee•lee•tsih•yah*	police

Money

ESSENTIAL

Where's…?	**Где…?** *gdyeh…*
the ATM	**банкомат** *bahn·kah·maht*
the bank	**банк** *bahnk*
the currency exchange office	**обмен валюты** *ahb·myen vah·lyoo·tih*
What time does the bank open/close?	**Во сколько открывается/закрывается банк?** *va skol'·kah aht·krih·vah·ee·tsah/ zah·krih·vah·ee·tsah bahnk*
I'd like to change dollars/pounds into rubles.	**Я хотел m /хотела f бы обменять доллары/фунты на рубли.** *yah khah·tyel/ khah·tyeh·lah bih ahb·mee·nyaht' dol·lah·rih/ foon·tih nah roob·lee*
I want to cash some traveler's checks.	**Я хочу обменять дорожные чеки.** *yah khah·choo ahb·mee·nyaht' dah·rozh·nih·ee cheh·kee*

At the Bank

Can I exchange foreign currency here?	**Можно обменять валюту здесь?** *mozh·nah ahb·mee·nyaht' vah·lyoo·too zdyes'*
What's the exchange rate?	**Какой курс?** *kah·koy koors*
How much is the fee?	**Сколько процентов комиссионный сбор?** *skol'·kah prah·tsen·tahf kah·mees·see·on·niy zbor*
I think there's a mistake.	**Я думаю, здесь ошибка.** *yah du·ma·yoo zdes' ash·eeb·kah*

I've lost my traveler's checks [cheques].	**Я потерял** *m* /**потеряла** *f* **дорожные чеки.**
	yah pah•tee•ryahl/pah•tee•ryah•lah dah•rozh•nih•ee cheh•kee
My card was lost.	**Я потерял** *m* /**потеряла** *f* **свою карточку.**
	yah pah•tee•ryahl/pah•tee•ryah•lah svah•yoo kahr•tahch•koo
My credit cards have been stolen.	**У меня украли кредитные карточки.**
	oo mee•nyah ook•rah•lee kree•deet•nih•ee kahr•tahch•kee
My card doesn't work.	**Моя карточка не работает.** *mah•yah kahr•tahch•kah nee rah•boh•tah•eet*
The ATM ate my card.	**Банкомат забрал мою карту.**
	bahn•kah•maht zahb•rahl moh•yoo kahr•too

For Numbers, see page 157.

Contact your travel agent or the Russian embassy before your trip to determine the latest regulations regarding how much foreign currency you can bring into the country. In major towns and cities, currency exchange offices can be found in banks, hotels, stores and even street kiosks. Some operate 24 hours a day.

Others are open from early morning to late evening, with a break for lunch. All currency exchange offices accept U.S. dollars and euro, and some pounds sterling; however, notes that are not clean and crisp are often rejected and you may be required to show your passport. You may have difficulty changing notes issued before 1993. For other currencies and traveler's checks, it's best to use banks and large hotels.

Warning: You may be approached by someone on the street offering attractive exchange rates. It is highly inadvisable to take up such offers.

YOU MAY SEE...

ВСТАВЬТЕ КАРТУ _fstahf'·tyeh kahr·too_	insert card
ОТМЕНИТЬ _aht·mee·neet'_	cancel
ОЧИСТИТЬ _ah·chees·teet'_	clear
ВВОД _vvot_	enter
ПИН-КОД _peen·kot_	PIN
СНИМАТЬ _snee·maht'_	withdraw funds
С ТЕКУЩЕГО СЧЕТА _s tee·koo·shchee·vah shchoh·tah_	from checking [current] account
СО СБЕРЕГАТЕЛЬНОГО СЧЕТА _sah zbee·ree·gah·teel'·nah·vah shchoh·tah_	from savings account
ЧЕК _chehk_	receipt

YOU MAY SEE...

The monetary unit is the ruble (**рубль** _roobl'_), which is divided into 100 kopecks (**копеек** _kah·pyeh·yek_).
Coins: 1, 5, 10, 50 **kopecks**; 1, 2, 5 **rubles**
Notes: 10, 50, 100, 500, 1000 **rubles**

Getting Around

ESSENTIAL

How do I get to town?	**Как мне добраться до города?** _kahk mnyeh dah·brah·tsah dah goh·rah·dah_
Where's...?	**Где...?** _gdyeh..._
the airport	**аэропорт** _ah·eh·rah·port_
the train [railway] station	**вокзал** _vahg·zahl_

the bus station	**автовокзал** ahf·tah·vahg·<u>zahl</u>
the metro [underground] station	**станция метро** <u>stahn</u>·tsih·yah mee·<u>troh</u>
How far is it?	**Как далеко это отсюда?** kahk dah·lee·<u>koh</u> eh·tah aht·<u>syoo</u>·dah
Where can I buy tickets?	**Где можно купить билеты?** gdyeh <u>mozh</u>·nah koo·<u>peet'</u> bee·<u>lyeh</u>·tih
A one-way [single]/ return-trip ticket.	**Билет в один конец/туда и обратно.** bee·<u>lyet</u> v ah·<u>deen</u> kah·<u>nyets</u>/too·<u>dah</u> ee ahb·<u>raht</u>·nah
How much?	**Сколько?** <u>skol'</u>·kah
Are there any discounts?	**Есть какая-нибудь скидка?** yehst' kah·<u>kah</u>·yah·nee·<u>boot'</u> <u>skeet</u>·kah
Which gate/line?	**Какой выход/путь?** kah·<u>koy</u> <u>vih</u>·khaht/poot'
Which platform?	**Какая платформа?** kah·<u>kah</u>·yah plaht·<u>for</u>·mah
Where can I get a taxi?	**Где можно взять такси?** gdyeh <u>mozh</u>·nah vzyaht' tahk·<u>see</u>
Please take me to this address.	**Пожалуйста, отвезите меня по этому адресу.** pah·<u>zhahl</u>·stah aht·vee·<u>zee</u>·tee mee·<u>nyah</u> pah eh·tah·moo <u>ahd</u>·ree·soo
Where can I rent a car?	**Где можно взять машину напрокат?** gdyeh <u>mozh</u>·nah vzyaht' mah·<u>shih</u>·noo nah·prah·<u>kaht</u>
Could I have a map?	**Можно мне карту?** <u>mozh</u>·nah mnyeh <u>kahr</u>·too

Tickets

When's…to Moscow?	**Когда…в Москву?** kahg·<u>dah</u>… v mahs·<u>kvoo</u>
the (first) bus	**(первый) автобус** (<u>pyer</u>·viy) ahf·<u>toh</u>·boos
the (next) flight	**(следующий) рейс** (<u>slyeh</u>·doo·yoo·shcheey) reys

the (last) train	**(последний) поезд** (pahs·lyed·neey) poh·eest
Where can I buy tickets?	**Где можно купить билеты?** gdyeh mozh·nah koo·peet' bee·lyeh·tih
One ticket/Two tickets, please.	**Один билет/Два билета, пожалуйста.** ah·deen bee·lyet/dvah bee·lyeh·tah pah·zhahl·stah
For today/tomorrow.	**На сегодня/завтра.** nah see·vod·nyah/ zahf·trah
A first/economy class ticket.	**Билет на первый/туристический класс.** bee·lyet nah pyer·viy/too·rees·tee·chees·keey klahss
A…ticket.	**Билет...** bee·lyeht
one-way	**в один конец** v ah·deen kah·nyets
return trip	**туда и обратно** too·dah ee ahb·raht·noh
business class	**бизнес-класс** biz·nes klahss
How much?	**Сколько?** skol'·kah
Is there a discount for…?	**Есть скидка…?** yest' skeet·kah…
children	**на детей** nah dee·tyey
students	**студентам** stoo·dyen·tahm
senior citizens	**пенсионерам** peen·see·ah·nyeh·rahm
tourists	**туристам** too·rees·tahm
I have an e-ticket.	**У меня электронный билет.** oo mee·nyah ee·leek·tron·niy bee·lyet
Can I buy a ticket on the bus/train?	**Я могу купить билет в автобусе/ поезде?** yah mah·goo koo·peet' bee·lyet v ahf·toh·boo·see/poh·eez·dee
Do I have to stamp the ticket before boarding?	**Нужно ли перед посадкой компостировать билет?** noozh·nah lee peret pah·saht·koy kam·pas·tee·ro·vat' bee·lyet

19

How long is this ticket valid?	**Как долго действителен билет?** *kahk dol•go dey•stvee•tee•lyen bee•lyet*
Can I return on the same ticket?	**Могу я вернуться по этому билету?** *mah•goo yah vyer•noo•tsah poh yeh•tah•moo bee•lye•too*
I'd like to...my reservation.	**Я хотел m /хотела f бы...свой предварительный заказ.** *yah khah•tyel/ khah•tyeh•lah bih...svoy preed•vah•ree•teel'•niy zah•kahz*
cancel	**отменить** *aht•mee•neet'*
change	**изменить** *eez•mee•neet'*
confirm	**подтвердить** *paht•tveer•deet'*

For Days, see page 160.

For Time, see page 159.

Plane

Airport Transfer

How much is a taxi to the airport?	**Сколько стоит такси в аэропорт?** *skol'•kah stoh•eet tahk•see v ah•eh•rah•port*
To...Airport, please.	**В аэропорт..., пожалуйста.** *v ah•eh•rah•port... pah•zhahl•stah*
My airline is...	**Я лечу самолётом авиакомпании...** *yah lee•choo sah•mah•lyoh•tahm ah•vee•ah•kahm•pah•nee•ee...*
My flight leaves at...	**Мой рейс отправляется в...** *moy reys aht•prahv•lyah•ee•tsah v...*
I'm in a rush.	**Я спешу.** *yah spee•shoo*
Can you take an alternate route?	**Вы можете поехать другим путём?** *vih moh•zhih•tee pah•yeh•khaht' droo•geem poo•tyom*
Can you drive faster/slower?	**Не могли бы вы ехать быстрее/ медленнее?** *nee mahg•lee bih vih yeh•khat' bihs•tryeh•yeh/myed•leen•nee•yeh*

YOU MAY HEAR...

Рейсом какой авиакомпании вы летите? What airline are you
rey·sahm kah·koy ah·vee·ah·kahm·pah·nee·ee flying?
vih lee·tee·tyeh

Внутренний или международный? Domestic or
vnoot·reen·neey ee·lee meezh·doo·nah·rod·niy International?

Какой терминал? *kah·koy teer·mee·nahl* What terminal?

YOU MAY SEE...

ПРИБЫТИЕ *pree·bih·tee·yeh*	arrivals
ОТПРАВЛЕНИЕ *aht·prahv·lyeh·nee·yeh*	departures
ВЫДАЧА БАГАЖА *vih·dah·chah bah·gah·zhah*	baggage claim
ВНУТРЕННИЕ РЕЙСЫ *vnoo·treen·nee·yeh* *rey·sih*	domestic flights
МЕЖДУНАРОДНЫЕ РЕЙСЫ *meezh·doo·nah·rod·nih·yeh rey·sih*	international flights
РЕГИСТРАЦИОННАЯ СТОЙКА *ree·gee·strah·tsih·on·nah·yah stoy·kah*	check-in desk
РЕГИСТРАЦИЯ ЭЛЕКТРОННЫХ БИЛЕТОВ *ree·gee·strah·tsih·yah ee·leek·tron·nihkh bee·lyeh·tahf*	e-ticket check-in
ВЫХОД НА ПОСАДКУ *vih·khaht nah pah·saht·koo*	departure gates

Checking In

Where is check-in?	**Где регистрация?** gdyeh ree·gees·<u>trah</u>·tsih·yah
My name is…	**Меня зовут…** mee·<u>nyah</u> zah·<u>voot</u>…
I'm going to…	**Я лечу в…** yah lyee·<u>choo</u> v…
I have…	**У меня есть…** oo mye·<u>nyah</u> yest'
one suitcase	**один чемодан** ah·<u>deen</u> chee·mah·<u>dahn</u>
two suitcases	**два чемодана** dvah chee·mah·<u>dah</u>·nah
one piece of hand luggage	**одна единица ручной клади** od·<u>nah</u> yeh·dee·<u>nee</u>·tsa rooch·<u>noy</u> <u>klah</u>·dee
How much luggage is allowed?	**Сколько багажа разрешается провозить?** <u>skol'</u>·kah bah·gah·<u>zhah</u> rahz·ree·<u>shah</u>·ee·tsah prah·vah·<u>zeet'</u>
Is that pounds or kilos?	**Это в фунтах или килограммах?** <u>eh</u>·tah v <u>foon</u>·tah ee·lee kee·lo·<u>gram</u> mahkh
Which gate does flight…leave from?	**У какого выхода посадка на рейс…?** oo kah·<u>koh</u>·vah <u>vih</u>·khah·dah pah·<u>saht</u>·kah nah reys…
Which terminal?	**Какой терминал?** kah·<u>koy</u> tyer·mee·<u>nal</u>
I'd like a window/ an aisle seat.	**Я бы хотел m /хотела f место у окна/ прохода.** yah bih khah·<u>tyel</u>/khah·<u>tyeh</u>·lah <u>myes</u>·tah oo ahk·<u>nah</u>/prah·<u>khoh</u>·dah
When do we leave/ arrive?	**Во сколько мы вылетаем/прилетаем?** vah <u>skol'</u>·kah mih vih·lee·<u>tah</u>·eem/ pree·lee·<u>tah</u>·eem
Is there any delay on flight…?	**Рейс в…задерживается?** reys v… zah·<u>dyer</u>·zhih·vah·ee·tsah
How late will it be?	**На сколько задерживается?** nah <u>skol'</u>·kah zah·<u>dyer</u>·zhih·vah·ee·tsah

For Numbers, see page 157.

YOU MAY HEAR...

Следующий! _slyeh·doo·yoo·shcheey_ — Next!

Ваш билет/паспорт, пожалуйста. _vahsh bee·lyet/pahs·pahrt pah·zhahl·stah_ — Your ticket/passport, please.

Сколько у Вас мест багажа? _skol'·kah oo vahs myest bah·gah·zhah_ — How much luggage do you have?

У Вас перевес багажа. _oo vahs pee·ree·vyes bah·gah·zhah_ — You have excess luggage.

Этот слишком тяжёлый/большой для ручной клади. _eh·taht sleesh·kahm tee·zhoh·liy/bahl'·shoy dlyah rooch·noy klah·dee_ — That's too heavy/large for a carry-on [to carry on board]

Вы сами упаковывали багаж? _vih sah·mee oo·pah·koh·vih·vah·lee bah·gahsh_ — Did you pack these bags yourself?

Вас просили что-нибудь перевезти? _vahs prah·see·lee shtoh·nee·boot' pee·ree·vees·tee_ — Did anyone give you anything to carry?

Выньте всё из карманов. _vihn'·tee fsyoh ees kahr·mah·nahf_ — Empty your pockets.

Снимите обувь. _snee·mee·tee oh·boof'_ — Take off your shoes.

Производится посадка на рейс... _prah·eez·voh·dee·tsah pah·saht·kah nah reys..._ — Now boarding flight...

Luggage

Where is/are...?	**Где...?** _gdyeh..._
the luggage trolleys	**багажные тележки** _bah·gahzh·nih·ee tee·lyesh·kee_
the luggage lockers	**камеры хранения** _kah·mee·rih khrah·nyeh·nee·yah_
the baggage claim	**выдача багажа** _vih·dah·chah bah·gah·zhah_

My luggage has been lost/stolen.	**У меня пропал/украли багаж.** *oo mee•nyah prah•pahl/oo•krah•lee bah•gahsh*
My suitcase was damaged.	**Мне повредили чемодан.** *mnyeh pah•vree•dee•lee chee•mah•dahn*

Finding your Way

Where is...?	**Где...?** *gdyeh...*
the currency exchange office	**обмен валюты** *ahb•myen vah•lyoo•tih*
the car hire	**прокат автомобилей** *prah•kaht ahf•tah•mah•bee•ley*
the exit	**выход** *vih•khaht*
the taxis	**такси** *tahk•see*
Is there...into town?	**Есть...в город?** *yest'... v goh•raht*
a bus	**автобус** *ahf•toh•boos*
a train	**поезд** *poh•eest*
a metro [subway]	**метро** *mee•troh*

For Asking Directions, see page 34.

Train

How do I get to the train station?	**Как мне добраться до вокзала?** *kahk mnyeh dah•brah•tsah dah vahg•zah•lah*
Is it far?	**Это далеко?** *eh•tah dah•lee•koh*
Where is/are...?	**Где...?** *gdyeh...*
the ticket office	**билетные кассы** *bee•lyet•nih•ee kah•sih*
the information desk	**бюро информации** *byoo•roh een•fahr•mah•tsee•ee*
the luggage lockers	**камеры хранения** *kah•mee•rih khrah•nyeh•nee•yah*
the platforms	**платформы** *plaht•for•mih*
Could I have a schedule [timetable]?	**Можно расписание?** *mozh•nah rahs•pee•sah•nee•yeh*

How long is the trip?	**Сколько длится поездка?** _skol'•kah dlee•tsah_ _pah•yest•kah_
Is it a direct train?	**Это прямой поезд?** _eh•tah pryah•moy poh•yest_
Do I have to change trains?	**Мне надо делать пересадку?** _mnyeh nah•dah dyeh•laht' pee•ree•saht•koo_
Is the train on time?	**Поезд приедет вовремя?** _poh•yest pree•ye•dit voh•vre•myah_

For Asking Directions, see page 34.

For Tickets, see page 18.

YOU MAY SEE...

К ПЛАТФОРМАМ _k plaht•for•mahm_	platforms
ИНФОРМАЦИЯ _een•fahr•mah•tsih•yah_	information
ЗАКАЗ БИЛЕТОВ _zah•kahz bee•lyeh•tahf_	reservations
ЗАЛ ОЖИДАНИЯ _zahl oh•zhee•dah•nee•yah_	waiting room
ПРИБЫТИЕ _pree•bih•tee•yeh_	arrivals
ОТПРАВЛЕНИЕ _aht•prahv•lyeh•nee•yeh_	departures

An often-quoted line by the great Russian writer Nikolai Gogol (1809-1852) states that Russia's roads are one of its greatest misfortunes. While the state of Russian roads is still a source of national frustration, the excellent rail system built during the Soviet era provides a good alternative to automobile travel. Unfortunately, Russia's train stations have become less safe than they were in the past.

Departures

Which platform does the train to…leave from?	**С какой платформы отходит поезд до…?** s kah-_koy_ plaht-_for_-mih aht-_khoh_-deet _poh_-eest dah…
Is this the track [platform] to…?	**С этой платформы поезд на…?** s _eh_-tie plaht-_for_-mih _poh_-eest nah…
Where is track [platform]…?	**Где платформа…?** gdyeh plaht-_for_-mah…
Where do I change for…?	**Где мне делать пересадку на…?** gdyeh mnyeh _dyeh_-laht' pee-ree-_saht_-koo nah…

On Board

Can I sit here/open the window?	**Можно здесь сидеть/открывать окно?** _mo_-zhno zdyes see-_dyet_'/at-krih-_vat_' ahk-_noh_
Is this seat taken?	**Это место занято?** _eh_-tah _myes_-tah _zah_-nee-tah
I think that's my seat.	**Мне кажется, это моё место.** mnyeh _kah_-zhih-tsah _eh_-tah mah-_yoh myes_-tah
Here's my reservation.	**Вот моя бронь.** Vot ma-_yah_ brohn'

YOU MAY HEAR…

Посадка заканчивается! pah-_saht_-kah zah-_kahn_-chee-vah-ee-tsah	All aboard!
Пожалуйста, предъявите билеты. pah-_zhahl_-stah preed-yah-_vee_-tee bee-_lyeh_-tih	Tickets, please.
Вам надо делать пересадку в… vahm _nah_-dah _dyeh_-laht' pee-ree-_saht_-koo v…	You have to change at…
Следующая остановка… _slyeh_-doo-yoo-shchah-yah ahs-tah-_nof_-kah…	Next stop…

Bus

Where's the bus station?	**Где автобусная станция?** *gdyeh ahf·toh·boos·nah·yah stahn·tsih·yah*
How far is it?	**Как далеко это?** *kahk dah·lee·koh eh·tah*
How do I get to…?	**Как мне доехать до…?** *kahk mnyeh dah·yeh·khaht' dah…*
Does the bus stop at…?	**Этот автобус останавливается в…?** *eh·taht ahf·toh·boos ah·stah·nahv·lee·vah·ee·tsah v…*
Could you tell me when to get off?	**Вы скажете мне, где выходить?** *vih skah·zhih·tee mnyeh gdyeh vih·khah·deet'*
Do I have to change buses?	**Мне нужно делать пересадку?** *mnyeh noozh·nah dyeh·laht' pee·ree·saht·koo*
Stop here, please!	**Остановите здесь, пожалуйста!** *ah·stah·nah·vee·tee zdyes' pah·zhahl·stah*

For Tickets, see page 18.

Buses offer a standard fare no matter how far you're going but you can't change buses on the same ticket. In big cities, a system of magnetized fare cards that can be used on buses and trolleybuses (electric buses powered by two overhead wires) as well as the metro (where such cards can be purchased) is in operation. In smaller cities you will need to purchase **талоны** *tah·loh·nih* (paper tickets that you have to stamp) from a conductor on the bus or from kiosks.

A popular alternative to buses are fixed-route taxis called **маршрутные такси** *mahrsh·root·nih·yeh tahk·see* or mini-buses, **маршрутки** *mahrsh·root·kee*, that follow a fixed route, usually the same as bus routes.

YOU MAY SEE...

АВТОБУСНАЯ ОСТАНОВКА	bus stop
ahf·<u>toh</u>·boos·nah·yah ahs·tah·<u>nof</u>·kah	
ОСТАНОВКА ПО ТРЕБОВАНИЮ	request stop
os·tah·<u>nov</u>·kah po <u>tree</u>·bo·vah·nee·yoo	
ВХОД/ВЫХОД fkhot/<u>vih</u>·khaht	enter/exit
ПРОКОМПОСТИРУЙТЕ ТАЛОН	stamp your ticket
prah·kahm·pah·<u>stee</u>·rooy·tyeh tah·<u>lon</u>	

Metro

Where's the nearest metro [underground] station?	**Где ближайшая станция метро?** gdyeh blee·<u>zhie</u>·shah·yah <u>stahn</u>·tsih·yah meet·<u>roh</u>
Could I have a map of the metro [underground]?	**Можно мне схему метро?** <u>mozh</u>·nah mnyeh <u>skhyeh</u>·moo meet·<u>roh</u>
Which line for...?	**По какой линии ехать до...?** pah kah·<u>koy</u> <u>lee</u>·nee·ee <u>yeh</u>·khaht' dah...
Which direction?	**В каком направлении?** f kah·<u>kom</u>·nap·rah·<u>vlye</u>·nee·ee
Where do I change for...?	**Где делать пересадку до...?** gdyeh <u>dyeh</u>·laht' pee·ree·<u>saht</u>·koo dah...
Is this the right train for...?	**Этот поезд идёт до...?** <u>eh</u>·taht <u>poh</u>·eest ee·<u>dyot</u> dah...
How many stops to...?	**Сколько остановок до ...?** <u>skol'</u>·kah as·tah·<u>noh</u>·vahk doh
Where are we?	**Где мы находимся?** gdyeh mih nah·<u>khoh</u>·deem·syah

For Tickets, see page 18.

МЕТРО *meet·roh* (subway) is the fastest and most convenient way to get around town. Moscow, St. Petersburg and a few other major cities have subway systems. Moscow has the most extensive system; its older stations are sights worth visiting in their own right, featuring a blend of ornate neoclassicism and Socialist Realism. The subway operates from 6:00 a.m. to 1:00 a.m. There is a set fare regardless of the distance traveled. If you plan to use public transit a lot, you may decide to buy a pass (**единый билет** *yee·dee·niy bee·lyet*), valid for 8 days, 16 days or a month, for travel on the metro, bus, trolleybus and tram.

Boat & Ferry

When is the ferry to…?	**Когда паром до…?** *kahg·dah pah·rom dah…*	
Where are the life jackets?	**Где спасательные жилеты?** *gdyeh spah·sah·teel'·nih·ee zhih·lyeh·tih*	

For Tickets, see page 18.

YOU MAY SEE…

СПАСАТЕЛЬНАЯ ШЛЮПКА *spah·sah·teel'·nah·yah shlyoop·kah*	life boat
СПАСАТЕЛЬНЫЙ ЖИЛЕТ *spah·sah·teel'·niy zhih·lyeht*	life jacket

---

Taxi

Where can I get a taxi?	**Где можно взять такси?** *gdyeh mozh·nah vzyaht' tahk·see*
Can you send a taxi?	**Не могли бы Вы прислать такси?** *nee mogh·lee bih vih pree·slat'tahk·see*

What is the number for a taxi?	**Как вызвать такси по телефону?** *kahk vihz•vaht' tahk•see pah tee•lee•foh•noo*
I'd like a taxi now/ for tomorrow at…	**Мне нужно такси сейчас/на завтра на…** *mnyeh noozh•nah tahk•see see•chahs/nah zahf•trah nah…*
Pick me up at (place/time)…	**Подъезжайте за мной к/в…** *pahd•yeh•zhie•tee zah mnoy k/v…*
Please take me to…	**Пожалуйста, отвезите меня…** *pah•zhahl•stah aht•vee•zee•tee mee•nyah…*
this address	**по этому адресу** *pah eh•tah•moo ahd•ree•soo*
the airport	**в аэропорт** *v ah•eh•rah•port*
the train station	**на вокзал** *nah vahg•zahl*
I'm late.	**Я опаздываю.** *yah ah•pahz•dih•vah•yoo*
Can you drive faster/slower?	**Не могли бы вы ехать быстрее/ медленнее?** *nee mahg•lee bih vih yeh•khaht' bihs•tryeh•yeh/myed•leen•nee•yeh*
Stop/Wait here.	**Остановитесь/Подождите здесь.** *ah•stah•nah•vee•tees'/pah•dahzh•dee•tee zdyes'*

YOU MAY HEAR…

Куда? *koo•dah*	Where to?
Какой адрес? *kah•koy ahd•rees*	What's the address?
Здесь положен дополнительный аэропортовый сбор/сбор за ночное время. *zdyes' po•lo•zhihn doh•pohl•nee•tyel'•nih ah•eh•rah•por•toh•viy sbohr/sbohr za noch•no•eh vreh•myah*	There's a nighttime/ airport surcharge.

How much will it cost?	**Сколько это будет стоить?** _skol'_·kah _eh_·tah _boo_·deet _stoh_·eet'
You said…rubles.	**Вы сказали…рублей.** vih skah·_zah_·lee… roob·_lyey_
Keep the change.	**Оставьте сдачу.** ah·_stahf'_·tee _zdah_·choo
A receipt, please.	**Можно чек, пожалуйста.** _mozh_·nah chehk pah·_zhahl_·stah

You'll find mainly private taxi services throughout Russia. It is common practice for Russians to hail private cars in the street, but foreigners, especially those who know little Russian and are unfamiliar with their surroundings, should exercise extreme caution. Before entering a private car, make sure that the driver understands where you want to go and agree on a price.
Warning: Never enter a car if somebody besides the driver is in it. Be especially careful after dark.

Bicycle & Motorbike

I'd like to hire…	**Я хотел m /хотела f бы взять напрокат…** yah khah·_tyel_/khah·_tyeh_·lah bih vzyaht' nah·prah·_kaht_…
a bicycle	**велосипед** vee·lah·see·_pyet_
a moped	**мопед** mah·_pyet_
a motorcycle	**мотоцикл** mah·tah·_tsihkl_
How much per day/week?	**Сколько стоит в день/неделю?** _skol'_·kah _stoh_·eet v dyen'/nee·_dyeh_·lyoo
Can I have a helmet/lock?	**Могу я получить шлем/замок?** mah·_goo_ yah pah·loo·_cheet'_ shlyem/zah·_mok_

Car Hire

Where can I rent a car?	**Где можно взять машину напрокат?** _gdyeh mozh·nah vzyaht' mah·shih·noo nah·prah·kaht_
I'd like to rent [hire]…	**Я хотел** _m_ **/хотела** _f_ **бы взять напрокат…** _yah khah·tyel/khah·tyeh·lah bih vzyaht' nah·prah·kaht…_
a cheap/small car	**недорогую/небольшую машину** _nih·do·ro·goo·yoo/nye·bol'·shoo·yoo mah·shih·noo_
a 2-/4-door car	**двух/четырёх дверную машину** _dvookh/chee·tih·ryokh dvyer·noo·yoo mah·shih·noo_
an automatic/manual car	**машину с автоматической/ручной трансмиссией** _mah·shih·noo s ahf·tah·mah·tee·chees·koy/rooch·noy trahns·mee·see·yey_
a car with air-conditioning	**машину с кондиционером** _mah·shih·noo s kahn·dee·tsih·ah·nyeh·rahm_
a car with a car seat	**машину с детским сидением** _mah·shih·noo s dyets·keem see·dyen'·yem_
How much…?	**Сколько…?** _skol'·kah…_
per day/week	**в день/неделю** _v dyen'/nee·dyeh·lyoo_
per kilometer	**за километр** _zah kee·lah·myetr_
for unlimited mileage	**за неограниченный пробег** _zah nee·ahg·rah·nee·cheen·niy prah·byek_
with insurance	**со страховкой** _sah strah·khof·kie_
Are there any special weekend rates?	**Есть особый тариф по выходным?** _yest' ah·soh·biy tah·reef pah vih·khahd·nihm_

Fuel Station

Where's the nearest fuel station?	**Где ближайшая заправочная станция?** _gdyeh blee·zhie·shah·yah zah·prah·vahch·nah·yah stahn·tsih·yah_

YOU MAY HEAR...

У Вас есть международное водительское удостоверение? *oo vahs yest' meezh·doo·nah·rod·nah·yeh vah·dee·teel'·skah·yeh oo·dahs·tah·vee·ryeh·nee·yeh*

Do you have an international driver's license?

Ваш паспорт, пожалуйста. *vahsh pahs·pahrt pah·zhahl·stah*

Your passport, please.

Вам нужна страховка? *vahm noozh·nah strah·khof·kah*

Do you want insurance?

Нужен залог... *noo·zhihn zah·log...*

There is a deposit of...

Распишитесь здесь. *rahs·pee·shih·tees' zdyes'*

Please sign here.

Fill it up, please.
Полный бак, пожалуйста. *pol·niy bahk pah·zhahl·stah*

...liters, please.
...литров бензина, пожалуйста. *...leet·rahf been·zee·nah pah·zhahl·stah*

I'll pay in cash/ by credit card.
Я заплачу наличными/по кредитной карточке. *yah zah·plah·choo nah·leech·nih·mee/ pah kree·deet·nie kahr·tahch·kyeh*

YOU MAY SEE...

бензин А-98 *been·zeen ah dee·vyah·nos·tah voh·seem'*	super
бензин А-93 *been·zeen ah dee·vyah·nos·tah tree*	regular
дизельное топливо *dee·zeel'·nah·yeh top·lee·vah*	diesel

Asking Directions

Is this the right road to...?	**Это дорога на...?** *eh*·tah dah·*roh*·gah nah...
How far is it to...?	**Далеко до...отсюда?** *dah·lee·koh* dah... aht·*syoo*·dah
Where's...?	**Где...?** *gdyeh*...
...Street	**улица...** *oo*·lee·tsah...
this address	**этот адрес** *eh*·taht ahd·rees
the highway [motorway]	**шоссе** shahs·*seh*
Can you show me on the map?	**Можете показать мне на карте?** *moh*·zhih·tee pah·kah·*zaht'* mnyeh nah *kahr*·tee
I'm lost.	**Я заблудился** *m* **/заблудилась** *f.* yah zah·bloo·*deel*·syah/zah·bloo·*dee*·lahs'

YOU MAY HEAR...

прямо *pryah*·mah	straight ahead
слева *slyeh*·vah	on the left
справа *sprah*·vah	on the right
на углу/за углом nah oo·*gloo*/zah oo·*glohm*	on/around the corner
напротив nah·*proh*·teef	opposite
позади pah·zah·*dee*	behind
рядом с *ryah*·dahm s	next to
после *pos*·lee	after
север/юг *syeh*·veer/yook	north/south
восток/запад vahs·*tok*/*zah*·paht	east/west
у светофора oo svee·tah·*foh*·rah	at the traffic light
на перекрестке nah pee·ree·*kryost*·kee	at the intersection

YOU MAY SEE...

 ОБГОН ЗАПРЕЩЕН *ahb•gon zah•pree•shchon* — no passing

 СТОП *stop* — stop

 ОДНОСТОРОННЕЕ ДВИЖЕНИЕ *ahd•nah•stah•ron•nyeh•yeh dvee•zheh•nee•yeh* — one-way street

 УСТУПИ ДОРОГУ *oos•too•pee dah•roh•goo* — yield [give way]

 ВЪЕЗД ЗАПРЕЩЕН *vyezd zah•pree•shchon* — no entry

 СТОЯНКА ЗАПРЕЩЕНА *stah•yahn•kah zah•pree•shchee•nah* — no parking

 ОПАСНЫЙ ПОВОРОТ *ah•pahs•niy pah•vah•rot* — dangerous curve

 ПЕШЕХОДНЫЙ ПЕРЕХОД *pee•shih•khod•niy pee•ree•khot* — pedestrian crossing

 ОГРАНИЧЕНИЕ СКОРОСТИ *ah•grah•nee•cheh•nee•yeh skoh•rahs•tee* — maximum speed limit

Parking

Can I park here?	**Здесь можно поставить машину?** *zdyes' mozh•nah pah•stah•veet' mah•shih•noo*
Where is the nearest parking garage/parking lot [car park]?	**Здесь рядом есть крытая стоянка/ автостоянка?** *zdyes' ryah•dahm yest' krih•tah•yah stah•yahn•kah/ ahf•tah•stah•yahn•kah*

Where's the parking meter?	**Где счётчик времени стоянки?** *gdyeh shchot·cheek vreh·meh·nee stah·yahn·kee*
How much…?	**Сколько…?** *skol'·kah…*
per hour	**в час** *f chahs*
per day	**в день** *v dyen'*
overnight	**за ночь** *zah nahch*

Parking is usually unrestricted, except in central areas of Moscow and St. Petersburg, where parking meters and no-parking zones can be found. Illegally parked cars are subject to clamping and towing.

Breakdown & Repair

My car broke down/won't start.	**У меня сломалась/не заводится машина.** *oo mee·nyah slah·mah·lahs'/nee zah·voh·dee·tsah mah·shih·nah*
Can you fix it?	**Можно починить?** *mozh·nah pah·chee·neet'*
When will it be ready?	**Когда будет готово?** *kahg·dah boo·deet gah·toh·vah*
How much will it cost?	**Сколько это будет стоить?** *skol'·kah eh·tah boo·deet stoh·eet'*
I have a puncture/flat tyre (tire).	**У меня проколота шина/спущено колесо** *oo meh·nya proh·koh·loh·tah shee·nah/spoo·shchyeh·noh koh·leh·soh*

Accidents

There has been an accident.	**Произошла авария.** *prah·ee·zah·shlah ah·vah·ree·yah*
Call an ambulance/the police.	**Вызовите скорую помощь/милицию.** *vih·zah·vee·tee skoh·roo·yoo poh·mahshch'/mee·lee·tsih·yoo*

ESSENTIAL

Can you recommend a hotel?	**Можете порекомендовать гостиницу?** _moh•zhih•tee pah•ree•kah•meen•dah•vaht' gahs•tee•nee•tsoo_
I have a reservation.	**У меня заказ.** _oo mee•nyah zah•kahs_
My name is…	**Меня зовут…** _mee•nyah zah•voot…_
Do you have a room…?	**У вас есть номер…?** _oo vahs yest' noh•meer…_
for one/two	**на одного/двоих** _nah ahd•nah•voh/dvah•eekh_
with a bathroom	**с ванной** _s vahn•nie_
with air-conditioning	**с кондиционером** _s kahn•dee•tzih•ah•nyeh•rahm_
For tonight.	**На эти сутки.** _nah eh•tee soot•kee_
For two nights.	**На два дня.** _nah dvah dnyah_
For one week.	**На неделю.** _nah nee•dyeh•lyoo_
How much?	**Сколько?** _skol'•kah_
Do you have anything cheaper?	**Есть что-нибудь подешевле?** _yest' shtoh•nee•boot' pah•dee•shev•lee_
When's check-out?	**Во сколько надо освободить номер?** _vah skol'•kah nah•dah ah•svah•bah•deet' noh•meer_
Can I leave this in the safe?	**Можно оставить это в сейфе?** _mozh•nah ah•stah•veet' eh•tah f sey•fee_
Can I leave my bags?	**Можно я оставлю сумки?** _mozh•nah yah ah•stahv•lyoo soom•kee_
Can I have the bill/a receipt?	**Можно счёт/чек?** _mozh•nah shchot/chehk_
I'll pay in cash/by credit card.	**Я заплачу наличными/по кредитной карточке.** _yah zah•plah•choo nah•leech•nih•mee/ pah kree•deet•noy kahr•tahch•kee_

Because of the many rules governing foreigners in Russia, it is easiest to make travel, housing and visa arrangements through a tour or travel agency. A Russian visa can be obtained once you have either a hotel reservation or an official invitation (**приглашение** _pree•glah•sheh•nee•yeh_) from a friend, business associate or relative in Russia.

Wherever you stay, you will need to make sure you are given an official registration paper, which you will need to relinquish when you exit the country.

If you stay in a hotel, the staff will take your passport from you while they process this registration. Be sure to obtain a receipt for your passport and carry it with you, as you can be stopped by the police and fined for not having a passport with you. If you stay with friends or relatives, you will need to obtain this registration from **ОВИР** _ah•veer_ (the Department of Visas and Registration) within 72 hours of your arrival.

Somewhere to Stay

Can you recommend...	**Можете порекомендовать... ?** _moh•zhih•tee pah•ree•kah•meen•dah•vaht'_
a hotel	**гостиницу** _gahs•tee•nee•tsoo_
a hostel	**общежитие** _ahp•shchee•zhih•tee•yeh_
a campsite	**палаточный лагерь** _pah•lah•toch•niy lah•geer'_
a bed and breakfast	**гостиницу типа «ночлег и завтрак»** _gahs•tee•nee•tsoo tee•pah noch•lyeg ee zavt•rahk_
What is it near?	**Что находится рядом?** _shtoh nah•khoh•dee•tsah ryah•dahm_
How do I get there?	**Как туда добраться?** _kahk too•dah dah•brah•tsah_

If at all possible, arrange to be met at the airport by a representative from your hotel. Some travel agencies, such as Intourist, will meet you when you exit customs. If you are not being met, try to use public transportation to get to your hotel. Be very cautious about getting into a taxi.

Intourist no longer holds a monopoly on accommodations in Russia, and in major cities an increasing number of new or newly renovated hotels are now jointly operated with Western companies. These first-class ventures offer a new, if pricey, option for tourists. If you are on an Intourist package tour you can state your hotel preference, but the final arrangements rest with Intourist.

Hotels also usually have service bureaus (**бюро обслуживания** *byoo•roh ahp•sloo•zhih•vah•nee•yah*) manned by multilingual staff, who provide information, arrange outings and excursions, make reservations and provide general assistance.

London Berlin Moscow Ulan-Ude Tokyo New York

At the Hotel

I have a reservation.	**У меня заказ.**	oo mee-_nyah_ zah-_kahs_
My name is…	**Моя фамилия…**	mee-_nyah_ zah-_voot_…
Do you have a room…?	**У вас есть номер…?**	oo vahs yest' _noh_-meer…
with a bathroom [toilet]/shower	**с ванной/душем**	s _vahn_-nie/_doo_-shehm
with air-conditioning	**с кондиционером**	s kahn-dee-tsih-ah-_nyeh_-rahm
that's smoking/ non-smoking	**для курящих/некурящих**	dlyah koo-_ryah_-shcheekh/nee-koo-_ryah_-shcheekh
For…	**На…**	nah…
tonight.	**эти сутки.**	_eh_-tee _soot_-kee
two nights.	**два дня.**	dvah dnyah
one week.	**неделю.**	nee-_dyeh_-lyoo
Does the hotel have…?	**В гостинице есть…?**	v gahs-_tee_-nee-tseh yest'…
a computer	**компьютер**	kahm-_pyoo_-ter
an elevator [lift]	**лифт**	leeft
(wireless) internet service	**(беспроводной) интернет**	(bees-prah-vahd-_noy_) een-ter-_net_
room service	**обслуживание номеров**	ahp-_sloo_-zhih-vah-nee-yeh nah-mee-_rof_
a gym	**спортзал**	sport-_zahl_

a pool	**бассейн** *bah·seyn*
I need…	**Мне нужно…** *mnyeh noozh·nah…*
an extra bed	**ещё одну кровать** *ee·shchoh ahd·noo krah·vaht'*
a cot	**раскладушку** *rahs·klah·doosh·koo*
a crib [child's cot]	**детскую кроватку** *dyets·koo·yoo krah·vaht·koo*

YOU MAY HEAR…

Ваш паспорт/Вашу кредитную карточку, Your passport/Your
пожалуйста. *vahsh pahs·pahrt/vah·shoo* credit card, please.
pah·zhahl·stah kree·deet·noo·yoo kahr·tahch·koo

Заполните бланк. *zah·pol·nee·tyeh blahnk* Fill out this form.

распишитесь здесь. *rahs·pee·shih·tyes'* Sign here.
zdyes'

Price

How much per night/week?	**Сколько в сутки/неделю?** *skol'·kah f soot·kee/nee·dyeh·lyoo*
Does the price include breakfast/ sales tax [VAT]?	**Цена включает завтрак/НДС?** *tsih·nah klyoo·chah·eet zahf·trahk/en·deh·es*
Are there any discounts?	**Есть скидки?** *yest' skih·dkih*

Preferences

Can I see the room?	**Могу я посмотреть номер?** *mah·goo yah pos·maht·ret' noh·mehr*
I'd like a…room.	**Мне нужен номер…** *mneh noo·zhyen noh·mehr*
better	**лучше** *loo·chshye*
bigger	**больше** *bol'·shye*

cheaper	**дешевле** deh·shyev·leh
quieter	**тише** tih·shye
I'll take it.	**Я сниму его.** yah snee·moo·eh·voh
No, I won't take it.	**Я не буду его снимать.** yah neh boo·doo ehvoh snih·maht'

Questions

Where's…?	**Где…?** gdyeh…
the bar	**бар** bahr
the toilets	**туалет** too·ah·lyet
the elevator [lift]	**лифт** leeft
Can I have…?	**Можно мне…?** mozh·nah mnyeh…
a blanket	**одеяло** ah·dee·yah·lah
an iron	**утюг** oo·tyook
the room key/ key card	**ключ/ключ-карта от номера** klyooch/klyooch kahr·tah ot noh·meh·rah
a pillow	**подушку** pah·doosh·koo
soap	**мыло** mih·lah

YOU MAY SEE…

ОТ СЕБЯ/НА СЕБЯ aht see·byah/nah see·byah	push/pull
ТУАЛЕТ too·ah·lyet	restroom [toilet]
ДУШ doosh	shower
ЛИФТ leeft	elevator [lift]
ЛЕСТНИЦА lyes·nee·tsah	stairs
ПРАЧЕЧНАЯ prah·cheech·nah·yah	laundry
НЕ БЕСПОКОИТЬ nyeh bees·pah·koh·eet'	do not disturb
АВАРИЙНЫЙ ВЫХОД ah·vah·reey·niy vih·khaht	emergency exit
ВЫХОД vih·khaht	exit
БУДИЛЬНИК boo·deel'·neek	wake-up call

toilet paper	**туалетную бумагу** too·ah·_lyet_·noo·yoo boo·_mah_·goo
a towel	**банное полотенце** _bahn_·nah·yeh pah·lah·_tyen_·tseh
Do you have an adapter for this?	**У вас есть адаптер для этого?** oo vahs yest' ah·_dahp_·ter dlyah eh·tah·vah
How do I turn on the lights?	**Как мне включить свет?** kahk mnyeh fklyoo·_cheet'_ svyet
Wake me at…	**Разбудите меня в…** rahz·boo·_dee_·tee mee·_nyah_ v…
Could I have my things from the safe?	**Можно взять вещи из сейфа?** _mozh_·nah vzyaht' _vyeh_·shchee ees _sey_·fah
Is there mail/ a message for me?	**Есть почта/сообщение для меня?** yest' _poch_·tah/sah·ahp·_shchyeh_·nee·yeh dlyah mee·_nyah_
Do you have a laundry service?	**У Вас есть прачечная?** oo vahs yest' _prah_·cheech·nah·yah

Problems

There's a problem.	**Есть проблема.** yest' prah·_blyeh_·mah
I've lost my key/key card.	**Я потерял** *m* **/потеряла** *f* **ключ/электронный ключ.** yah pah·tee·_ryahl_/pah·tee·_ryah_·lah klyooch/ee·leek·_tron_·niy klyooch
I've locked myself out of my room.	**Я случайно захлопнул** *m* **/захлопнула** *f* **дверь.** yah sloo·_chie_·nah zah·_khlop_·nool/ zah·_khlop_·noo·lah dvyer'
There's no hot water/toilet paper.	**Нет горячей воды/туалетной бумаги.** nyet gah·_ryah_·chey vah·_dih_/too·ah·_lyet_·nie boo·_mah_·gee
The room is dirty.	**В комнате грязно.** f _kom_·nah·tyeh gryahz·nah
There are bugs in our room.	**У нас в комнате насекомые.** oo nahs f _kom_·nah·tyeh nah·see·_koh_·mih·yeh

The...has broken down.	**...не работает.**	...nee rah·*boh*·tah·yet
Can you fix...?	**Можно починить...?**	*mozh*·nah pah·chee·*neet'*...
the air-conditioning	**кондиционер**	kahn·dee·tsih·ah·*nyer*
the fan	**вентилятор**	veen·tee·*lyah*·tahr
the heat [heating]	**отопление**	ah·tahp·*lyeh*·nee·yeh
the light	**свет**	svyet
the TV	**телевизор**	tee·lee·*vee*·zahr
the toilet	**туалет**	too·ah·*lyet*
I'd like to move to another room.	**Я хотел m /хотела f бы другую комнату.**	yah khah·tyel/khah·*tyeh*·lah bih droo·*goo*·yoo *kom*·nah·too

While 220 volt AC tends to be standard in Russia, you'll still find 110-120 volt AC in some places. Russian outlets differ from Western ones, but large hotels often have outlets that will take Western plugs. Since suitable adapters are sometimes hard to find in Russia, especially outside major cities, it is prudent to travel with one. If you are traveling with electronics built to support multiple voltages, you may want to bring a surge protector suitable for Russian outlets. If your electronics do not support 220 volt current, you will need both an adapter and a step-down transformer.

Checking Out

When's check-out?	**Во сколько надо освободить комнату?** vah *skol'*·kah *nah*·dah ah·svah·bah·*deet'* *kom*·nah·too
Could I leave my bags here until...?	**Можно мне оставить вещи здесь до...?** *mozh*·nah mnyeh ah·*stah*·veet' *vyeh*·shchee zdyes' dah...

Can I have an itemized bill/ a receipt?	**Можно детальный счёт/чек?** _mozh_•nah dee•_tahl_'•niy shchot/chehk
I think there's a mistake in this bill.	**Мне кажется, в счёте ошибка.** mnyeh _kah_•zhee•tsah v _shchoh_•tee ah•_shihp_•kah
I'll pay in cash/by credit card.	**Я заплачу наличными/по кредитной карточке.** yah zah•plah•_choo_ nah•_leech_•nih•mee/ pah kree•_deet_•nie _kahr_•tahch•kyeh

Tips of 10-20% are generally appropriate in restaurants and taxis, depending on the level of service. Porters and maids will certainly expect and appreciate a dollar or two (or the ruble equivalent) for each bag they carry or day that they clean.

As anywhere else, generous tippers will often get better service than those who tip poorly or not at all. Tour guides and their drivers, especially if they have gone 'above and beyond' to get you into restaurants and museums, will expect to be compensated somewhat above the agreed rate.

Renting

I've reserved an apartment/a room.	**Я заказывал** *m* **/заказывала** *f* **квартиру/комнату.** yah zah•*kah*•zih•vahl/ zah•*kah*•zih•vah•lah kvahr•*tee*•roo/*kom*•nah•too
My name is...	**Меня зовут...** mee•*nyah* zah•*voot*...
Can I have the key/key card?	**Можно получить ключ/электронный ключ?** *mozh*•nah pah•loo•*cheet'* klyooch/ ee•leek•*tron*•niy klyooch

Are there...?	**Есть...?** yest'...
dishes and utensils	**посуда** pah•*soo*•dah
pillows	**подушки** pah•*doosh*•kee
sheets	**простыни** proh•stih•nee
towels	**полотенца** pah•lah•*tyen*•tsah

When/Where do I put out the bins?	**Когда/Куда выносить мусор?** kahg•*dah*/ koo•*dah* vih•nah•*seet'* moo•sahr
...is broken.	**...не работает.** ...nee rah•*boh*•tah•yet
How does...work?	**Как работает...?** kahk rah•*boh*•tah•yet...
the air-conditioner	**кондиционер** kahn•dee•tsih•ah•*nyer*
the dishwasher	**посудомоечная машина** pah•soo•dah•*moh*•eech•nah•yah mah•*shih*•nah
the freezer	**морозильная камера** mah•rah•*zeel'*•nah•yah *kah*•mee•rah
the heater	**обогреватель** ah•bah•gree•*vah*•teel'
the microwave	**микроволновка** meek•rah•vahl•*nof*•kah
the refrigerator	**холодильник** khah•lah•*deel'*•neek
the stove	**плита** plee•*tah*
the washing machine	**стиральная машина** stee•*rahl'*•nah•yah mah•*shih*•nah

Domestic Items

I need...	**Мне нужно...** mnyeh _noozh_·nah...
an adapter	**адаптер** ah·_dahp_·ter
aluminum [kitchen] foil	**фольга** fahl'·_gah_
a bottle opener	**открывалка** aht·krih·_vahl_·kah
a broom	**веник** _vyeh_·neek
a can opener	**консервный нож** kahn·_syerv_·niy nosh
cleaning supplies	**моющие средства** _moh_·yoo·shchee·yeh _sryet_·stvah
a corkscrew	**штопор** _shtoh_·pahr
detergent	**стиральный порошок** stee·_rahl_'·niy pah·rah·_shok_
dishwashing liquid	**жидкость для мытья посуды** _zhiht_·kahst' dlyah mih·_tyah_ pah·_soo_·dih
bin bags	**мешки для мусора** meesh·_kee_ dlyah _moo_·sah·rah
a light bulb	**лампочка** _lahm_·pahch·kah
matches	**спички** _speech_·kee
a mop	**швабра** _shvahb_·rah
napkins	**салфетки** sahl·_fyet_·kee

paper towels	**бумажные полотенца** boo·_mahzh_·nih·ee pah·lah·_tyen_·tsah	
I need…	**Мне нужно…** mnyeh noozh·nah…	
plastic wrap [cling film]	**продуктовая плёнка** prah·dook·_toh_·vah·yah _plyon_·kah	
a plunger	**вантуз** _vahn_·toos	
scissors	**ножницы** _nozh_·nee·tsih	
a vacuum cleaner	**пылесос** pih·lee·_sos_	

For In the Kitchen, see page 78.

At the Hostel

Do you have any places left for tonight?	**Есть свободные места на сегодня?** yest' svah·_bod_·nih·yeh mee·_stah_ nah see·_vod_·nyah
Can I have…?	**Можно мне…?** _mozh_·nah mnyeh…
a single/double room	**одноместный/двухместный номер** ahd·nah·_myes_·niy/dvookh·_myes_·niy _noh_·meer
a blanket	**одеяло** ah·dee·_yah_·lah
a pillow	**подушку** pah·_doosh_·koo
sheets	**простыни** _proh_·stih·nee
a towel	**полотенце** pah·lah·_tyen_·tseh
Do you have lockers?	**У Вас есть запирающиеся шкафчики?** oo vahs yest' zah·pee·_rah_·yoo·shcheeyeh·sya _shkaf_·chee· kee
What time do you lock up?	**Во сколько закрывается вход?** vah _skol'_·kah zah·krih·_vah_·ee·tsah fkhot

Спутник _spoot_·neek (Sputnik), the Russian youth travel association, organizes group tours for students with accommodation in **молодёжная турбаза** mah·lah·_dyozh_·nah·yah toor·_bah_·zah (youth hostels).

Do I need a membership card?	**Нужна ли мне членская карта?** *noozh·nah lee mneh chlehn·skaya kahr·tah*
Here's my international student card.	**Вот мой международный студенческий билет.** *vot moy meezh·doo·nah·rod·niy stoo·dehn·chyes·keey bee·lyet*

Going Camping

Can I camp here?	**Здесь можно разбить лагерь?** *zdyes' mozh·nah rahz·beet' lah·geer'*
Is there a campsite near here?	**Здесь есть кемпинг поблизости?** *zdyes' yest' kehm·peenk pah·blee·zahs·tee*
What is the charge per day/week?	**Сколько стоит в день/неделю?** *skol'·kah stoh·eet v dyen'/nee·dyeh·lyoo*
Are there...?	**Есть...?** *yest'...*
cooking facilities	**кухня** *kookh·nyah*
electrical outlets	**электроточки** *ee·lyek·trah·toch·kee*
laundry facilities	**прачечная** *prah·cheech·nah·yah*
showers	**душ** *doosh*
tents for hire	**палатки напрокат** *pah·laht·kee nah·prah·kaht*
Where can I empty the chemical toilet?	**Куда мне выбросить содержимое химического туалета?** *koo·dah mnyeh vih·brah·seet' sah·deer·zhih·mah·yeh khee·mee·chees·kah·vah too·ah·lyeh·tah*

For Domestic Items, see page 47.

YOU MAY SEE...

ПИТЬЕВАЯ ВОДА *peet'·ee·vah·yah vah·dah*	drinking water
СТОЯНКА ЗАПРЕЩЕНА *stah·yahn·kah zah·pree·shchee·nah*	no camping
КОСТРЫ ЗАПРЕЩЕНЫ *kahst·rih zah·pree·shchee·nih*	no fires

Communications

ESSENTIAL

Where's an internet cafe?	**Где находится интернет-кафе?** *gdyeh nah-khoh-dee-tsah een-ter-net kah-feh*
Can I access the internet here/ check e-mail?	**Здесь можно войти в Интернет/ проверить электронную почту?** *zdyes' mozh-nah vie-tee v een-ter-net/prah-vyeh-reet' ee-leek-tron-noo-yoo poch-too*
How much per half hour/hour?	**Сколько за полчаса/час?** *skol'-kah zah pol-chee-sah/chahs*
How do I connect/ log on?	**Как мне подключиться/зарегистрироваться?** *kahk mnyeh paht-klyoo-chee-tsah/ zah-ree-gee-stree-rah-vah-tsah*
I'd like a phone card, please.	**Телефонную карточку, пожалуйста.** *tee-lee-fon-noo-yoo kahr-tahch-koo pah-zhahl-stah*
Can I have your phone number?	**Можно Ваш номер телефона?** *mozh-nah vahsh noh-meer tee-lee-foh-nah*
Here's my number/ e-mail address.	**Вот мой номер/адрес электронной почты.** *vot moy noh-meer/ahd-rees ee-leek-tron-nie poch-tih*
Call me.	**Звоните.** *zvah-nee-tee*
E-mail me.	**Напишите мне по электронной почте.** *nah-pee-shih-tee mnyeh pah ee-leek-tron-nie poch-tyeh*
Hello. This is...	**Алло. Это...** *ah-loh eh-tah...*
I'd like to speak to...	**Я хотел m /хотела f бы поговорить с...** *yah khah-tyel/khah-tyeh-lah bih pah-gah-vah-reet' s...*
Repeat that, please.	**Повторите, пожалуйста.** *pahf-tah-ree-tee pah-zhahl-stah*

I'll call back later.	**Я перезвоню попозже.** yah pee•ree•zvah•nyoo pah•pozh•zheh
Bye.	**До свидания.** dah svee•dah•nee•yah
Where is the nearest/main post office?	**Где здесь ближайшая почта/главпочтамт?** gdyeh zdyes' blee•zhie•shah•yah poch•tah/glahf•pahch•tamt
I'd like to send this to…	**Я хотел m /хотела f бы отправить это в…** yah khah•tyel/khah•tyeh•lah bih aht•prah•veet' eh•tah v…

Online

Where's an internet cafe?	**Где находится интернет-кафе?** gdyeh nah•khoh•dee•tsah een•ter•net kah•feh
Does it have wireless internet?	**Есть беспроводной Интернет?** yest' bees•prah•vahd•noy een•ter•net
What is the WiFi password?	**Какой пароль от WiFi?** kah•koy pah•rol' ot WiFi
Is the WiFi free?	**WiFi бесплатный?** WiFi behs•plaht•niy
Do you have bluetooth?	**У Вас есть bluetooth?** oo vas yest' bluetooth
How do I turn the computer on/off?	**Как мне включить/выключить компьютер?** kahk mnyeh fklyoo•cheet'/vih•klyoo•cheet' kahm•pyoo•ter
Can I…?	**Я смогу…?** yah smah•goo…
access the internet here	**войти в Интернет здесь** vie•tee v een•ter•net zdyes'
check e-mail	**проверить электронную почту** prah•vyeh•reet' ee•leek•tron•noo•yoo poch•too
print	**распечатать** rahs•pee•chah•taht'
plug in/charge my laptop/iPhone/	**подключить/зарядить ноутбук/iPhone/iPad/BlackBerry?** pod•klyoo•cheet'/zah•rya•deet'

iPad/BlackBerry?	*notebook /iPhone/iPad/BlackBerry*
access Skype?	**войти в Skype?** *voy·tee v Skype*
How much per hour/half hour?	**Сколько за час/полчаса?** *skol'·kah zah chahs/pol·chah·sah*
How do I...?	**Как мне...?** *kahk mnyeh...*
connect/disconnect	**подключиться/отключиться** *paht·klyoo·chee·tsah/aht·klyoo·chee·tsah*
log on/off	**войти/выйти** *vie·tee/viy·tee*
type this symbol	**напечатать этот символ** *nah·pee·chah·taht 'eh·taht seem·vahl*
What's your e-mail?	**Какой у вас адрес электронной почты?** *kah·koy oo vahs ahd·rees ee·leek·tron·nie poch·tih*
My e-mail is...	**Мой адрес электронной почты...** *moy ahd·rees ee·leek·tron·nie poch·tih...*
Do you have a scanner?	**У Вас есть сканер?** *oo vas est' skah·nehr*

Social Media

Are you on Facebook/Twitter?	**Вы есть в Facebook/Twitter?** *vih est' v Facebook/Twitter*
What's your user name?	**Какое у Вас имя пользователя?** *kah·koh·eh oo vas ee·mya pol'·zo·vah·tyeh·lya*
I'll add you as a friend.	**Я добавлю Вас в друзья.** *yah doh·bahv·lyoo vas v drooz'·ya*
I'll follow you on Twitter.	**Я присоединюсь к Вам в Twitter.** *yah pree·soh·eh·dee·nyus' k vam v Twitter*
Are you following...?	**Вы присоединились...?** *vih pree·soh· eh·dee·nee·lees'*
I'll put the pictures on Facebook/Twitter.	**Я выложу фотографии на Facebook/Twitter.** *yah vih· lah·zhoo·fo·to·grah·fee·ee na Facebook/Twitter*
I'll tag you in the pictures.	**Я отмечу Вас на фотографиях.** *yah ot·meh·choo vas na foh·to·grah·fee·yakh*

YOU MAY SEE…

ЗАКРОЙТЕ zah·<u>kroy</u>·tee	close
УДАЛИТЕ oo·dah·<u>lee</u>·tee	delete
ЭЛЕКТРОННАЯ ПОЧТА ee·leek·<u>tron</u>·nah·yah <u>poch</u>·tah	e-mail
ВЫХОД <u>vih</u>·khaht	exit
СПРАВКА <u>sprahf</u>·kah	help
МГНОВЕННЫЙ ОБМЕН СООБЩЕНИЯМИ mgnah·<u>vyen</u>·niy ahb·<u>myen</u> sah·ahp·<u>shchyeh</u>·nee·yah·mee	instant messenger
ИНТЕРНЕТ een·ter·<u>net</u>	internet
ВХОД В СИСТЕМУ fhot f sees·<u>tyeh</u>·moo	login
НОВОЕ (СООБЩЕНИЕ) <u>noh</u>·vah·yeh (sah·ahp·<u>shchyeh</u>·nee·yeh)	new (message)
ВКЛ/ВЫКЛ fkl/vihkl	on/off
ОТКРЫТЬ aht·<u>kriht'</u>	open
РАСПЕЧАТАТЬ rahs·pee·<u>chah</u>·taht'	print
СОХРАНИТЬ sah·khrah·<u>neet'</u>	save
ОТПРАВИТЬ aht·<u>prah</u>·veet'	send
ИМЯ ПОЛЬЗОВАТЕЛЯ/ПАРОЛЬ <u>ee</u>·myah <u>pol'</u>·zah·vah·tee·lyah/pah·<u>rol'</u>	username/ password
БЕСПРОВОДНОЙ ИНТЕРНЕТ bees·prah·vahd·<u>noy</u> een·ter·<u>net</u>	wireless internet

Phone

A phone card/ prepaid phone, please.	**Телефонную карточку/оплаченный телефон, пожалуйста.** tee·lee·<u>fon</u>·noo·yoo <u>kahr</u>·tahch·koo/ ah·<u>plah</u>·cheen·niy tee·lee·<u>fon</u> pah·<u>zhahl</u>·stah
How much?	**Сколько?** <u>skol'</u>·kah
Where's the pay phone?	**Где есть таксофон?** gdeh est' tah·xo·<u>fohn</u>

What's the area/ country code for…?	**Какой код города/страны для…?** *kah·koy kot goh·rah·dah/strah·nih dlyah…*
What's the number for Information?	**Какой номер справочной службы?** *kah·koy noh·meer sprah·vahch·nie sloozh·bih*
I'd like the number for…	**Мне нужен номер…** *mnyeh noo·zhihn noh·meer…*
I'd like to call collect [reverse the charges].	**Я хочу позвонить за счет абонента [удержать оплату].** *yah kho·choo poz·voh·neet' zah shchot ah·boh·nehn·tah [oo·dehr·zhat' op·lah·too]*
My phone doesn't work here.	**Мой телефон здесь не работает.** *moy tee·lee·fon zdyes' nee rah·boh·tah·eet*
What network are you on?	**К какой сети Вы подключены?** *k kah·koy sye·tee vih pod· klyoo·cheh·nih*
Is it 3G?	**Это 3G?** *eh·tah 3G*
I have run out of credit/ minutes.	**У меня закончились единицы/минуты.** *oo meh·nya zah·kohn·chee·lees' eh·dee·nee· tsih/ mee·noo·tih*
Can I buy some credit?	**Могу я приобрести единицы?** *moh·goo yah pree·obrye·stee ye·dee·nee·tsih*
Do you have a phone charger?	**У Вас есть зарядное устройство для телефона?** *u vas est' zah·ryad·no·he oost·roy·stvoh dlya teh·leh·foh·nah*
Can I have your number?	**Можно Ваш номер телефона?** *mozh·nah vahsh noh·meer tee·lee·foh·nah*
Here's my number.	**Вот мой телефон.** *vot moy tee·lee·fon*
Call me.	**Звоните.** *zvah·nee·tee*
Text me.	**Пришлите СМС.** *pree·shlee·tee es·em·es*
I'll call you.	**Я позвоню Вам.** *yah pah·zvah·nyoo vahm*
I'll text you.	**Я пришлю Вам СМС.** *yah pree·shlyoo vahm es·em·es*

For Numbers, see page 157.

Telephone Etiquette

Hello. This is…	**Алло. Это…** *ah·loh eh·tah…*
I'd like to speak to…	**Я хотел** *m* **/хотела** *f* **бы поговорить с…** *yah khah·tyel/khah·tyeh·lah bih pah·gah·vah·reet' s…*
Extension…	**Добавочный номер…** *dah·bah·vahch·niy noh·meer…*
Speak louder/more slowly, please.	**Говорите громче/медленнее, пожалуйста.** *gah·vah·ree·tee grom·cheh/myed·leen·nee·yeh pah·zhahl·stah*

YOU MAY HEAR…

Кто говорит? *ktoh gah·vah·reet*	Who's calling?
Подождите, пожалуйста. *pah·dah·zhdee·tee pah·zhahl·stah*	Hold on, please.
Соединяю. *sah·ee·dee·nyah·yoo*	I'll put you through.
Боюсь, что его/её нет. *bah·yoos' shtoh yee·voh/yee·yoh nyet*	I'm afraid he's/ she's not in.
Он/Она не может подойти к телефону. *on/ah·nah nee moh·zhiht pah·die·tee k tee·lee·foh·noo*	He/She can't come to the phone.
Хотите оставить сообщение? *khah·tee·tee ah·stah·veet' sah·ahp·shcheh·nee·yeh*	Would you like to leave a message?
Перезвоните позже/через десять минут. *pee·ree·zvah·nee·tee pozh·zheh/cheh·reez dyeh·seet' mee·noot*	Call back later/in 10 minutes.
Он/Она может перезвонить Вам? *on/ah·nah moh·zhiht pee·ree·zvah·neet' vahm*	Can he/she call you back?
Можно Ваш номер телефона? *mozh·nah vahsh noh·meer tee·lee·foh·nah*	What's your number?

Repeat that, please.	**Повторите, пожалуйста.** pahf·tah·<u>ree</u>·tee pah·<u>zhahl</u>·stah
I'll call back later.	**Я перезвоню попозже.** yah pee·ree·zvah·<u>nyoo</u> pah·<u>pozh</u>·zheh
Bye.	**До свидания.** dah svee·<u>dah</u>·nee·yah

For Business Travel, see page 134.

Fax

Can I send/receive a fax here?	**Я могу здесь получить/отправить факс?** yah mah·<u>goo</u> zdyes' pah·loo·<u>cheet'</u>/ aht·<u>prah</u>·veet' fahks
What's the fax number?	**Какой номер факса?** kah·<u>koy</u> <u>noh</u>·meer <u>fahk</u>·sah
Fax this to…	**Отправьте это по факсу, номер…** aht·<u>prahf'</u>·tee <u>eh</u>·tah pah <u>fahk</u>·soo <u>noh</u>·meer…

Post

Where's the post office/mailbox?	**Где почта/почтовый ящик?** gdyeh <u>poch</u>·tah/pahch·<u>toh</u>·viy <u>yah</u>·shcheek
A stamp for this postcard/letter, please.	**Дайте марку на эту открытку/это письмо, пожалуйста.** <u>die</u>·tee <u>mahr</u>·koo nah <u>eh</u>·too aht·<u>kriht</u>·koo/<u>eh</u>·tah pees'·<u>moh</u> pah·<u>zhahl</u>·stah
How much?	**Сколько?** <u>skol</u>'·kah
I want to send this package by airmail/express.	**Я хочу послать эту посылку авиа/экспресс почтой.** yah khah·<u>choo</u> pah·<u>slaht'</u> <u>eh</u>·too pah·<u>sihl</u>·koo <u>ah</u>·vee·ah/eeks·<u>press</u> poch·toy
A receipt, please.	**Дайте чек, пожалуйста.** die·<u>tee</u> chek pah·<u>zhahl</u>·stah

YOU MAY HEAR...

Пожалуйста, заполните таможенную
декларацию. *pah·zhahl·stah zah·pol·nee·tee*
tah·moh·zhihn·noo·yoo dee·klah·rah·tsih·yoo
Какая стоимость? *kah·kah·yah*
stoh·ee·mahst'
Что там? *shtoh tahm*

Please fill out
the customs
declaration form.
What's the value?

What's inside?

The main post offices in Moscow and St. Petersburg offer round-the-clock service. Other post offices are generally open Monday through Saturday from 8:00 a.m. to 7:00 p.m. and Sunday from 9:00 a.m. to 7:00 p.m. Major hotels have their own postal and telephone services. Both incoming and outgoing international mail is slow, so allow plenty of time. While DHL has the greatest presence in Russia among Western express shipping companies, FedEx, UPS and other companies also provide service to and from Russia.

Food & Drink

Куряга Шоколадная

Урюк от сердечных
болезней

Урюк Чай
аромат

ESSENTIAL

Can you recommend a good restaurant/bar?	**Можете посоветовать хороший ресторан/ бар?** <u>moh</u>•zhih•tee pah•sah•<u>vyeh</u>•tah•vaht' khah•<u>roh</u>•shiy ree•stah•<u>rahn</u>/bahr
Is there a traditional Russian/an inexpensive restaurant near here?	**Здесь есть традиционный русский/ недорогой ресторан поблизости?** zdyes' yest' trah•dee•tsih•<u>on</u>•niy <u>roos</u>•keey/nee•dah•rah•<u>goy</u> ree•stah•<u>rahn</u> pah•<u>blee</u>•zahs•tee
A table for..., please.	**Столик на..., пожалуйста.** <u>stoh</u>•leek nah... pah•<u>zhal</u>•stah
Could we sit...?	**Можно нам сесть...?** <u>mozh</u>•nah nahm syehst'...
here/there	**здесь/там** zdyehs'/tahm
outside	**на улице** nah <u>oo</u>•lee•tseh
in a non-smoking area	**где не курят** gdyeh nee <u>koo</u>•ryaht
I'm waiting for someone.	**Я кое-кого жду.** yah <u>koh</u>•ee kah•<u>voh</u> zhdoo
Where are the toilets?	**Где туалет?** gdyeh too•ah•<u>lyeht</u>
A menu, please.	**Меню, пожалуйста.** mee•<u>nyoo</u> pah•<u>zhal</u>•stah
What do you recommend?	**Что вы посоветуете?** shtoh vih pah•sah•<u>vyeh</u>•too•ee•tee
I'd like...	**Я хотел** *m* **/хотела** *f* **бы...** yah khah•<u>tyel</u>/ khah•<u>tyeh</u>•lah bih...
Some more..., please.	**Можно ещё..., пожалуйста.** <u>mozh</u>•nah ee•<u>shchoh</u>...pah•<u>zhal</u>•stah
Enjoy your meal!	**Приятного аппетита!** pree•<u>yaht</u>•nah•vah ah•pee•<u>tee</u>•tah

The check [bill], please.	**Счёт, пожалуйста.** *shchoht pah·zhahl·stah*
Is service included?	**Счёт включает обслуживание?** *shchot fklyoo·chah·eet ahp·sloo·zhih·vah·nee·yeh*
Can I pay by credit card?	**Можно платить кредитной карточкой?** *mozh·nah plah·teet' kree·deet·noy kahr·tahch·kie*
Can I have a receipt?	**Можно чек?** *mozh·nah chek*
Thank you!	**Спасибо!** *spah·see·bah*

Where to Eat

Can you recommend...?	**Вы можете порекомендовать…?** *vih moh·zhih·tee pah·ree·kah·meen·dah·vaht'…*
a restaurant	**ресторан** *ree·stah·rahn*
a bar	**бар** *bahr*
a cafe	**кафе** *kah·feh*
a fast-food place	**кафе быстрого обслуживания** *kah·feh bihs·trah·vah ahp·sloo·zhih·vah·nee·yah*
a cheap restaurant	**недорогой ресторан** *neh·doh·roh·goy rehs·toh·rahn*
an expensive restaurant	**дорогой ресторан** *doh·roh·goy rehs·toh·rahn*
a restaurant with a good view	**ресторан с хорошим видом из окна** *rehs·toh·rahn s kho·roh·sheem vee·dohm eez ohk·nah*
an authentic/ a non-touristy restaurant	**национальный/не туристический ресторан** *nah·tsee·oh·nahl' niy/neh too·rees·tee·chehs·kiy reh·stoh·rahn*
a blini bar	**блинную** *bleen·noo·yoo*

A vast array of fast-food options have sprung up in Russia's major cities, and, in addition to international fast-food chains, many home-grown restaurants that serve traditional Russian food can be found, such as Russkoe Bistro, Yolki-Palki Taverns and Mu-Mu.

Reservations & Preferences

I'd like to reserve a table...	**Я хотел *m* /хотела *f* бы заказать столик...** yah khah·_tyel_/khah·_tyeh_·lah bih zah·kah·_zaht'_ _stoh_·leek...
for two	**на двоих** nah dvah·_eekh_
I'd like to reserve a table...	**Я хотел *m* /хотела *f* бы заказать столик...** yah khah·_tyel_/khah·_tyeh_·lah bih zah·kah·_zaht'_ _stoh_·leek...
for this evening	**на сегодня на вечер** nah see·_vod_·nyah nah _vyeh_·cheer
for tomorrow at...	**на завтра на...** nah _zahf_·trah nah...
A table for two, please.	**Столик на двоих, пожалуйста.** _stoh_·leek nah dvah·_eekh_ pah·_zhahl_·stah
We have a reservation.	**У нас заказ.** oo nahs zah·_kahs_
My name is...	**Меня зовут...** mee·_nyah_ zah·_voot_...

Can we sit...?	**Можем мы сесть ...?** _moh_·zhehm mih sehst'
here/there	**здесь/там** zdyes'/tahm
outside	**снаружи** snah·_roo_·zhih
in a non-smoking area	**в некурящем зале** v nye·koo·_rya_·shcheem _zah_·leh
by the window	**возле окна** _voz_·leh okh·_nah_
in the shade	**в тени** v teh·_nee_
in the sun	**на солнце** nah _sohln_·tseh
Where is the restroom [toilet]?	**Где туалет?** gdyeh too·ah·_lyet_

YOU MAY HEAR...

У вас заказан столик? oo vahs zah·_kah_·zahn _stoh_·leek	Do you have a reservation?
Сколько? _skol_'·kah	How many?
Для курящих или некурящих? dlyah koo·_ryah_·shcheekh ee·lee nee·koo·_ryah_·shcheekh	Smoking or non-smoking?
Будете заказывать? _boo_·dee·tee zah·_kah_·zih·vaht"	Are you ready to order?
Что вы желаете? shtoh vih zhih·_lah_·ee·tee	What would you like?
Я бы рекомендовал m **/рекомендовала** f yah bih ree·kah·meen·dah·_vahl_/ ree·kah·meen·dah·_vah_·lah	I recommend...
Приятного аппетита! pree·_yaht_·nah·vah ah·pee·_tee_·tah	Enjoy your meal!

How to Order

| Waiter!/Waitress! | **Официант!/Девушка!** ah·fee·tsih·_ahnt_/ _dyeh_·voosh·kah |

We're ready to order. **Мы готовы сделать заказ.** *mih gah·toh·vih zdyeh·laht' zah·kahs*

May I see the wine list? **Можно посмотреть карту вин?** *mozh·nah pah·smah·tryet' kahr·too veen*

I'd like... **Я хотел** *m* **/хотела** *f* **бы...** *yah khah·tyel/ khah·tyeh·lah bih...*

a bottle of... **бутылку...** *boo·tihl·koo...*

a carafe of... **графин...** *grah·feen...*

a glass of... **бокал...** *bah·kahl...*

The menu, please. **Меню, пожалуйста.** *mee·nyoo pah·zhahl·stah*

Do you have...? **У вас есть...?** *oo vahs yest'...*

a menu in English **меню на английском** *mee·nyoo nah ahn·gleeys·kahm*

a fixed-price menu **комплексное меню** *kom·pleeks·nah·yeh mee·nyoo*

a children's menu **детское меню** *dyets·kah·yeh mee·nyoo*

What do you recommend? **Что вы посоветуете?** *shtoh vih pah·sah·vyeh·too·ee·tee*

What's this? **Что это?** *shtoh eh·tah*

What's in it? **Что туда входит?** *shtoh too·dah fkhoh·deet*

Is it spicy? **Это острое?** *eh·tah os·trah·yeh*

I'd like... **Я хотел** *m* **/хотела** *f* **бы...** *yah khah·tyel/ khah·tyeh·lah bih...*

More...please. **Можно ещё...пожалуйста.** *mozh·nah yee·shchoh...pah·zhahl·stah*

With/Without... **С/Без...** *s/byes...*

I can't have... **Мне нельзя есть...** *mnyeh neel'·zyah yest'...*

rare **с кровью** *s krov'·yoo*

medium **средне прожаренный** *sryed·nee prah·zhah·ree·niy*

well-done **хорошо прожаренный** *khah·rah·shoh prah·zhah·ree·niy*

It's to go [take away]. **Это с собой.** *eh·tah s sah·boy*

YOU MAY SEE...

НАЦЕНКА nah•tsen•kah	cover charge
КОМПЛЕКСНЫЙ МЕНЮ kom•plyeks•niy меню	fixed-price menu
МЕНЮ ДНЯ mee•nyoo dnyah	menu of the day
ОБСЛУЖИВАНИЕ (НЕ) ВКЛЮЧЕНО	service (not)
ahp•sloo•zhih•vah•nee•yeh (nee) fklyoo•chee•noh	included
БЛЮДО ДНЯ blyoo•dah dnyah	specials

Cooking Methods

baked	**печеный** pee•choh•niy	
boiled	**варёный** vah•ryoh•niy	
braised	**тушёный** too•shoh•niy	
breaded	**панированный** pah•nee•roh•vah•niy	
creamed	**со сливками** soh sleev•kah•mee	
diced	**нарезанный мелкими кубиками**	
	nah•ryeh•zah•niy myel•kee•mee koo•bee•kah•mee	
filleted	**филе** fee•lyeh	
fried	**жареный** zhah•ree•niy	
grilled	**жареный на** гриле zhah•ree•niy nah gree•lee	
poached	**отварной** aht•vahr•noy	
roasted	**запечёный** zah•pee•choh•nih	
sautéed	**соте** sah•teh	
smoked	**копчёный** kahp•choh•niy	
steamed	**паровой** pah•rah•voy	
stewed	**тушёный** too•shoh•niy	
stuffed	**фаршированный** fahr•shih•roh•vah•niy	

Dietary Requirements

I'm diabetic.	**Я диабетик.** *yah dee•ah•byeh•teek*
I'm lactose intolerant.	**У меня непереносимость лактозы.** *oo mee•nyah nee•pee•ree•nah•see•mahst' lahk•toh•zih*
I'm vegetarian.	**Я вегетарианец.** *yah vee•gee•tah•ree•ah•neets*
I'm vegan.	**Я вегетарианец.** *yah vee•gee•tah•ree•ah•neets*
I'm allergic to…	**У меня аллергия на…** *oo mee•nyah ah•leer•gee•yah nah…*
I can't eat…	**Мне нельзя есть…** *mnyeh neel'•zyah yest'…*
dairy	**молочные продукты** *mah•loch•nih•yeh prah•dook•tih*
gluten	**растительный белок** *rahs•tee•tyel'•niy bee•lok*
nuts	**орехи** *ah•ryeh•khee*
pork	**свинину** *svee•nee•noo*
shellfish	**раков** *rah•kahf*
spicy foods	**острую пищу** *os•troo•yoo pee•shchoo*
wheat	**пшеничную муку** *pshih•neech•noo•yoo moo•koo*
Is it halal/kosher?	**Это халяль/кошерное?** *eh•tah khah•lyahl'/kah•sher•nah•yeh*
Do you have…?	**У Вас есть…?** *oo vas est'*

skimmed milk	**обезжиренное молоко** oh•bez•_zhee_•reh•noh•ye _moh_•loh•_koh_
whole milk	**цельное молоко** _tsehl_'•noye moh•loh•_koh_
soya milk	**соевое молоко** _soh_•yeh•voh•ye moh•loh•_koh_

Dining with Children

Do you have children's portions?	**У вас есть детские порции?** oo vahs yest' _dyets_•kee•yeh _por_•tsih•ee
A highchair/child's seat, please.	**Высокий детский стульчик/Детское сидение, пожалуйста.** vih•_soh_•keey _dyets_•keey _stool_'•cheek/_dyets_•kah•yeh see•_dyeh_•nee•yeh pah•_zhahl_•stah
Where can I feed/ change the baby?	**Где мне покормить/переодеть ребёнка?** gdyeh mnyeh pah•kahr•_meet_'/pee•ree•ah•_dyet_' ree•_byon_•kah
Can you warm this?	**Вы можете подогреть это?** vih _moh_•zhih•tee pah•dah•_gryet_' _eh_•tah

For Traveling with Children, see page 136.

How to Complain

How much longer will our food be?	**Сколько ещё ждать?** _skol_'•kah ee•_shchoh_ zhdaht'
We can't wait any longer.	**Мы не можем больше ждать.** mih nee _moh_•zhem _bol_'•sheh zhdaht'
We're leaving.	**Мы уходим.** mih oo•_khoh_•deem
I didn't order this.	**Это не то, что я заказывал** m / **заказывала** f. _eh_•tah nee toh shtoh yah zah•_kah_•zih•vahl/zah•_kah_•zih•vah•lah
I ordered…	**Я просил** m /**просила** f… yah prah•_seel_/ prah•_see_•lah…

I can't eat this.	**Это невозможно есть.** *eh•tah nee•vahz•mozh•nah yest'*
This is too…	**Это слишком…** *eh•tah slee•shkam…*
cold/hot	**холодное/горячее** *khah•lod•nah•yeh/ gah•ryah•chee•yeh*
salty/spicy	**солёное/острое** *sah•lyoh•nah•yeh/os•trah•yeh*
tough/bland	**жёсткое/мягкое** *zhost•kah•yeh/myahkh•kah•yeh*
This isn't clean/ fresh.	**Это грязное/несвежее.** *eh•tah gryahz•nah•yeh/nee•svyeh•zhih•yeh*

Paying

The check [bill], please.	**Счёт, пожалуйста.** *shchot pah•zhahl•stah*
We'd like to pay separately.	**Мы будем платить отдельно.** *mih boo•deem plah•teet' ahd•dyel'•nah*
It's all together.	**Всё вместе.** *fsyoh vmyes•tee*
Is service included?	**Счёт включает обслуживание?** *shchot fklyoo•chah•eet ahp•sloo•zhih•vah•nee•yeh*
What's this amount for?	**А это за что?** *ah eh•tah zah shtoh*
I didn't have that.	**Я это не заказывал m /заказывала f.** *yah eh•tah nee zah•kah•zih•vahl/zah•kah•zih•vah•lah*
I had…	**У меня было…** *oo mee•nyah bih•lah…*
Can I pay by credit card?	**Можно платить кредитной карточкой?** *mozh•nah plah•teet' kree•deet•nie kahr•tahch•kie*
Can I have an itemized bill/a receipt?	**Можно детальный счёт/чек?** *mozh•nah dee•tahl'•niy shchot/chek*
That was a very good meal.	**Всё было очень вкусно.** *fsyoh bih•lah oh•cheen' fkoos•nah*
I've already paid.	**Я уже оплатил.** *yah oo•zheh oplah•teel*

Meals & Cooking

The country's geographic, climatic and ethnic variety is reflected in a rich and varied cuisine. Russians have a sweet tooth and are very fond of desserts and pastries, as well as their excellent ice cream. Eating plays an important part in Russian social life, and it is while dining that you'll find Russians at their most hospitable. Don't forget to wish your table companions a hearty appetite: **Приятного аппетита!** pree·*yaht*·nah·vah ah·pee·*tee*·tah. At the end of a meal Russians will often thank those who dined with them. The proper response is **На здоровье!** nah zdah·*rov'*·yeh.

Breakfast

boiled egg	**вареное яйцо**	vah·*ryoh*·nah·yeh yie·*tsoh*
bread	**хлеб**	khlyep
fried eggs	**яичница**	yah·*eesh*·nee·tsah
fruit juice	**фруктовый сок**	frook·*toh*·viy sok
grapefruit juice	**грейпфрутовый сок**	greyp·*froo*·tah·viy sok
ham and eggs	**яичница с ветчиной**	yah·*eesh*·nee·tsah s veet·chee·*noy*
honey	**мёд**	myot
jam	**джем**	dzhem
oatmeal	**овсянка**	ahf·*syahn*·kah
orange juice	**апельсиновый сок**	ah·peel'·*see*·nah·viy sok
scrambled eggs	**яичница-болтунья**	yah·*eesh*·nee·tsah bahl·*toon'*·yah
toast	**тост**	tost
yogurt	**йогурт**	yoh·*goort*

Appetizers

assorted meat	**ассорти мясное**	*ah·sahr·tee myahs·noh·yeh*
assorted fish	**ассорти рыбное**	*ah·sahr·tee rihb·nah·yeh*
caviar	**икра**	*eek·rah*
ham	**ветчина**	*veet·chee·nah*
herring	**сельдь**	*syel't'*
mushrooms	**грибы**	*gree·bih*
hot pancake filled with cheese (Georgian dish)	**хачапури**	*khah·chah·poo·ree*
pancakes...	**блины...**	*blee·nih...*
with caviar	**с икрой**	*s eek·roy*
with jam	**с вареньем**	*s vah·ryen'·yem*
with salmon	**с сёмгой**	*s syom·gie*
with sheep's cheese	**с брынзой**	*s brihn·zie*
with sour cream	**со сметаной**	*sah smee·tah·nie*
paté (mostly liver)	**паштет**	*pahsh·tyet*
pie	**пирог**	*pee·rok*
sausage	**колбаса**	*kahl·bah·sah*
shrimp [prawns]	**креветки**	*kree·vyet·kee*
spiced herring	**кильки**	*keel'·kee*
sturgeon	**осетрина**	*ah·seet·ree·nah*

Appetizers are often divided into hot and cold. If you want to indicate that a particular item will be an appetizer, just indicate that it is **На закуску** *nah zah·koos·koo*.

Блины *blee·nih* (pancakes) are often made with yeast and stuffed with different fillings. Smaller and thicker than western pancakes, they are usually served with sour cream (**сметана** *smee·tah·nah*) and/or butter (**масло** *mahs·lah*).

Soup

beet soup (borsch)	**борщ** *borshch*
beet soup with extra bacon	**московский** *mahs·kof·skeey*
chicken soup	**суп из курицы** *soop ees koo·ree·tsih*
cold beet soup	**холодник** *khah·lahd·neek*
cold soup made from kvass, cucumbers, eggs, onions and sour cream	**окрошка** *ah·krosh·kah*
fish soup	**уха** *oo·khah*
spicy Georgian soup made with mutton and rice	**харчо** *khahr·choh*
mushroom soup	**грибной суп** *greeb·noy soop*
pea soup	**гороховый суп** *gah·roh·khah·viy soop*
potato soup	**картофельный** *kahr·toh·feel'·niy soop*
soup made with salted cucumbers and olives	**солянка** *sah·lyahn·kah*
thick soup made with cabbage or sauerkraut	**щи** *shchee*

Uzbek mutton soup with bacon and tomatoes	**шурпа** shoor•*pah*
Ukrainian beet soup with garlic	**украинский борщ** oo•krah•*een*•skeey borshch

Fish & Seafood

carp	**карп** kahrp
crab	**краб** krahp
halibut	**палтус** *pahl*•toos
herring	**сельдь** syel't'
lobster	**омар** ah•*mahr*
mackerel	**макрель** mahk•*ryel'*
oysters	**устрицы** *oos*•tree•tsih
pike perch fried in butter/poached	**судак жареный в тесте/отварной** soo•*dahk* zhah•ree•niy f *tyes*•tee/aht•vahr•*noy*
shrimp [prawns]	**креветки** kree•*vyet*•kee
salmon	**сёмга** *syom*•gah
sprats	**шпроты** *shproh*•tih
trout	**форель** fah•*ryel'*
tuna	**тунец** too•*nyets*
sturgeon...	**осетрина...** ah•seet•*ree*•nah...
served with a white sauce	**под белым соусом** pahd *byeh*•lihm *soh*•oo•sahm
poached	**по-русски** pah *roos*•kee
steamed	**паровая** pah•rah•*vah*•yah

Meat & Poultry

beef	**говядина** gah•*vyah*•dee•nah
beef stroganoff	**бефстроганов** beef•*stroh*•gah•nahf
braised beef with aromatic vegetables	**говядина тушёная** gah•*vyah*•dee•nah too•*shoh*•nah•yah

cabbage stuffed with meat and rice	**голубцы** _gah·loop·tsih_
chicken	**курица** _koo·ree·tsah_
chopped meat in a savory sauce	**азу** _ah·zoo_
duck	**утка** _oot·kah_
duck roasted with apples	**утка тушёная с яблоками** _oot·kah too·shoh·nah·yah s yahb·lah·kah·mee_
goose	**гусь** _goos'_
lamb	**молодая баранина** _mah·lah·dah·yah bah·rah·nee·nah_
lamb kebabs	**шашлык** _shahsh·lihk_
liver	**печёнка** _pee·chon·kah_
pork	**свинина** _svee·nee·nah_
rabbit	**кролик** _kroh·leek_
stuffed breast of chicken	**котлеты по-киевски** _kaht·lyeh·tih pah kee·eef·skee_
stuffed pasta	**пельмени** _peel'·myeh·nee_
turkey	**индейка** _een·dyey·kah_
veal	**телятина** _tee·lyah·tee·na_

Vegetables & Staples

beans	**фасоль** _fah·sol'_
beet	**свёкла** _svyok·lah_
bread	**хлеб** _khlyep_
cabbage	**капуста** _kah·poos·tah_
carrots	**морковь** _mahr·kof'_
cauliflower	**цветная капуста** _tsveet·nah·yah kah·poos·tah_
cucumber	**огурец** _ah·goo·ryets_
eggplant [aubergine]	**баклажан** _bahk·lah·zhahn_
mushrooms	**грибы** _greeb·ih_
noodles	**лапша** _lahp·shah_

onion	**лук** *look*	
pasta	**макароны** *mah·kah·<u>roh</u>·nih*	
stuffed pasta	**пельмени** *peel'·<u>myeh</u>·nee*	
small pastries with various sweet or savoury fillings	**пирожки** *pee·rahsh·<u>kee</u>*	
peas	**горох** *gah·<u>rokh</u>*	
pepper	**перец** *<u>pyeh</u>·reets*	
porridge	**каша** *<u>kah</u>·shah*	
potato	**картофель** *kahr·<u>toh</u>·feel'*	
rice	**рис** *rees*	
spaghetti	**спагетти** *spah·<u>gyeh</u>·tee*	
sweet corn	**сладкая кукуруза** *<u>slaht</u>·kah·yah koo·koo·<u>roo</u>·zah*	
tomato	**помидор** *pah·mee·<u>dor</u>*	
zucchini [courgette]	**молодой кабачок** *mah·lah·<u>doy</u> kah·bah·<u>chok</u>*	

Fruit

apple	**яблоко** *<u>yahb</u>·lah·kah*
apricot	**абрикос** *ab·ree·<u>kos</u>*
banana	**банан** *bah·<u>nahn</u>*
cherry	**черешня** *chee·<u>ryesh</u>·nyah*
currants	**смородина** *smah·<u>roh</u>·dee·nah*
gooseberry	**крыжовник** *krih·<u>zhov</u>·neek*
grapes	**виноград** *vee·nah·<u>graht</u>*
lemon	**лимон** *lee·<u>mon</u>*
melon	**дыня** *<u>dih</u>·nyah*
orange	**апельсин** *ah·peel'·<u>seen</u>*
peach	**персик** *<u>pyer</u>·seek*
pear	**груша** *<u>groo</u>·shah*
pineapple	**ананас** *ah·nah·<u>nahs</u>*
plum	**слива** *<u>slee</u>·vah*

| strawberry | **клубника** *kloob·nee·kah* |
| watermelon | **арбуз** *ahr·boos* |

Cheese

baked sour milk, often served chilled	**ряженка** *ryah·zhihn·kah*
...cheese	**сыр...** *sihr...*
Latvian	**латвийский** *laht·veey·skeey*
Poshekhonsky	**пошехонский** *pah·shih·khon·skeey*
Russian	**российский** *rah·seey·skeey*
sharp ewe's milk cheese	**брынза** *brihn·zah*
fresh white cheese or spread	**сырок** *sih·rok*
white unsalted cheese similar to cottage cheese	**творог** *tvah·rok*

Dessert

apple baked in pastry	**яблоко в тесте** *yahb·lah·kah f tyes·tee*
cottage cheese pastry	**ватрушка** *vah·troosh·kah*
Ukrainian dumplings filled with white cheese	**вареники** *vah·ryeh·nee·kee*
fruit compote	**компот** *kahm·pot*
fruit jelly-like drink	**кисель** *kee·syel'*
...ice cream	**...мороженое** *...mah·roh·zhih·nah·yeh*
chocolate	**шоколадное** *shah·kah·lad·nah·yeh*
fruit	**фруктовое** *frook·toh·vah·yeh*
vanilla	**ванильное** *vah·neel'·nah·yeh*

pie...	**пирог...** _pee·rok_...
with cottage cheese	**с творогом** s tvah·rah·_gom_
with fruit	**с фруктами** s _frook_·tah·mee
with lemon	**с лимоном** s lee·_moh_·nahm
rice pudding	**рисовый пудинг** _ree_·sah·viy _poo_·deenk
small apple pancakes	**оладьи с яблоками** ah·_lahd'_·yee s _yahb_·lah·kah·mee
small pancakes served with jam	**блинчики с вареньем** _bleen_·chee·kee s vah·_ryen'_·yem
sponge roll	**рулет** roo·_lyet_
whipped cream	**взбитые сливки** vzbee·tih·yeh _sleef_·kee
yeast cake saturated in liquor	**ромовая баба** _roh_·mah·vah·yah _bah_·bah
white cheese fritters served with sour cream	**сырники со сметаной** _sihr_·nee·kee sah smee·_tah_·nie

Sauces & Condiments

mustard	**горчица** gahr·_chee_·tsah
pepper	**перец** _pyeh_·reets
salt	**соль** sol'
sugar	**сахар** _sah_·khahr
ketchup	**кетчуп** _Keht_·choop

At the Market

Where are the trolleys/baskets?	**Где здесь тележки/корзинки?** gdyeh zdyes' tee·_lyesh_·kee/kahr·_zeen_·kee
Where is...?	**Где...?** gdyeh...
I'd like some of that/those.	**Дайте, пожалуйста, вон то/те.** _die_·tee pah·_zhahl_·stah von toh/tyeh
Can I taste it?	**Можно это попробовать?** _mozh_·nah _eh_·tah pah·_proh_·bah·vaht'

I'd like...	**Дайте, пожалуйста,...** _die_·tee pah·_zhahl_·stah...
a kilo/half-kilo of...	**кило/полкило...** kee·_loh_/_pol_·kee·_loh_...
a liter/half-liter of...	**литр/пол-литра...** leetr/pol·_leet_·rah...
a piece of...	**кусочек...** koo·_soh_·cheek...
a slice of...	**ломтик...** _lom_·teek...
More./Less.	**Побольше./Поменьше.** pah·_bol_'·sheh/ pah·_myen_'·sheh
How much?	**Сколько?** _skol_'·kah
Where do I pay?	**Куда платить?** koo·_dah_ plah·_teet_'
A bag, please.	**Пакет, пожалуйста.** pah·_kyet_ pah·_zhahl_·stah
I'm being helped.	**Меня уже обслуживают.** mee·_nyah_ oo·_zheh_ ahp·_sloo_·zhih·vah·yoot

For Conversion Tables, see page 163.

Measurements in Russia are metric — and that applies to the weight of food too. If you tend to think in pounds and ounces, it's worth brushing up on what the metric equivalent is before you go shopping for fruit and veg in markets and supermarkets. Five hundred grams, or half a kilo, is a common quantity to order, and that converts to just over a pound (17.65 ounces, to be precise).

YOU MAY HEAR...

Я вас слушаю. yah vahs _sloo_·shah·yoo	Can I help you?
Что вы хотите? shtoh vih khah·_tee_·tee	What would you like?
Что ещё? shtoh ee·_shchoh_	Anything else?
Это...рублей. _eh_·tah...roob·_lyey_	That's...rubles.

Today, Russia's cities feature supermarkets very much like those in western Europe and the United States. The business and tourism districts of Moscow and St. Petersburg now feature small stores very much like the American convenience store, where you can buy a drink and snack.

YOU MAY SEE...

ГОДЕН ДО... _goh·deen dah..._	best if used by...
КАЛОРИЙ _kah·loh·reey_	calories
ОБЕЗЖИРЕННЫЙ _ah·beezh·zhih·ree·niy_	fat free
ХРАНИТЬ В ХОЛОДИЛЬНИКЕ _khrah·neet' f khah·lah·deel'·nee·kee_	keep refrigerated
МОЖЕТ СОДЕРЖАТЬ СЛЕДЫ... _moh·zhiht sah·deer·zhaht' slee·dih..._	may contain traces of...
РЕАЛИЗОВАТЬ ДО... _ree·ah·lee·zah·vaht' dah..._	sell by...
ВЕГЕТАРИАНСКОЕ ПИТАНИЕ _vee·gee·tah·ree·ahn·skah·yeh pee·tah·nee·yeh_	suitable for vegetarians

In the Kitchen

bottle opener	**открывалка** aht·krih·<u>vahl</u>·kah
bowl	**миска** <u>mees</u>·kah
can opener	**консервный нож** kahn·<u>syerv</u>·niy nosh
corkscrew	**штопор** <u>shtoh</u>·pahr
cup	**чашка** <u>chahsh</u>·kah
fork	**вилка** <u>veel</u>·kah
frying pan	**сковорода** skah·vah·rah·<u>dah</u>
glass	**стакан** stah·<u>kahn</u>
knives	**ножи** nah·<u>zhih</u>
measuring cup/	**мерная чашка/ложка** <u>myer</u>·nah·yah
spoon	<u>chahsh</u>·kah/<u>losh</u>·kah
napkin	**бумажные салфетки** boo·<u>mahzh</u>·nih·yeh
	sahl·<u>fyet</u>·kee
plate	**тарелка** tah·<u>ryel</u>·kah
pot	**высокая кастрюля** vih·<u>soh</u>·kah·yah
	kahs·<u>tryoo</u>lyah
saucepan	**кастрюля** kahs·<u>tryoo</u>·lyah
spatula	**лопаточка** lah·<u>pah</u>·tahch·kah
spoons	**ложки** <u>losh</u>·kee

Drinks

ESSENTIAL

May I see the wine list/drink menu?	**Можно посмотреть карту вин/меню напитков?** <u>mozh</u>·nah pah·smah·<u>tryet'</u> <u>kahr</u>·too veen/mee·<u>nyoo</u> nah·<u>peet</u>·kahf
What do you recommend?	**Что вы порекомендуете?** shtoh vih pah·ree·kah·meen·<u>doo</u>·ee·tee

I'd like a bottle/ glass of red/white wine.	**Я хотел** *m* **/хотела** *f* **бы бутылку/бокал красного/белого вина.** *yah khah•tyel/ khah•tyeh•lah bih boo•tihl•koo/bah•kahl krahs•nah•vah/byeh•lah•vah vee•nah*
The house wine, please.	**Вино ресторана, пожалуйста.** *vee•noh ree•stah•rah•nah pah•zhahl•stah*
Another bottle/ glass, please.	**Ещё одну бутылку/один бокал, пожалуйста.** *yee•shchoh ahd•noo boo•tihl•koo/ah•deen bah•kahl pah•zhahl•stah*
I'd like a local beer.	**Я хотел** *m* **/хотела** *f* **бы местного пива.** *yah khah•tyel/khah•tyeh•lah bih myes•nah•vah pee•vah*
Let me buy you a drink.	**Позвольте вам предложить что-нибудь выпить.** *pahz•vol'•tee vahm preed•lah•zhiht' shtoh•nee•boot' vih•peet'*
Cheers!	**За ваше здоровье!** *za vah•sheh zdah•rov'•yeh*
A coffee/tea, please.	**Кофе/Чай, пожалуйста.** *koh•fye/chie pah•zhahl•stah*
Black.	**Чёрный.** *chor•niy*
With…	**С…** *s…*
milk	**молоком** *mah•lah•kom*
sugar	**сахаром** *sah•khah•rahm*
artificial sweetener	**заменителем сахара** *zah•mee•nee•tee•lyem sah•khah•rah*
…, please.	**…, пожалуйста.** *…pah•zhahl•stah*
Juice	**Сок** *sok*
Soda	**Содовую** *soh•dah•voo•yoo*
Sparkling/Still water	**Воду с газом/без газа** *voh•doo z gah•zahm/beez gah•zah*
Is the tap water safe to drink?	**Безопасно ли пить воду из крана?** *bee•zah•pahs•nah lee peet' voh•doo ees krah•nah*

Non-alcoholic Drinks

apple/orange juice	**яблочный/апельсиновый сок**
	yahb•lahch•niy/ah•peel'•see•nah•viy sok
coffee...	**кофе...** _koh•fyeh..._
black	**чёрный** _chor•niy_
decaffeinated	**без кафеина** _bees kah•fee•ee•nah_
with milk	**с молоком** _s mah•lah•kom_
iced tea	**чай со льдом** _chie sah l'dom_
kvass, soft drink made from yeast	**квас** _kvahss_
lemonade	**лимонад** _lee•mah•naht_
milk	**молоко** _mah•lah•koh_
milk shake	**молочный коктейль** _mah•loch•niy kahk•teyl'_
mineral water	**минеральная вода** _mee•nee•rahl'•nah•yah vah•dah_
soda	**содовая** _soh•dah•vah•yah_
tea	**чай** _chie_
water	**вода** _vah•dah_

Stores and kiosks in large towns and cities are full of imported and locally produced soft drinks, fruit juice and mineral water. Ice cream cafes offer something called **коктейль** _kahk•teyl'_ (cocktail), a non-alcoholic drink made from fruit juice or lemonade, to which ice cream and sometimes whipped cream is added.

Квас _kvahs_ is a popular traditional Russian soft drink and a good thirst quencher in the summer. Kvass, which looks like beer, is made from black bread and yeast.

YOU MAY HEAR...

Вам принести что-нибудь попить? *vahm pree·nees·tee shtoh·nee·boot' pah·peet'* — Can I get you a drink?

С молоком/сахаром? *s mah·lah·kom/ sah·khah·rahm* — With milk/sugar?

Воду с газом или без газа? *voh·doo z gah·zahm ee·lee beez gah·zah* — Sparkling or still water?

Aperitifs, Cocktails & Liqueurs

brandy (cognac)	**коньяк**	*kahn'·yahk*
gin	**джин**	*dzhihn*
liqueur	**ликёр**	*lee·kyor*
rum	**ром**	*rom*
sherry	**херес**	*khyeh·rees*
vodka	**водка**	*vot·kah*
whisky	**виски**	*vees·kee*

Russian vodka is world famous. Kremlevskaya, Stolichnaya, Moskovskaya and some other brands are well-known internationally. Make sure you buy alcohol from a licensed seller, in order to avoid purchasing a low-quality counterfeit.

Beer

Moscow beer	**московское** *mahs·kof·skah·ye*
Russian beer	**жигулёвское** *zhih·goo·lyof·skah·ye*
Riga beer	**рижское** *reesh·skah·yeh*
dark/light	**темное/светлое** *tyom·noh·ye/sveht·loye*
local/imported	**местное/импортное** *mehst·noh·ye/ eem·port·noye*
bottled/draft	**в бутылках/разливное** *v boo·tihl·kahkh/ rahz·leev·noh·eh*
non-alcoholic	**безалкогольное** *behz·ahl·koh·gohl' noh·eh*

Wine

champagne	**шампанское** *sham·pahn·sko·ye*
dry	**сухое** *soo·khoh·yeh*
sparkling wine (like champagne)	**игристое** *eeg·rees·tah·yeh*
red wine	**красное вино** *krahs·nah·yeh vee·noh*
rosé wine	**розовое вино** *roh·zah·vah·yeh vee·noh*
sweet	**сладкое** *slaht·kah·yeh*
white wine	**белое вино** *byeh·lah·yeh vee·noh*

International brands of wine are available throughout Russia. It
is sometimes easier to find French, Californian and Italian wines
than to find old favorites from Georgia.
Russian sparkling wine is a popular drink. Dry, it can accompany almost
any meal; sweet, it is usually enjoyed after meals or with dessert.
Quality and price vary for wine with the same label. In general, it is
better to buy alcohol in a liquor store than from a kiosk or street vendor.

On the Menu

aperitif	**аперитив** *ah·pee·ree·teef*
apple	**яблоко** *yahb·lah·kah*
apple baked in pastry	**яблоко в тесте** *yahb·lah·kah f tyes·tee*
apricot	**абрикос** *ahb·ree·kos*
artificial sweetener	**заменитель сахара** *zah·mee·nee·teel' sah·khah·rah*
chopped meat in a savory sauce	**азу** *ah·zoo*

bacon	**грудинка** *groo·deen·kah*
banana	**банан** *bah·nahn*
beans	**фасоль** *fah·sol'*
beef stroganoff	**бефстроганов** *beef·stroh·gah·nahf*
beef	**говядина** *gah·vyah·dee·nah*
beer	**пиво** *pee·vah*
beet [beetroot]	**свёкла** *svyok·lah*
beet soup (borsch)	**борщ** *borshch*
braised beef with aromatic vegetables	**говядина тушёная с кореньями** *gah·vyah·dee·nah too·shoh·nah·yah s kah·ryen'·yah·mee*
brandy	**бренди** *bren·dee*
bread	**хлеб** *khlyep*
butter	**масло** *mahs·lah*
cabbage	**капуста** *kah·poos·tah*
cake (large)	**торт** *tort*
cake (small)	**пирожное** *pee·rozh·nah·yeh*
carrots	**морковь** *mahr·kof'*
caviar	**икра** *eek·rah*
cereal	**каша** *kah·shah*
champagne	**шампанское** *shahm·pahn·skah·yeh*
cheese	**сыр** *sihr*
cherry	**вишня** *veesh·nyah*
stuffed breast of chicken	**котлеты по-киевски** *kaht·lyeh·tih pah kee·eef·skee*
chicken soup	**суп из курицы** *soop ees koo·ree·tsih*
chicken	**курица** *koo·ree·tsah*
chocolate	**шоколад** *shah·kah·laht*
chop	**отбивная** *aht·beev·nah·yah*
chopped meat	**рубленое мясо** *roob·lee·nah·yeh myah·sah*
coffee	**кофе** *koh·fyeh*

cold cuts [charcuterie]	**мясная закуска** myahs-*nah*-yah zah-*koos*-kah
cold soup made from kvass, cucumbers, eggs, onions and sour cream	**окрошка** ah-*krosh*-kah
cornmeal	**кукурузная мука** koo-koo-*rooz*-nah-yah moo-*kah*
cottage cheese tart	**ватрушка** vaht-*roosh*-kah
cottage cheese	**творог** tvah-*rok*
crab	**краб** krahp
crabmeat	**мясо краба** *myah*-sah *krah*-bah
cracker	**крекер** *kryeh*-kyer
cream	**сливки** *sleef*-kee
cucumber	**огурец** ah-goo-*ryets*
cumin	**тмин римский** tmeen *reem*-skeey
currants	**смородина** smah-*roh*-dee-nah
duck	**утка** *oot*-kah
dumpling	**клёцка** *klyots*-kah
egg	**яйцо** *yie*-tsoh
eggplant [aubergine]	**баклажан** bahk-lah-*zhahn*
fish soup	**уха** oo-*khah*
fish	**рыба** *rih*-bah
fresh white cheese	**сырок** sih-*rok*
fritter	**оладья** ah-*lahd'*-yah
fruit compote	**компот** kahm-*pot*
fruit jelly	**кисель** kee-*syel'*
fruit	**фрукты** *frook*-tih
garlic sauce	**чесночный соус** chees-*noch*-niy *soh*-oos
garlic	**чеснок** chees-*nok*

gin	**джин** *dzhihn*
ginger	**имбирь** *eem•beer'*
goat cheese	**сыр из козьего молока** *sihr ees koz'•yeh•vah mah•lah•kah*
goat	**козлятина** *kahz•lyah•tee•nah*
cabbage stuffed with rice and meat	**голубцы** *gah•loop•tsih*
goose	**гусь** *goos'*
gooseberry	**крыжовник** *krih•zhov•neek*
grapefruit	**грейпфрут** *greyp•froot*
grapefruit juice	**сок из грейпфрута** *sok eez greyp•froo•tah*
grapes	**виноград** *vee•nahg•raht*
halibut	**палтус** *pahl•toos*
ham	**ветчина** *veet•chee•nah*
hamburger	**гамбургер** *gahm•boor•geer*
herbs	**травы** *trah•vih*
herring	**сельдь** *syel't'*
honey	**мёд** *myot*
ice (cube)	**кубик льда** *koo•beek l'dah*
ice cream	**мороженое** *mah•roh•zhih•nah•yeh*
jam	**варенье** *vah•ryen'•yeh*
jelly	**желе** *zhih•lyeh*
juice	**фруктовый сок** *frook•toh•viy sok*
kidney	**почка** *poch•kah*
lamb	**молодая баранина** *mah•lah•dah•yah bah•rah•nee•nah*
lamb kebabs	**шашлык** *shahsh•lihk*
lemon	**лимон** *lee•mon*
lemonade	**лимонад** *lee•mah•naht*
liqueur	**ликёр** *lee•kyor*
liver	**печень** *pyeh•cheen'*

lobster	**омар**	*ah-mahr*
mackerel	**макрель**	*mahk-ryel'*
meat	**мясо**	*myah-sah*
melon	**дыня**	*dih-nyah*
milk shake	**молочный коктейль**	*mah-loch-niy kahk-teyl'*
milk	**молоко**	*mah-lah-koh*
mineral water	**минеральная вода**	*mee-nee-rahl'-nah-yah vah-dah*

mushroom	**гриб**	*greep*
mustard	**горчица**	*gahr-chee-tsah*
mutton	**баранина**	*bah-rah-nee-nah*
noodles	**лапша**	*lahp-shah*
nuts	**орехи**	*ah-ryeh-khee*
olive	**оливка**	*ah-leef-kah*
onions	**лук**	*look*
orange juice	**апельсиновый сок**	*ah-peel'-see-nah-viy sok*
orange liqueur	**апельсиновый ликёр**	*ah-peel'-see-nah-viy lee-kyor*
orange	**апельсин**	*ah-peel'-seen*
oyster	**устрица**	*oost-ree-tsah*
pancakes	**блины**	*blee-nih*
pasta	**макароны**	*mah-kah-roh-nih*
pastry	**кондитерские изделия**	*kahn-dee-teer-skee-yeh eez-dyeh-lee-yah*
pâté	**паштет**	*pahsh-tyet*
peach	**персик**	*pyer-seek*
peanut	**арахис**	*ah-rah-khees*
pear	**груша**	*groo-shah*
peas	**горошек**	*gah-roh-shek*
pepper	**перец**	*pyeh-reets*

pie or tart served with a variety of fruit or cheese fillings	**пирог** *pee·rok*
pike perch fried in batter	**судак жареный в тесте** *soo·dahk zhah·ree·niy f tyes·tee*
pike perch poached	**судак отварной** *soo·dahk aht·vahr·noy*
pineapple	**ананас** *ah·nah·nahs*
plum	**слива** *slee·vah*
pork	**свинина** *svee·nee·nah*
potato chips [crisps]	**чипсы** *cheep·sih*
potatoes	**картофель** *kahr·toh·feel'*
rabbit	**кролик** *kroh·leek*
red currant	**красная смородина** *krahs·nah·yah smah·roh·dee·nah*
rice pudding	**рисовый пудинг** *ree·sah·viy poo·deenk*
rice	**рис** *rees*
roast beef	**ростбиф** *rost·beef*
roast duck with apples	**утка тушёная с яблоками** *oot·kah too·shoh·nah·yah s yahb·lah·kah·mee*
roast pork with plums	**жаркое из свинины с черносливом** *zhahr·koh·yeh ees svee·nee·nih s cheer·nah·slee·vahm*
roast	**жаркое** *zhahr·koh·yeh*
roll	**булочка** *boo·lahch·kah*
rum	**ром** *rom*
Russian soft drink	**квас** *kvahs*
salmon	**лосось** *lah·sos'*
salt	**соль** *sol'*
sauce	**соус** *soh·oos*
sausage	**колбаса** *kahl·bah·sah*

shellfish	**моллюски**	mah-_lyoos_-kee
sherry	**херес**	_kheh_-rees
shrimp	**креветка**	kree-_vyet_-kah
small apple pancakes	**оладьи с яблоками**	ah-_lahd'_-yee s _yahb_-lah-kah-mee
small pancakes with jam	**блинчики с вареньем**	_bleen_-chee-kee s vah-_ryen'_-yem
snack	**лёгкая закуска**	_lyokh_-kah-yah zah-_koos_-kah
soup	**суп**	soop
sour cream	**сметана**	smee-_tah_-nah
spaghetti	**спагетти**	spah-_gyeh_-tee
spices	**приправы**	pree-_prah_-vih
spicy Georgian soup made with mutton and rice	**харчо**	khahr-_choh_
spirits	**спиртные напитки**	speert-_nih_-yeh nah-_peet_-kee
sponge roll	**рулет**	roo-_lyet_
steak	**бифштекс**	beef-_shteks_
strawberries	**клубника**	kloob-_nee_-kah
stuffed pasta	**пельмени**	peel'-_myeh_-nee
sturgeon poached	**осетрина по-русски**	ah-seet-_ree_-nah pah _roos_-kee
sturgeon served with a white sauce	**осетрина под белым соусом**	ah-seet-_ree_-nah pahd _byeh_-lihm _soh_-oo-sahm
sturgeon steamed	**осетрина паровая**	ah-seet-_ree_-nah pah-rah-_vah_-yah
sugar	**сахар**	_sah_-khahr
sweet corn	**сладкая кукуруза**	_slaht_-kah-yah koo-koo-_roo_-zah
syrup	**сироп**	see-_rop_
tea	**чай**	chie

thick soup made with cabbage or sauerkraut	**щи** *shchee*
toast	**тост** *tost*
tomato	**помидор** *pah·mee·<u>dor</u>*
trout	**форель** *fah·<u>ryel'</u>*
tuna	**тунец** *too·<u>nyets</u>*
turkey	**индейка** *een·<u>dyey</u>·kah*
Uzbek soup made with mutton, bacon and tomato	**шурпа** *shoor·<u>pah</u>*
vanilla	**ваниль** *vah·<u>neel'</u>*
veal	**телятина** *tee·<u>lyah</u>·tee·nah*
vegetables	**овощи** *<u>oh</u>·vah·shchee*
vodka	**водка** *<u>vot</u>·kah*
water	**вода** *vah·<u>dah</u>*
watermelon	**арбуз** *arh·<u>boos</u>*
wheat	**пшеница** *pshih·<u>nee</u>·tsah*
whipped cream	**взбитые сливки** *vzbee·tih·yeh <u>sleef</u>·kee*
whisky	**виски** *<u>vees</u>·kee*
wine	**вино** *vee·<u>noh</u>*
yeast cake saturated in liquor	**ромовая баба** *<u>roh</u>·mah·vah·yah <u>bah</u>·bah*
yogurt	**йогурт** *<u>yoh</u>·goort*
zucchini [courgette]	**цуккини** *tsoo·<u>kee</u>·nee*

People

Conversation

ESSENTIAL

Hello./Hi!	**Здравствуйте./Привет!** <u>zdrah</u>·stvooy·tee/ pree·<u>vyet</u>
How are you?	**Как дела?** kahk dee·<u>lah</u>
Fine, thanks.	**Спасибо, хорошо.** spah·<u>see</u>·bah khah·rah·<u>shoh</u>
Excuse me!	**Извините!** eez·vee·<u>nee</u>·tee
Do you speak English?	**Вы говорите по-английски?** vih gah·vah·<u>ree</u>·tee pah ahn·<u>gleey</u>·skee
What's your name?	**Как Вас зовут?** kahk vahz zah·<u>voot</u>
My name is…	**Меня зовут…** mee·<u>nyah</u> zah·<u>voot</u>…
Pleased to meet you.	**Очень приятно.** <u>oh</u>·cheen' pree·<u>yaht</u>·nah
Where are you from?	**Откуда вы приехали?** aht·<u>koo</u>·dah vih pree·<u>yeh</u>·khah·lee
I'm from the U.S./U.K.	**Я из США/Великобритании.** yah ees seh sheh <u>ah</u>/vee·lee·kah·bree·<u>tah</u>·nee·ee
What do you do?	**Ваша профессия?** <u>vah</u>·shah prah·<u>fyeh</u>·see·yah
I work for…	**Я работаю в…** yah rah·<u>boh</u>·tah·yoo v…
I'm a student.	**Я студент.** yah stoo·<u>dyehnt</u>
I'm retired.	**Я на пенсии.** yah nah <u>pyehn</u>·see·ee
Do you like…?	**Вы любите…?** vih <u>lyoo</u>·bee·tee…
Goodbye.	**До свидания.** dah svee·<u>dah</u>·nee·yah
See you later.	**Увидимся.** oo·<u>vee</u>·deem·syah

It is polite to address people you know by their first name and patronymic, derived from the father's name. So, Nikolay, whose father's name is Ivan, would be called Nikolay Ivanovich; Natalia, whose father's name is Alexander, would be called Natalia Alexandrovna.

Like many other languages, Russian has two forms of the pronoun you: the informal (singular) **ты** *tih* and the formal (plural) **вы** *vih*. **Ты** is used between members of the same family, close friends and to address young children; **вы** *vih* is the polite form of address when you are talking to a person you do not know well or who is older or senior to you. When you are addressing more than one person, **вы** must always be used.

The pre-revolutionary **господин** *gahs·pah·deen* (Mr.) and **госпожа** *gahs·pah·zhah* (Mrs. or Miss) has re-entered usage in Russia.

Language Difficulties

Do you speak English?	**Вы говорите по-английски?** *vih gah·vah·ree·tee pah ahn·gleey·skee*
Does anyone here speak English?	**Кто-нибудь говорит по-английски?** *ktoh nee·bood' goh·voh·reet poh ahn·gleey·skee*
I don't speak Russian.	**Я не говорю по-русски.** *yah nyeh gah·vah·ryoo pah·roos·kee*
I don't speak much Russian.	**Я плохо говорю по-русски.** *yah ploh·khah gah·vah·ryoo pah·roos·kee*
Speak slowly, please.	**Говорите медленнее, пожалуйста.** *gah·vah·ree·tee myed·lee·nee·yeh pah·zhahl·stah*
Repeat that, please.	**Повторите, пожалуйста.** *pahf·tah·ree·tee pah·zhahl·stah*

Excuse me?	**Простите?** *prah·stee·tee*
What was that?	**Что такое?** *shtoh tah·koh·yeh*
Can you spell it?	**Вы можете это написать?** *vih moh·zheh·teh eh·toh nah·pee·saht'*
Write it down, please.	**Напишите, пожалуйста.** *nah·pee·shih·tee pah·zhahl·stah*
Translate this for me, please.	**Переведите мне это, пожалуйста.** *pee·ree·vee·dee·tee mnyeh eh·tah pah·zhahl·stah*
What does this/that mean?	**Что это/то значит?** *shtoh eh·tah/toh znah·cheet*
I (don't) understand.	**Я (не) понимаю.** *yah (nee) pah·nee·mah·yoo*
Do you understand?	**Вы понимаете?** *vih pah·nee·mah·ee·tee*

YOU MAY HEAR...

Я плохо говорю по-английски. *yah ploh·khah gah·vah·ryoo pah·ahn·gleey·skee*	I speak only a little English.
Я не говорю по-английски. *yah nee gah·vah·ryoo pah·ahn·gleey·skee*	I don't speak English.

Making Friends

Hello./Hi!	**Здравствуйте./Привет!** *zdrah·stvooy·tee/pree·vyet*
Good morning.	**Доброе утро.** *doh·brah·yeh oot·rah*
Good afternoon.	**Добрый день.** *doh·briy dyen'*
Good evening.	**Добрый вечер.** *doh·briy vyeh·cheer*
My name is...	**Меня зовут...** *mee·nyah zah·voot...*
What's your name?	**Как Вас зовут?** *kahk vahz zah·voot*
I'd like to introduce you to...	**Хочу познакомить Вас с...** *khah·choo pah·znah·koh·meet' vahs s...*

Nice to meet you.	**Очень приятно.** _oh_·cheen' pree·_yaht_·nah
How are you?	**Как дела?** kahk dee·_lah_
Fine, thanks.	**Спасибо, хорошо.** spah·_see_·bah khah·rah·_shoh_
And you?	**А как вы?** ah kahk vih

At first meeting **Здравствуйте!** _zdrah_·stvooy·tee (Hello!) is the preferred greeting; you can use the informal **Здравствуй!** _zdrah_·stvooy to address children. **Привет!** pree·_vyet_ (Hi!) is less formal and may sound rude if used in the wrong context.

Travel Talk

I'm here…	**Я здесь…** yah zdyes'…
on business	**в командировке** f kah·mahn·dee·_rof_·kyeh
on vacation [holiday]	**в отпуске** v _ot_·poos·kyeh
studying	**учусь** oo·_choos'_
I'm staying for…	**Я здесь на…** yah zdyes' nah…
I've been here…	**Я здесь уже…** yah zdyes' oo·_zheh_…
a day	**день** dyen'
a week	**неделю** nee·_dyeh_·lyoo
a month	**месяц** _myeh_·syahts
Where are you from?	**Откуда вы?** aht·_koo_·dah vih
I'm from…	**Я из…** yah eez…

For Numbers, see page 157.

Personal

Who are you with?	**С кем вы?** s kyem vih
I'm on my own.	**Я один** _m_ /**одна** _f_. yah ah·_deen_/ahd·_nah_

I'm with…	**Я с…** *yah s…*
my husband/wife	**моим мужем/моей женой** *mah·eem moo·zhihm/mah·yey zhee·noy*
my boyfriend/ girlfriend	**моим другом/моей подругой** *mah·eem droo·gahm/mah·yey pah·droo·gie*
I'm with…	**Я с…** *yah s…*
a friend/friends	**другом/друзьями** *droo·gahm/drooz'·yah·mee*
a colleague/ colleagues	**коллегой/коллегами** *kah·lyeh·gie/ kah·lyeh·gah·mee*
When's your birthday?	**Когда Ваш день рождения?** *kahg·dah vahsh dyen' rahzh·dyeh·nee·yah*
How old are you?	**Сколько Вам лет?** *skol'·kah vahm lyet*
I'm…	**Мне…** *mnyeh…*
I'm…	**Я…** *yah…*
single	**холост** *m* **/не замужем** *f* *yah khoh·lahst/ nee zah·moo·zhihm*
in a relationship	**с партнёром** *s pahrt·nyoh·rahm*
engaged	**Я помолвлен** *m* **/помолвлена** *f* *yah pah·mohl·vlen/pah·mohl·vle·nah*
married	**женат** *m* **/замужем** *f* *zhih·naht/ zah·moo·zhihm*
divorced	**разведён** *m* **/разведена** *f* *rahz·vee·dyon/ rahz·vee·dee·nah*
separated	**не живу с женой** *m* **/мужем** *f* *nee zhih·voo s zhih·noy/moo·zhihm*
I'm widowed.	**Я вдовец** *m* **/вдова** *f.* *yah vdah·vyets/ vdah·yah*
Do you have children/ grandchildren?	**У Вас есть дети/внуки?** *oo vahs yest' dyeh·tee/vnoo·kee*

For Numbers, see page 157.

Work & School

What do you do?	**Ваша профессия?** _yah_•shah prah•_fyeh_•see•yah
What are you studying?	**Что вы изучаете?** shtoh vih ee•zoo•_chah_•ee•tee
I'm studying...	**Я изучаю...** yah ee•zoo•_chah_•yoo...
I...	**Я...** yah
work full-/	**работаю полный/неполный день**
part-time	rah•_boh_•tah•yu _pohl_•niy/neh•_pohl_•niy dehn'
am unemployed	**Я безработный** _m_ **/безработная** _f_ yah
	bez•rah•_boht_•nee/bez•rah•_boht_•na•yah
work at home	**работаю дома** rah•_boh_•tah•yu _doh_•mah
Who do you work for?	**Где вы работаете?** gdyeh vih rah•_boh_•tah•ee•tee
I work for...	**Я работаю в...** yah rah•_boh_•tah•yoo v...
Here's my business card.	**Вот моя визитка.** vot mah•yah vee•_zeet_•kah

For Business Travel, see page 134.

Weather

What is the weather forecast?	**Какой прогноз погоды?** kah•_koy_ prahg•_nos_ pah•_goh_•dih
What beautiful/ terrible weather!	**Какая чудесная/ужасная погода!** kah•_kah_•yah choo•_dyes_•nah•yah/ oo•_zhahs_•nah•yah pah•_goh_•dah
It's cool./warm.	**Прохладно./Тепло.** prah•_khlahd_•nah/teep•_loh_
It's hot./cold.	**Жарко./Холодно.** _zhahr_•kah/hoh•lahd•nah
It's rainy./sunny.	**Дождливо./Солнечно.** dahzh•_dlee_•vah/ _sol_•neech•nah
It's snowy/icy.	**Идёт снег./Гололёд.** ee•_dyot_ snyek/ gah•lah•_lyot_
Do I need a jacket?	**Нужно надевать куртку?** _noozh_•nah nah dee•_vaht'_ _koort_•koo
Do I need an umbrella?	**Нужно брать зонт?** _noozh_•nah braht' zont

For Temperature, see page 164.

Romance

ESSENTIAL

Would you like to go out for a drink/meal?	**Не хотите выпить/поесть где-нибудь?** nee khah·<u>tee</u>·tee vih·peet'/pah·<u>yest'</u> <u>gdyeh</u>·nee·boot'
What are your plans for tonight/tomorrow?	**Какие у вас планы на сегодняшний вечер/завтра?** kah·<u>kee</u>·yeh oo vahs <u>plah</u>·nih nah see·<u>vod</u>·neesh·neey vyeh·cheer/<u>zahf</u>·trah
Can I have your number?	**Можно Ваш номер телефона?** <u>mozh</u>·nah vahsh <u>noh</u>·meer tee·lee·<u>foh</u>·nah
Can I join you?	**Можно к Вам присоединиться?** <u>mozh</u>·nah k vahm pree·sah·ee·dee·<u>nee</u>·tsah
Let me buy you a drink.	**Позвольте вам предложить что-нибудь выпить.** pahz·<u>vol'</u>·tee vahm preed·lah·<u>zheet'</u> <u>shtoh</u>·nee·boot' vih·peet'
I like you.	**Вы мне нравитесь.** vih mnyeh <u>nrah</u>·vee·tees'
I love you.	**Я Вас люблю.** yah vahs lyoob·<u>lyoo</u>

The Dating Game

Would you like to…?	**Хотите…?** khah·<u>tee</u>·tee…
go out for coffee	**выпить кофе где-нибудь** <u>vih</u>·peet' <u>koh</u>·fyeh <u>gdyeh</u>·nee·boot'
go for a drink	**пойти выпить где-нибудь** pie·<u>tee</u> vih·peet' <u>gdyeh</u>·nee·boot'
go for a meal	**пойти поесть где-нибудь** pie·<u>tee</u> pah·<u>yest'</u> <u>gdyeh</u>·nee·boot'
What are your plans for…?	**Какие у вас планы на…?** kah·<u>kee</u>·yeh oo vahs <u>plah</u>·nih nah…

today	**сегодня** *seh•vohd•nya*
tonight	**сегодняшний вечер** *see•vod•neesh•neey vyeh•cheer*
tomorrow	**завтра** *zahf•trah*
this weekend	**эти выходные** *eh•tee vih•khahd•nih•yeh*
Where would you like to go?	**Куда вы хотите пойти?** *koo•dah vih khah•tee•tee pie•tee*
I'd like to go to…	**Я хотел *m* /хотела *f* бы пойти в…** *yah khah•tyel **m**/khah•tyeh•lah **f** bih pie•tee v…*
Do you like…?	**Вы любите…?** *vih lyoo•bee•tee…*
Can I have your number/e-mail?	**Можно Ваш номер телефона/электронный адрес?** *mozh•nah vahsh noh•meer tee•lee•foh•nah/ee•leek•tron•niy ahd•rees*
Are you on facebook/Twitter?	**Вы есть в facebook/Twitter?** *vih est' v facebook/Twitter*
Can I join you?	**Можно к Вам присоединиться?** *mozh•nah k vahm pree•sah•ee•dee•nee•tsah*
You're very attractive.	**Вы прекрасно выглядите.** *vih pree•krahs•nah vih•glee•dee•tee*
Shall we go somewhere quieter?	**Пойдём куда-нибудь в тихое место?** *pie•dyom koo•dah•nee•boot' f tee•khah•yeh myes•tah*

For Communications, see page 50.

Accepting & Rejecting

Thank you! I'd love to.	**Спасибо! Я с удовольствием.** *spah•see•bah yah s oo•dah•vol'•stvee•yem*
Where shall we meet?	**Где встретимся?** *gdyeh fstryeh•teem•syah*
I'll meet you at the bar/your hotel.	**Встретимся в баре/вашем отеле.** *fstryeh•teem•syah v bah•ryeh/vah•shem ah•teh•lee*

I'll come by at…	**Я зайду в…** _yah zayh-doo v…_
Thank you, but I'm busy.	**Спасибо, но я занят _m_ /занята _f_.**
	spah-see-bah noh yah zah-nyaht/zah-nyah-tah
I'm not interested.	**Меня это не интересует.** _mee-nyah eh-tah_
	nee een-tee-ree-soo-eet
Leave me alone.	**Оставьте меня в покое.** _ah-stahf'-tee_
	mee-nyah f pah-koh-yeh
Stop bothering me!	**Перестаньте мне надоедать!**
	pee-ree-stahn'-tee mnyeh nah-dah-ee-daht'

Getting Intimate

Can I hug/kiss you?	**Можно тебя обнять/поцеловать?** _mozh-nah_
	tee-byah ahb-nyaht'/pah-tsih-lah-vaht'
Yes.	**Да.** _dah_
No.	**Нет.** _nyet_
Stop!	**Перестань!** _pee-ree-stahn'_
I love you.	**Я Вас люблю.** _yah vahs lyoob-lyoo_

Sexual Preferences

Are you gay?	**Ты гей _m_ /лесбиянка _f_ ?** _tih gyey/_
	lez-bee-yahn-kah
I'm…	**Я…** _yah…_
heterosexual	**гетеросексуал** _gyeh-teh-rah-sek-soo-ahl_
homosexual	**гомосексуал** _goh-mah-sek-soo-ahl_
bisexual	**бисексуал** _bee-sek-soo-ahl_
Do you like men/	**Вам нравятся мужчины/женщины?** _vam_
women?	_nrah-vyat-sya moo-zhchee-nih/zhehn-shchee-nih_

Leisure Time

Sightseeing

ESSENTIAL

Where's the tourist information office?	**Где турбюро?** *gdyeh* <u>*toor*</u>•*byoo*•<u>*roh*</u>
What are the main points of interest?	**Какие главные достопримечательности?** *kah*•<u>*kee*</u>•*yeh* <u>*glahv*</u>•*nih*•*yeh* *dah*•*stah*•*pree*•*mee*•<u>*chah*</u>•*teel'*•*nahs*•*tee*
Do you have tours in English?	**У вас есть экскурсии на английском?** *oo vahs yehst'* *ehks*•<u>*koor*</u>•*see*•*ee nah ahn*•<u>*gleey*</u>•*skahm*
Can I have a map/guide?	**Можно мне карту/путеводитель?** <u>*mozh*</u>•*nah* *mnyeh* <u>*kahr*</u>•*too/poo*•*tee*•*vah*•<u>*dee*</u>•*teel*

Tourist Information

Do you have any information on…?	**У Вас есть информация по…?** *oo vahs yest'* *een*•*fahr*•<u>*mah*</u>•*tsih*•*yah pah*…
Can you recommend…?	**Вы можете порекомендовать…?** *vih* <u>*moh*</u>•*zhih*•*tee pah*•*ree*•*kah*•*meen*•*dah*•<u>*vaht'*</u>…
a boat trip	**водную экскурсию** <u>*vod*</u>•*noo*•*yoo eks*•<u>*koor*</u>•*see*•*yoo*
an excursion	**экскурсию** *eks*•<u>*koor*</u>•*see*•*yoo*
a sightseeing tour	**обзорную экскурсию** *ahb*•<u>*zor*</u>•*noo*•*yoo* *eks*•<u>*koor*</u>•*see*•*yoo*

Intourist hotels have **бюро обслуживания** *byoo·roh ahp·sloo·zhih·vah·nee·yah* (service bureaus) manned by multilingual staff who provide information, arrange outings and excursions, make reservations and give general assistance. Other useful sources of information are the tourist information offices, English-language newspapers, *The Moscow Times* and *Where in St. Petersburg?*, found in many hotels and at kiosks.

On Tour

I'd like to go on the tour to…	**Я хотел *m* /хотела *f* бы поехать на экскурсию в…** *yah khah·tyel/khah·tyeh·lah bih pah·yeh·khaht' nah eks·koor·see·yoo v…*
When's the next tour?	**Когда будет следующая поездка?** *kahg·dah boo·deht sleh·doo·yu·shchah·ya poh·yehzd·kah*
Are there tours in English?	**Есть экскурсии на английском?** *yest' eks·koor·see·ee nah ahn·gleey·skahm*
Is there an English guide book/audio guide?	**Есть путеводитель/аудиокнига на английском языке?** *est' poo·teh·voh·dee·tehl'/ ah·oo·dee·oh·knee·gah nah ahng·leey·skohm yaz·ihkeh*
What time do we leave/return?	**Во сколько отправляемся/возвращаемся?** *vah skol'·kah aht·prahv·lyah·eem·syah/ vahz·vrah·shchah·eem·syah*
We'd like to have a look at the…	**Нам хотелось бы посмотреть…** *nahm khah·tyeh·las' bih pah·smah·tryet'…*
Can we stop here…?	**Можно здесь остановиться, чтобы…?** *mozh·nah zdyes' ah·stah·nah·vee·tsah shtoh·bih…*
to take photographs	**пофотографировать** *pah·fah·tah·grah·fee·rah·vaht'*

to buy souvenirs	**купить сувениры** koo·<u>peet</u>' soo·vee·<u>nee</u>·rih
to use the restroom [toilet]	**сходить в туалет** skhah·<u>deet</u>' f too·ah·<u>lyet</u>
Is there access for the disabled?	**Есть условия для инвалидов?** yest' oos·<u>loh</u>·vee·yah dlyah een·vah·<u>lee</u>·dahf

For Tickets, see page 18.

Seeing the Sights

Where is...?	**Где...?** gdye...
the battleground	**место сражения** <u>myes</u>·tah srah·<u>zheh</u>·nee·yah
the botanical garden	**ботанический сад** bah·tah·<u>nee</u>·chees·keey saht
the castle	**замок** <u>zah</u>·mahk
the downtown area	**центр города** tsentr <u>goh</u>·rah·dah
the fountain	**фонтан** fahn·<u>tahn</u>
the library	**библиотека** bee·blee·ah·<u>tyeh</u>·kah
the market	**рынок** <u>rih</u>·nahk
the museum	**музей** moo·<u>zey</u>
the old town	**старый город** <u>stah</u>·riy <u>goh</u>·raht
the opera house	**опера** <u>oh</u>·peh·rah
the palace	**дворец** dvah·<u>ryets</u>
the park	**парк** pahrk

the ruins	**руины** roo·*een*·y
the shopping area	**торговый район** tahr·*goh*·viy rah·*yon*
the town square	**центральная площадь** tsihn·*trahl'*·nah·yah *ploh*·shchaht'
Show me on the map	**Покажите мне на карте.** pah·kah·*zhih*·tee mnyeh nah *kahr*·tye
It's…	**Это…** *eh*·tah…
amazing	**удивительно** oo·dee·*vee*·tehl'·noh
beautiful	**прекрасно** pree·*krahs*·nah
boring	**скучно** *skoosh*·nah
It's…	**Это…** *eh*·tah…
interesting	**интересно** een·tee·*ryes*·nah
magnificent	**великолепно** vee·lee·kah·*lyep*·nah
romantic	**романтично** rah·mahn·*teech*·nah
strange	**странно** *strah*·noh
terrible	**ужасно** oo·*zhahs*·nah
ugly	**безобразно** bee·zah·*brahz*·nah
I (don't) like it.	**Мне это (не) нравится.** mnyeh *eh*·tah (nee) *nrah*·vee·tsah

For Asking Directions, see page 34.

Religious Sites

Where's…?	**Где…?** gdyeh…
the Catholic/ Protestant church	**церковь католическая/протестантская** *tser*·kahf' kah·toh·lee·che·ska·ya/pro·tye·stahn·ska·ya
the mosque	**мечеть** mee·*chet'*
the shrine	**обитель** ah·*bee*·teel'
the synagogue	**синагога** see·nah·*goh*·gah
the temple	**храм** khrahm
What time is mass/ the service?	**Когда будет месса/служба?** kahg·dah boo·deet *myes*·sah/*sloozh*·bah

Shopping

ESSENTIAL

Where is the shop/mall?	**Где магазин/торговый центр?** *gdyeh mah-gah-zeen/tahr-goh-viy tsehntr*
I'm just looking.	**Я просто смотрю.** *yah proh-stah smath-ryoo*
Can you help me?	**Можете мне помочь?** *moh-zhih-tee mnyeh pah-mohch*
I'm being helped.	**Меня уже обслуживают.** *mee-nyah oo-zheh ahp-sloo-zhih-vah-yoot*
How much?	**Сколько?** *skol'-kah*
That one.	**Вон то.** *vohn toh*
That's all, thanks.	**Это всё, спасибо.** *eh-tah fsyoh spah-see-bah*
Where do I pay?	**Куда платить?** *koo-dah plah-teet'*
I'll pay in cash/by credit card.	**Я заплачу наличными/по кредитной карточке.** *yah zah-plah-choo nah-leech-nih-mee/pah kree-deet-noy kahr-tahch-kee*
A receipt, please.	**Чек, пожалуйста.** *chehk pah-zhahl-stah*

Shopping in Moscow and St. Petersburg now looks very much like shopping in New York and London, at least in the city centers and malls. Moscow does its serious shopping in the mega-stores along the outer ring-road, where names like Ikea and Marks & Spencer can be found. The Tyoply Stan mega mall claims to be Europe's busiest shopping center. Both cities also offer thriving and rich open-air markets, for example, Moscow's Izmailovsky Market, near Partizanskaya metro station, or St. Petersburg's market, near the Nevsky Prospect metro station. These are great places to pick up souvenirs.

At the Shops

Where is…?	**Где…?** gdyeh…	
the antiques store	**антикварный магазин** ahn·tee·<u>kvahr</u>·niy mah·gah·<u>zeen</u>	
the bakery	**булочная** <u>boo</u>·lahch·nah·yah	
the bank	**банк?** bahnk	
the bookstore	**книжный магазин** <u>kneezh</u>·niy mah·gah·<u>zeen</u>	
Where is…?	**Где…?** gdyeh…	
the clothing store	**магазин одежды** mah·gah·<u>zeen</u> ah·dyezh·dih	
the delicatessen	**гастроном** gah·stroh·<u>nohm</u>	
the department store	**универмаг** oo·nee·veer·<u>mahk</u>	
the gift shop	**магазин подарков** mah·gah·<u>zeen</u> poh·<u>dahr</u>·kohv	
the jeweler	**ювелирный магазин** yoo·vee·<u>leer</u>·niy mah·gah·<u>zeen</u>	
the liquor store [off-license]	**винный магазин** <u>veen</u>·niy mah·gah·<u>zeen</u>	
the market	**рынок** <u>rih</u>·nahk	
the music store	**музыкальный магазин** moo·zih·<u>kahl'</u>·niy mah·gah·<u>zeen</u>	
the pastry store	**кондитерская** kahn·<u>dee</u>·teer·skah·yah	
the pharmacy	**аптека** ahp·<u>tyeh</u>·kah	
the shoe store	**обувной магазин** ah·boov·<u>noy</u> mah·gah·<u>zeen</u>	
Where is…?	**Где…?** gdyeh…	
the shopping mall	**торговый центр** tahr·<u>goh</u>·viy tsehntr	
the souvenir store	**магазин сувениров** mah·gah·<u>zeen</u> soo·vee·<u>nee</u>·rahf	
the supermarket	**универсам** oo·nee·veer·<u>sahm</u>	
the tobacconist	**табачный киоск** tah·<u>bahch</u>·niy kee·<u>osk</u>	
the toy store	**магазин игрушек** mah·gah·<u>zeen</u> ee·<u>groo</u>·shek	

Ask an Assistant

What are the hours of operation?	**В какие часы работает?** *f kah•kee•yeh chah•sih rah•boh•tah•yet*
Where is…?	**Где…?** *gdyeh…*
the cashier [cash desk]	**касса** *kahs•sah*
the escalator	**эскалатор** *es•kah•lah•tahr*
the elevator [lift]	**лифт** *leeft*
the fitting room	**примерочная** *pree•myeh•rahch•nah•yah*
the store directory	**перечень отделов** *pyeh•ree•cheen' ahd•dyeh•lahf*
Help me, please.	**Помогите мне, пожалуйста.** *pah•mah•gee•tee mnyeh pah•zhahl•stah*
I'm just looking.	**Я просто смотрю.** *yah proh•stah smah•tryoo*
I'm being helped.	**Меня уже обслуживают.** *mee•nyah oo•zheh ahp•sloo•zhih•vah•yoot*
Do you have…?	**У Вас есть…?** *oo vahs yest'…*
Where is…?	**Где…?** *gdyeh…*
Could you show me…?	**Можете мне показать…?** *moh•zhih•tee mnyeh pah•kah•zaht'…*
Can you ship/wrap it?	**Вы можете доставить/завернуть это?** *vih moh•zhih•tee dah•stah•veet'/zah•veer•noot' eh•tah*
How much?	**Сколько?** *skol'•kah*
That's all, thanks.	**Это всё, спасибо.** *eh•tah fsyoh spah•see•bah*

For Clothes & Accessories, see page 116.

For Meals & Cooking, see page 68.

For Souvenirs, see page 120.

YOU MAY HEAR...

Я вас слушаю. yah vahs <u>sloo</u>·shah·yoo

Одну минуту. ahd·<u>noo</u> mee·<u>noo</u>·too

Что вы хотите? shtoh vih khah·<u>tee</u>·tee

Что ещё? shtoh ee·<u>shchoh</u>

Can I help you?

One moment.

What would you like?

Anything else?

YOU MAY SEE...

ОТКРЫТО/ЗАКРЫТО aht·<u>krih</u>·tah/ zah·<u>krih</u>·toh	open/closed
ЗАКРЫТО НА ОБЕД zah·<u>krih</u>·toh nah ah·<u>byed</u>	closed for lunch
ПРИМЕРОЧНАЯ pree·<u>meh</u>·rah·chnah·ya	fitting room
КАССА <u>kah</u>·sah	cashier
ТОЛЬКО НАЛИЧНЕ <u>tohl'</u>·koh nah·<u>lich</u>·nih·ee	cash only
ПРИНИМАЮТСЯ КРЕДИТНЫЕ КАРТЫ pree·nee·<u>mah</u>·yoot·sah kreh·<u>deet</u>·nihye <u>kahr</u>·tih	credit cards accepted
ЧАСЫ РАБОТЫ chah·<u>sih</u> rah·bohty	business hours
ВЫХОД <u>vih</u>·khaht	exit

Personal Preferences

I'd like something...	**Я хочу что-нибудь...** yah khah·<u>choo</u> <u>shtoh</u>·nee·boot'...
cheap/expensive	**дешёвое/дорогое** dee·<u>shoh</u>·vah·yeh/ dah·rah·<u>goh</u>·yeh
larger/smaller	**побольше/поменьше** pah·<u>bol'</u>·sheh/ pah·<u>myen'</u>·sheh
from this region	**из этого региона** eez <u>eh</u>·tah·vah reh·gih·<u>oh</u>·nah
around... rubles	**примерно... рублей** pree·<u>mehr</u>·noh ... roob·<u>lyey</u>

Is it real?	**Это настоящее?** _eh_•tah nahs•tah•_yah_•shchee•yeh
Could you show me this/that?	**Можете показать мне это/вон то?** _moh_•zhih•tee pah•kah•_zaht'_ mnyeh _eh_•tah/von toh
That's not quite what I want.	**Это не совсем то, что я хочу.** _eh_•tah nee sahf•_syem_ toh shtoh yah khah•_choo_
I don't like it.	**Это мне не нравится.** _eh_•tah mnyeh nee _nrah_•vee•tsah
That's too expensive.	**Это слишком дорого.** _eh_•tah _sleesh_•kahm _doh_•rah•gah
I'd like to think about it.	**Надо подумать.** _nah_•dah pah•_doo_•maht'
I'll take it.	**Я возьму это.** yah vahz'•_moo eh_•tah

Paying & Bargaining

How much?	**Сколько?** _skol'_•kah
I'll pay…	**Я заплачу…** yah zah•plah•_choo_…
in cash	**наличными** nah•_leech_•nih•mee

YOU MAY HEAR…

Как будете платить? kahk _boo_•dee•tee plah•_teet'_	How are you paying?
Кредитная карта не принята. kreh•_deet_•nah•ya _kahr_•tah neh _pree_•nya•tah	Your credit card has been declined.
Только наличные, пожалуйста. _tol'_•kah nah•_leech_•nih•yeh pah•_zhahl_•stah	Cash only, please.
удостоверение личности пожалуйста. oo•dahs•ta•_veer_•en•ye leech•nus•tee pah•_zhahl_•stah	ID, please.
У Вас есть деньги мельче? oo vahs yest' dyen'•gee _myel'_•cheh	Do you have any smaller change?

While credit cards are increasingly common in Russia and fairly safe to use, especially in large and mid-sized cities, you should avoid using them in places that do not inspire complete confidence.

by credit card	**по кредитной карточке** *pah kree·deet·noy kar·tach·kee*
by traveler's cheque	**дорожным чеком** *dah·rozh·nihm cheh·kahm*
A receipt, please.	**Можно чек, пожалуйста.** *mozh·nah chehk pah·zhahl·stah*
That's too much.	**Это слишком дорого.** *eh·tah sleesh·kahm doh·rah·gah*
I'll give you…	**Я дам вам…** *yah dahm vahm…*
I only have…rubles.	**У меня только…рублей.** *oo mee·nyah tol'·kah…roob·lyey*
Is that your best price?	**Это ваша последняя цена?** *eh·tah vah·shah pahs·lyed·nee·yah tsih·nah*
Can you give me a discount?	**Вы можете дать мне скидку?** *vih moh·zhih·tee daht' mnyeh skeet·koo*

Making a Complaint

I'd like…	**Я хотел *m* /хотела *f* бы…** *yah khah·tyel/ khah·tyeh·lah bih…*
to exchange this	**обменять это** *ahb·mee·nyaht' eh·tah*
to return this	**возвратить это** *vahz·vrah·teet' eh·tah*
a refund	**возврат денег** *vahz·vraht dye·neek*
to see the manager	**увидеть менеджера** *oo·vee·deet' myeh·ned·zhih·rah*

Services

Can you recommend...?	**Вы можете порекомендовать...?** *vih·moh·zhih·tee pah·ree·kah·meen·dah·vaht'...*
a barber	**парикмахерскую** *pah·reek·mah·kheer·skoo·yoo*
a dry cleaner	**химчистку** *kheem·cheest·koo*
a hairdresser	**парикмахерскую** *pah·reek·mah·kheer·skoo·yoo*
a laundromat [launderette]	**прачечную** *prah·cheech·noo·yoo*
a nail salon	**маникюрный салон** *mah·nee·kyoor·niy sah·lon*
a spa	**спа** *spah*
a travel agency	**бюро путешествий** *byoo·roh poo·tee·shest·veey*
Can you...this?	**Вы можете это...?** *vih moh·zhih·tee eh·tah...*
alter	**переделать** *pee·ree·dyeh·lat'*
clean	**почистить** *pah·chees·teet'*
mend	**заштопать** *zah·shtoh·paht'*
press	**погладить** *pah·glah·deet'*
When will it be ready?	**Когда будет готово?** *kahg·dah boo·deet gah·toh·vah*

Hair & Beauty

I'd like…	**Я хотел m /хотела f бы…** yah khah·<u>tyel</u>/ khah·tyeh·<u>lah</u> bih…
an appointment for today/tomorrow	**записаться на сегодня/завтра** zah·pee·<u>sah</u>·tsah nah see·<u>vod</u>·nyah/<u>zahf</u>·trah
some colour/ highlights	**покрасить волосы/сделать мелирование** pah·<u>kra</u>·seet' <u>voh</u>·loh·sih/<u>sdeh</u>·laht' meh·<u>lee</u>·roh·vah·nee·yeh
my hair styled/ blow-dried	**модельную стрижку/укладку феном** mah·<u>del</u>'·noo·yoo/ook·lahd·koo·feh·nohm <u>streesh</u>·koo
a haircut	**постричься** pah·<u>streech</u>·syah
an eyebrow/ bikini wax	**восковую эпиляцию бровей/зоны бикини** <u>vos</u>·kah·voo·yoo eh·pee·<u>lyah</u>·tsih·yoo brah·<u>vyey</u>/<u>zoh</u>·nih bee·<u>kee</u>·nee
a facial	**чистку лица** <u>cheest</u>·koo lee·<u>tsah</u>
a manicure/ pedicure	**маникюр/педикюр** mah·nee·<u>kyoor</u>/ pee·dee·<u>kyoor</u>
a (sports) massage	**(спортивный) массаж** (spahr·<u>teev</u>·niy) mahs·<u>sahsh</u>
a trim	**подравнивание** pahd·<u>rahv</u>·nee·vah·nee·yeh
Don't cut it too short.	**Не слишком коротко.** nee <u>sleesh</u>·kahm <u>koh</u>·raht·kah
Shorter here.	**Здесь покороче.** zdyes' pah·kah·<u>roh</u>·cheh
Do you do…?	**Вы делаете…?** vih <u>dyeh</u>·lah·ee·tee…
acupuncture	**иглотерапию** <u>eeg</u>·lah·tee·rah·<u>pee</u>·yoo
aromatherapy	**ароматерапию** ah·<u>roh</u>·mah·tee·rah·<u>pee</u>·yoo
oxygen treatment	**кислородотерапию** kees·lah·<u>roh</u>·dah·tee·rah·<u>pee</u>·yoo
Is there a sauna?	**Есть сауна?** yest' <u>sah</u>·oo·nah

113

Natural approaches to health and beauty include herb remedies and **баня** _bah_•nyah (Russian steam bath); these are deeply ingrained in Russian traditional folk medicine. Today these approaches have been combined with modern spa and wellness resources. Even outside of Moscow and St. Petersburg you will find a variety of day and overnight spas. Most hotels offer facials, massage and a number of other day spa services right on the premises. It is customary to tip from 10-20% depending on your satisfaction with services provided.

Antiques

How old is this?	**Какой возраст этой вещи?** kah•_koy_ voz•rahst _eh_•tie _vyeh_•shchee
Do you have anything from the...period?	**У Вас есть что-нибудь на период с ...?** oo vahs _yest'_ shtoh•nee•_boot'_ nah peh•ree•_ot_ s
Do I have to fill out any forms?	**Нужно заполнить формы?** _noozh_•nah zah•_pohl_•neet' _fohr_•mih
Will I have problems with customs?	**Могут быть проблемы на таможне?** moh•goot biht' prah•_blyeh_•mih nah tah•_mozh_•nee
Is there a certificate of authenticity?	**Есть сертификат подлинности?** yest' seer•tee•fee•_kaht_ pod•_lyeen_•nahs•tee
Can you ship/wrap it?	**Вы можете доставить/упаковать?** vih _moh_•zhih•tye dah•_stah_•veet'/oo•pah•kah•_vaht'_

Clothing

I'd like...	**Я хотел m /хотела f бы...** yah khah•_tyel_ m/ khah•_tyeh_•lah f bih...
Can I try this on?	**Можно это примерить?** _mozh_•nah _eh_•tah pree•_myeh_•reet'

It doesn't fit.	**Не подходит.** *nee paht·khoh·deet*
It's too big/small.	**Слишком велико/мало.** *sleesh·kahm vee·lee·koh/mah·loh*
It's too short/long.	**Слишком коротко/длинно.** *sleesh·kahm koh·raht·kah/dleen·nah*
It's too tight/loose.	**Слишком туго/слабо.** *slee·shkohm too·goh/slah·boh*
Do you have this in size…?	**У Вас есть размер…?** *oo vahs yest' rahz·myer…*
Do you have this in a bigger/smaller size?	**У Вас есть это большего/меньшего размера?** *oo vahs yest' eh·tah bol'·shee·vah/myen'·shee·vah rahz·myeh·rah*

For Numbers, see page 157.

YOU MAY HEAR…

That looks great on you.	**Вам очень идет** *vahm oh·chen' eed·yoht*
How does it fit?	**Как Вам нравится?** *kahk vahm nrah·vee·tsya*
We don't have your size.	**У нас нет Вашего размера.** *oo nahs neht vah·sheh·vah·rahz·meh·rah*

YOU MAY SEE…

МУЖСКАЯ ОДЕЖДА *moosh·skah·yah ah·dyezh·dah*	men's clothing
ЖЕНСКАЯ ОДЕЖДА *zhen·skah·yah ah·dyezh·dah*	women's clothing
ДЕТСКАЯ ОДЕЖДА *dyets·kah·yah ah·dyezh·dah*	children's clothing

Colors

I'm looking for something in...	**Я ищу что-нибудь...**	*yah ee·<u>shchoo</u> <u>shtoh</u>·nee·boot'...*
beige	**бежевое**	<u>byeh</u>·zhih·vah·yeh
black	**чёрное**	<u>chor</u>·nah·yeh
blue	**синее**	<u>see</u>·nee·yeh
brown	**коричневое**	kah·<u>reech</u>·nee·vah·yeh
green	**зелёное**	zee·<u>lyoh</u>·nah·yeh
gray	**серое**	<u>syeh</u>·rah·yeh
orange	**оранжевое**	ah·<u>rahn</u>·zhih·vah·yeh
pink	**розовое**	<u>roh</u>·zah·vah·yeh
purple	**фиолетовое**	fee·ah·<u>lyeh</u>·tah·vah·yeh
red	**красное**	<u>krahs</u>·nah·yeh
white	**белое**	<u>byeh</u>·lah·yeh
yellow	**жёлтое**	<u>zhol</u>·tah·yeh

Clothes & Accessories

a backpack	**рюкзак**	ryook·<u>zahk</u>
a belt	**ремень**	ree·<u>myen'</u>
a bikini	**бикини**	bee·<u>kee</u>·nee
a blouse	**блузка**	<u>bloos</u>·kah
a bra	**бюстгальтер**	byoost·<u>gahl</u>·teer
briefs [underpants]	**трусы**	<u>troo</u>·sih
a coat	**пальто**	pahl'·<u>toh</u>
a dress	**платье**	<u>plaht</u>'·yeh
a hat	**шапка**	<u>shahp</u>·kah
a jacket	**пиджак**	peed·<u>zhahk</u>
jeans	**джинсы**	<u>dzhihn</u>·sih
pajamas	**пижама**	pee·<u>zhah</u>·mah
pants [trousers]	**брюки**	<u>bryoo</u>·kee
pantyhose [tights]	**колготки**	kahl·<u>got</u>·kee

a purse [handbag]	**сумка** <u>soom</u>·kah
a raincoat	**плащ** plahshch
a scarf	**шарф** shahrf
a shirt	**рубашка** roo·<u>bahsh</u>·kah
shorts	**шорты** <u>shor</u>·tih
a skirt	**юбка** <u>yoop</u>·kah
socks	**носки** nahs·<u>kee</u>
a suit	**костюм** kahs·<u>tyoom</u>
sunglasses	**солнечные очки** <u>sol</u>·neech·nih·yeh ahch·<u>kee</u>
a sweater	**пуловер** poo·<u>loh</u>·veer
a sweatshirt	**свитер** <u>svee</u>·tehr
swimming trunks	**плавки** <u>plahf</u>·kee
a swimsuit	**купальник** koo·<u>pahl'</u>·neek
a T-shirt	**майка** <u>mie</u>·kah
a tie	**галстук** <u>gahls</u>·took
underwear	**нижнее бельё** <u>neezh</u>·nee·yeh bee·<u>lyoh</u>

Fabric

I'd like…	**Я хотел** *m* /**хотела** *f* **бы…** yah khah·<u>tyel</u>/ khah·<u>tyeh</u>·lah bih…
cotton	**хлопок** <u>khloh</u>·pahk
denim	**джинс** dzhihns
lace	**кружева** kroo·zhih·<u>vah</u>
leather	**кожа** <u>koh</u>·zhah
linen	**лен** lyon
silk	**шёлк** sholk
wool	**шерсть** sherst'
Is it machine washable?	**Это можно стирать в машине?** <u>eh</u>·tah <u>mozh</u>·nah stee·<u>raht'</u> v mah·<u>shih</u>·nyeh

Shoes

I'd like…	**Я хотел** *m* **/хотела** *f* **бы…** *yah khah•tyel/ khah•tyeh•lah bih…*
high-heeled/flat shoes	**туфли на высоком/низком каблуке** *toof•lee nah vih•soh•kahm/nees•kahm kahb•loo•kyeh*
boots	**сапоги** *sah•pah•gee*
loafers	**мокасины** *mah•kah•see•nih*
sandals	**сандалии** *sahn•dah•lee•ee*
shoes	**туфли** *toof•lee*
slippers	**тапочки** *tah•pahch•kee*
sneakers	**кроссовки** *krah•sof•kee*
In size…	**Размер…** *rahz•myer…*

For Numbers, see page 157.

Sizes

small (S)	**малый** *mah•liy*
medium (M)	**средний** *sryed•neey*
large (L)	**большой** *bahl'•shoy*
extra large (XL)	**очень большой** *oh•cheen' bahl'•shoy*
petite	**маленький** *mah•leen'•keey*
plus size	**для полных** *dlyah pol•nihkh*

Newsagent & Tobacconist

Do you sell English-language books/newspapers?	**Есть в продаже английские книги/газеты?** *yest' f prah·dah·zheh ahn·gleey·skee·yeh knee·gee/gah·zyeh·tih*
I'd like…	**Дайте…** *die·tee…*
candy	**конфеты** *kohn·feh·tih*
chewing gum	**жевательную резинку** *zhih·vah·teel·'noo·yoo ree·zeen·koo*
a chocolate bar	**плитку шоколада** *pleet·koo shoh·koh·lah·dah*
cigars	**сигары** *see·gah·rih*
a pack/carton of cigarettes	**пачку/блок сигарет** *pahch·koo/blok see·gah·ryet*
a lighter	**зажигалку** *zah·zhih·gahl·koo*
a magazine	**журнал** *zhoor·nahl*
matches	**спички** *speech·kee*
a newspaper	**газету** *gah·zyeh·too*
a pen	**ручку** *rooch·koo*
a road/town map of…	**карту автомобильных дорог/города…** *kahr·too ahf·tah·mah·beel'·nihkh dah·rok/goh·rah·dah…*
stamps	**марки** *mahr·kee*

Photography

I'm looking for…camera.	**Я ищу…фотоаппарат.** *yah ee·shchoo…fah·tah·ah·pah·raht*
an automatic	**автоматический** *ahf·tah·mah·tee·chees·keey*
a digital	**цифровой** *tsihf·rah·voy*
a disposable	**одноразовый** *ahd·nah·rah·zah·viy*
I'd like…	**Я хотел m /хотела f бы…** *yah khah·tyel/khah·tyeh·lah bih…*
a battery	**батарейку** *bah·tah·ryey·koo*

119

digital prints	**цифровые фотографии** tsihf·rah·_vih_·yeh fah·tah·_grah_·fee·ee
a memory card	**карту памяти** _kahr_·too pah·_myah_·tee
Can I print digital photos here?	**Здесь можно напечатать цифровые фотографии?** zdyes' _mozh_·nah nah·pee·_chah_·taht' tsihf·rah·_vih_·yeh fah·tah·_grah_·fee·ee

Souvenirs

amber	**янтарь** yeen·_tahr'_
balalaika (traditional musical instrument)	**балалайка** bah·lah·_lie_·ka
caviar	**икра** eek·_rah_
chess set	**шахматы** _shahkh_·mah·tih
fur hat	**меховая шапка** mee·khah·_vah_·yah _shahp_·kah
key ring	**брелок** bree·_lok_
nesting doll	**матрёшка** maht·_ryosh_·kah
Palekh box	**палехская шкатулка** _pah_·leekh·skah·yah shkah·_tool_·kah
postcard	**открытка** aht·_kriht_·kah
poster	**плакат** plah·_kaht_
rug from Tekin	**текинский ковер** tee·_keen_·skeey kah·_vyor_
samovar	**самовар** sah·mah·_vahr_
shawl	**шаль** shahl'
souvenir guide	**альбом** ahl'·_bom_
tea towel	**кухонное полотенце** _koo_·khahn·nah·yeh pah·lah·_tyen_·tseh
T-shirt	**майка** _mie_·kah
wood carving	**резьба по дереву** reez'·_bah_ pah _dyeh_·ree·voo
wooden spoons	**деревянные ложки** dee·ree·_vyan_·nih·yeh _losh_·kee
Can I see this/ that?	**Можно посмотреть это/вон то?** _mozh_·nah pah·smah·_tryet'_ eh·tah/von toh

It's the one in the window/display case.	**Это то, что на витрине/стеллаже.** _eh_·tah toh shtoh nah vee·_tree_·nyeh/stee·_lah_·zheh
I'd like…	**Я хотел *m* /хотела *f* бы…** yah khah·_tyel_/ khah·_tyeh_·lah bih…
a battery	**батарейку** bah·tah·_ryey_·koo
a bracelet	**браслет** brahs·_lyet_
a brooch	**брошь** brosh
earrings	**серьги** _syer'_·gee
a necklace	**ожерелье** ah·zhih·_ryel'_·yeh
a ring	**кольцо** kal'·_tsoh_
a watch	**часы** chah·_sih_
copper	**медь** myet'
crystal (quartz)	**хрусталь** khroo·_stahl'_
diamond	**брильянт** breel'·_yahnt_
white/yellow gold	**белое/желтое золото** _byeh_·lah·yhe/ _zhol_·tah·yeh _zoh_·lah·tah
pearl	**жемчуг** _zhem_·chook
pewter	**олово** _oh_·lah·vah
platinum	**платину** _plah_·tee·noo
sterling silver	**чистое серебро** _chees_·tah·yeh see·reeb·_roh_
Is this real?	**Это настоящее?** _eh_·tah nah·stah·_yah_·shchee·yeh
Can you engrave it?	**Вы можете сделать на нем гравировку?** vih _moh_·zhih·tee _zdyeh_·laht' nah nyom grah·vee·_rof_·koo

In the past shops called **Подарки** pah·_dahr_·kee (gifts) were the traditional places for Russians to buy souvenirs. There are similar departments in almost every department store nowadays. Worth a visit, these stores carry everything from crystal & jewelry to toiletries. Favorite gifts for Russians are flowers, chocolate, wine, cognac and crystal. Visitors take home matreshkas (nesting dolls), lacquered wood boxes, scarves, jewelry, etc.

Sport & Leisure

ESSENTIAL

When's the game?	**Во сколько игра?** vah _skohl'_·kah eeg·_rah_
Where's…?	**Где…?** gdyeh…
the beach	**пляж** plyahsh
the park	**парк** pahrk
the pool	**бассейн** bah·_syehyn_
Is it safe to swim/ dive here?	**Здесь не опасно плавать/нырять?** zdyehs' nee ah·_pahs_·nah _plah_·vaht'/nih·_ryaht'_
Can I hire golf clubs?	**Я могу взять напрокат клюшки для гольфа?** yah mah·_goo_ vzyaht' nah·prah·_kaht klyoosh_·kee dlyah _gohl'_·fah
How much per hour?	**Сколько стоит в час?** _skohl'_·kah _stoh_·eet f chahs
How far is it to…?	**Далеко до…отсюда?** dah·lee·_koh_ dah… aht·_syoo_·dah
Can you show me on the map?	**Можете показать мне на карте?** _moh_·zhih·tyeh pah·kah·_zaht'_ mnyeh nah _kahr_·tyeh

Watching Sport

When's…?	**Когда…?** *kahg·dah…*
the baseball game	**бейсбольный матч** *beys·bohl'·niy mahtch*
the basketball game	**баскетбольный матч** *bahs·keed·bol'·niy mahtch*
the boxing match	**боксёрский матч** *bahk·syor·skeey mahtch*
the cricket game	**игра в крикет** *eeg·rah v kree·kyet*
the cycling race	**велогонка** *vyeh·lah·gon·kah*
the golf tournament	**турнир по гольфу** *toor·neer pah gol'·foo*
the soccer [football] game	**футбольный матч** *foot·bol'·niy mahtch*
the tennis match	**теннисный матч** *teh·nees·niy mahtch*
the volleyball game	**волейбольный матч** *vah·leey·bol'·niy mahtch*
Which teams are playing?	**Какие команды играют?** *kah·kee·yeh kah·mahn·dih ee·grah·yoot*
Where's…?	**Где…?** *gdyeh…*
the horse track	**ипподром** *eep·pah·drom*
the racetrack	**автодром** *ahf·tah·drom*
the stadium	**стадион** *stah·dee·on*
Where can I place a bet?	**Где я могу сделать ставку?** *gdyeh yah mah·goo zdyeh·laht' stahf·koo*

The most popular sports in Russia are ice hockey, skiing and skating in winter, and soccer, volleyball and horseback riding in summer. Water sports, especially swimming, are very popular all year round, as are hunting and fishing.

A turkish-style public bath (**баня** *bah·nyah*) is a very popular form of relaxation and a fun way to meet people.

Playing Sport

Where's…?	**Где…?**	gdyeh…
the golf course	**поле для гольфа**	<u>poh</u>•lyeh dlyah <u>gol'</u>•fah
the gym	**спортзал**	sport•<u>zahl</u>
the park	**парк**	pahrk
the tennis courts	**теннисные корты**	<u>teh</u>•nees•nih•yeh <u>kor</u>•tih
How much…?	**Сколько стоит…?**	<u>skohl'</u>•kah <u>stoh</u>•eet…
per day	**в день**	v dyen'
per hour	**в час**	f chahs
per game	**за игру**	zah eeg•<u>roo</u>
per round	**за круг**	zah krook
Can I hire…?	**Я могу взять напрокат…?**	yah mah•<u>goo</u> vzyaht' nah•prah•<u>kaht</u>…
golf clubs	**клюшки для гольфа**	<u>klyoosh</u>•kee dlyah <u>gohl'</u>•fah
equipment	**снаряжение**	snah•ree•<u>zheh</u>•nee•yeh
a racket	**ракетку**	rah•<u>kyet</u>•koo

At the Beach/Pool

Where's the beach/pool?	**Где пляж/бассейн?** *gdyeh plyahsh/bah·seyn*
Is there...?	**Здесь есть...?** *zdyes' yest'...*
a kiddie pool	**детский бассейн** *dyets·keey bah·seyn*
an indoor/	**закрытый/открытый бассейн**
outdoor pool	*zah·krih·tiy/aht·krih·tiy bah·seyn*
a lifeguard	**спасатель** *spah·sah·teel'*
Is it safe...?	**Здесь не опасно...?** *zdyes' nee ah·pahs·nah...*
to swim	**плавать** *plah·vaht'*
to dive	**нырять** *nih·ryat'*
for children	**для детей** *dlyah dee·tyey*
I want to hire...	**Я хочу взять напрокат...** *yah khah·choo vzyaht' nah·prah·kaht...*
a deck chair	**шезлонг** *shez·lonk*
diving equipment	**водолазное снаряжение** *voh·doh·lahz·noh·ye snah·rya·zheh·nee·ye*
a jet-ski	**водный мотоцикл** *vod·niy mah·tah·tsihkl*
a motorboat	**моторную лодку** *mah·tor·noo·yoo lot·koo*
a rowboat	**лодку** *lot·koo*
snorkeling equipment	**снаряжение для подводного плавания** *snah·rya·zheh·nee·ye dlya pohd·vohd·navah plah·vahn'ya*
I want to hire...	**Я хочу взять напрокат...** *yah khah choo vzyaht' nah prah kaht...*
a surfboard	**доску для серфинга** *dahs·koo dlyah ser·feen·gah*
a towel	**полотенце** *pah·lah·tyen·tseh*
an umbrella	**зонт** *zont*
water skis	**водные лыжи** *vod·nih·yeh lih·zhih*
a windsurfer	**виндсерфер** *vind·syer·fehr*

For Traveling with Children, see page 136.

Although the Russian summer is short, it can be hot. During the warmer months, Russians head to local lakes and rivers to swim or to a number of popular resorts on the Black Sea. The tourist infrastructure that went into decline after the fall of the Soviet Union is gradually being updated and the Black Sea coast is becoming an appealing international vacation destination, especially the town of Sochi, host of the 2014 Winter Olympics.

Winter Sports

A lift pass for a day/five days, please.	**Абонемент на подъемник на день/пять дней, пожалуйста.** ah·bah·nee·<u>ment</u> nah pahd'·<u>yom</u>·neek nah dyen'/pyaht' dnyey pah·<u>zhahl</u>·stah
I want to hire…	**Я хотел** *m* **/хотела** *f* **бы взять напрокат…** **yah** khah·<u>tyel</u>/khah·tyeh·<u>lah</u> bih vzyaht' nah·prah·<u>kaht</u>…
boots	**лыжные ботинки** <u>lihzh</u>·nih·ee bah·<u>teen</u>·kee
a helmet	**шлем** shlyem
poles	**лыжные палки** <u>lihzh</u>·nih·ee <u>pahl</u>·kee
skis	**лыжи** <u>lih</u>·zhih
a snowboard	**сноуборд** <u>snoh</u>·oo·bort
snowshoes	**снегоступы** snee·gah·<u>stoo</u>·pih
These are too big/small.	**Это слишком велико/мало.** <u>eh</u>·tah <u>sleesh</u>·kahm vee·lee·<u>koh</u>/mah·<u>loh</u>
Are there lessons?	**Есть уроки?** yest' oo·<u>roh</u>·kee
I'm a beginner.	**Я новичок.** ya noh·vee·<u>chohck</u>
I'm experienced.	**Я опытный лыжник.** yah <u>oh</u>·piht·niy <u>lizh</u>·neek
A trail [piste] map, please.	**Схему трассы, пожалуйста.** <u>skhyeh</u>·moo <u>trah</u>·sih pah·<u>zhahl</u>·stah

Skiing, particularly cross-country, is a popular sport in Russia. Moscow even has two downhill ski slopes, one in Krylatskoye and one in Bitsevsky Park. Adventurous tourists can find guided skiing adventures in remote areas of the taiga, while others can rent skis in city parks, such as Moscow's Sokolniki and Bitsevsky. Skating is also very popular. There are ice rinks in large parks and squares. Russians also enjoy traditional horse-drawn sleighs.

YOU MAY SEE…

ПОДЪЁМНИК phad·<u>yom</u>·neek	drag lift
ВАГОН ПОДВЕСНОЙ ДОРОГИ vah·<u>gon</u> pahd·vees·<u>noy</u> dah·<u>roh</u>·gee	cable car
ПОДВЕСНОЙ ПОДЪЁМНИК pahd·vees·<u>noy</u> phad·<u>yom</u>·neek	chair lift
ДЛЯ НАЧИНАЮЩИХ dlyah nah·chee·<u>nah</u>·yoo·shcheekh	novice
ДЛЯ ОПЫТНЫХ dlyah <u>oh</u>·piht·nihkh	intermediate
ДЛЯ МАСТЕРОВ dlyah mahs·tee·rof	expert
ТРАССА ЗАКРЫТА <u>trah</u>·sah zah·<u>krih</u>·tah	trail [piste] closed

Out in the Country

I'd like a map of…	**Я хотел m /хотела f бы карту…** yah khah·<u>tyel</u>/khah·<u>tyeh</u>·lah bih <u>kahr</u>·too…
this region	**этого района** <u>eh</u>·tah·vah rah·<u>yoh</u>·nah
the walking routes	**пешеходных маршрутов** pee·shee·<u>khod</u>·nihkh mahrsh·<u>roo</u>·tahf

the bike routes	**велосипедных маршрутов**
	vee·lah·see·pyed·nihkh mahrsh·roo·tahf
the trails	**трасс** *trahs*
Is it easy/difficult?	**Он легкий/сложный?** *on lyokh·keey/slozh·niy*
Is it far/steep?	**Он длинный/крутой?** *on dleen·niy/kroo·toy*
How far is it to...?	**Какое расстояние до...?** *kah·koh·yeh*
	rah·stah·yah·nee·yeh dah...
Can you show me	**Можете показать мне на карте?** *moh·zhih·tee*
on the map?	*pah·kah·zaht' mnyeh nah kahr·tyeh*
I'm lost.	**Я заблудился *m* /заблудилась *f*.** *yah*
	zah·bloo·deel·syah/zah·bloo·dee·lahs'
Where's...?	**Где...?** *gdyeh...*
the bridge	**мост** *most*
the cave	**пещера** *pee·shchyeh·rah*
the cliff	**обрыв** *ah·brihf*
the farm	**ферма** *fyer·mah*
the field	**поле** *poh·leh*
the forest	**лес** *lyes*
the hill	**холм** *khohlm*
the lake	**озеро** *oh·zee·rah*
the mountain	**гора** *gah·rah*
the nature preserve	**заповедник** *zah·pah·vyed·neek*
the overlook	**смотровая площадка** *smah·trah·vah·yah*
	plah·shchaht·kah
the park	**парк** *pahrk*
the path	**тропинка** *trah·peen·kah*
the peak	**пик** *peek*
the picnic area	**площадка для пикника** *plah·shchaht·kah*
	dlyah peek·nee·kah
the pond	**пруд** *prood*
the river	**река** *ree·kah*

the sea	**море** <u>moh</u>•ryeh
the thermal spring	**минеральный источник** mee•nee•<u>rahl</u>'•nihy ees•<u>toch</u>•neek
the stream	**течение** tye•<u>chye</u>•nyeh
the valley	**долина** dah•<u>lee</u>•nah
the vineyard	**виноградник** vee•noh•<u>grahd</u>•nik
the waterfall	**водопад** vah•dah•<u>paht</u>

Going Out

ESSENTIAL

What is there to do in the evenings?	**Что здесь можно делать по вечерам?** shtoh zdyehs' <u>mozh</u>•nah <u>dyeh</u>•laht' pah vee•chee•<u>rahm</u>
Do you have a program of events?	**У Вас есть программа мероприятий?** oo vahs yehst' prah•<u>grah</u>•mah mee•rah•pree•<u>yah</u>•teey
What's playing at the movies [cinema] tonight?	**Что идёт в кинотеатре сегодня вечером?** shtoh ee•<u>dyot</u> f kee•nah•tee•<u>aht</u>•ree see•<u>vohd</u>•nyah <u>vyeh</u>•chee•rahm
Where's...?	**Где...?** gdyeh...
the downtown area	**центр города** tsehntr <u>goh</u>•rah•dah
the bar	**бар** bahr
the dance club	**дискотека** dees•kah•<u>tyeh</u>•kah
Is there a cover charge?	**Нужно платить за вход?** <u>noozh</u>•nah plah•<u>teet</u>' zah fkhot

Most Russian restaurants have traditionally featured music and dancing, and Russians are less shy than others about getting out of their chairs and letting loose. Women do not wait for an invitation; it is not uncommon to see women dancing together or friends dancing as a group.

Moscow and St. Petersburg are developing solid reputations among young jet-setters as first-class party cities with a number of exclusive nightclubs. Many nightclubs and dance clubs are located in popular hotels and casinos.

Entertainment

Can you recommend...?	**Вы можете порекомендовать...?** *vih moh‧zhih‧tee pah‧ree‧kah‧meen‧dah‧vaht'...*
a concert	**концерт** *kahn‧tsert*
a movie	**фильм** *feel'm*
an opera	**оперу** *oh‧pee‧roo*
a play	**пьесу** *pyeh‧soo*

When does it start/end?	**Когда начинается/заканчивается?** kahg·*dah* nah·chee·*nah*·ee·tsah/ zah·*kahn*·chee·vah·ee·tsah
What's the dress code?	**Какая форма одежды?** kah·*kah*·yah *for*·mah ah·*dyezh*·dih
I like...	**Я люблю...** yah lyoob·*lyoo*...
classical music	**классическую музыку** klah·*see*·chees·koo·yoo *moo*·zih·koo
folk music	**народную музыку** nah·*rod*·noo·yoo *moo*·zih·koo
jazz	**джаз** dzhahs
pop music	**поп-музыку** *pop*·moo·zih·koo
rap	**рэп** rep

For Tickets, see page 18.

131

There is extensive English-language information available on the internet about the schedules of performances at the Bolshoi Theater in Moscow and the Mariinsky Theater in St. Petersburg. Both theaters offer free courier service that can deliver tickets to your hotel or apartment.

YOU MAY HEAR...

| **Выключите Ваши мобильные телефоны, пожалуйста.** *vih*·klyoo·chee·tee *vah*·shee mah·*beel*'·nih·ee tee·lee·*foh*·nih pah·*zhahl*·stah | Turn off your cell [mobile] phones, please |

Nightlife

What is there to do in the evenings?	**Что здесь можно делать по вечерам?** *shtoh zdyehs' mozh·nah dyeh·laht' pah vee·chee·rahm*
Can you recommend...?	**Вы можете порекомендовать...?** *vih moh·zhih·tee pah·ree·kah·meen·dah·vaht'...*
a bar	**бар** *bahr*
a cabaret	**ресторан с эстрадным выступлением** *reh·stah·rahn s ehst·rahd·nihm vihs·toop·lehnyehm*
a casino	**казино** *kah·zee·noh*
a dance club	**дискотеку** *dees·kah·tyeh·koo*
a gay club	**гейклуб** *gyey·kloop*
a jazz club	**джазовый клуб** *dzhah·zoh·viy kloob*
a club with Russian music	**клуб с русской музыкой** *kloob s roos·koy moo·zih·koy*
a nightclub	**ночной клуб** *nahch·noy kloop*
Is there live music?	**Там есть живая музыка?** *tahm yest' zhih·vah·yah moo·zih·kah*
How do I get there?	**Как туда добраться?** *kahk too·dah dah·brah·tsah*
Is there a cover charge?	**Нужно платить за вход?** *noozh·nah plah·teet' zah fkhot*
Let's go dancing.	**Пойдём танцевать.** *pie·dyom tahn·tsih·vaht'*
Is this area safe at night?	**В этом районе ночью безопасно?** *v etohm rah·yoh·neh nohch'·yu beh·zoh·pahs·noh*

Special Requirements

Business Travel

ESSENTIAL

I'm here on business.	**Я здесь по делам.** *yah zdyehs' pah dee·lahm*
Here's my business card.	**Вот моя визитка.** *voht mah·yah vee·zeet·kah*
Can I have your card?	**Можно Вашу визитку?** *mozh·nah vah·shoo vee·zeet·koo*
I have a meeting with…	**У меня встреча с…** *oo mee·nyah fstreh·chah s…*
Where's…?	**Где…?** *gdyeh…*
the business center	**бизнес-центр** *beez·nehs tsehntr*
the convention hall	**конференц-зал** *kahn·fee·ryehnts zahl*
the meeting room	**комната для встреч** *kohm·nah·tah dlyah fstrehch*

On Business

I'm here to attend…	**Я приехал m /приехала f на…** *yah pree·yeh·khahl/pree·yeh·khah·lah nah…*
a seminar	**семинар** *see·mee·nahr*
a conference	**конференцию** *kahn·fee·ryen·tsih·yoo*
a meeting	**деловую встречу** *dee·lah·voo·yoo fstreh·choo*
My name is…	**Меня зовут…** *mee·nyah zah·voot…*
May I introduce my colleague…	**Разрешите представить моего m /мою f коллегу…** *rahz·ree·shih·tee preet·stah·veet' mah·ee·voh/mah·yoo kah·lyeh·goo…*
Pleasure to meet you.	**Был рад m /Была рада f встретиться с вами.** *bihl rahd/bih·lah rah·dah fstryeh·tee·tsah s vah·mee*
I'm sorry I'm late.	**Извините за опоздание.** *eez·vee·nee·tee zah ah·pahz·dah·nee·yeh*

I have a meeting/an appointment with …	**У меня встреча с…** *oo meh·nya vstreh·chah s*
I need an interpreter.	**Мне нужен переводчик.** *mnyeh noo·zhihn pee·ree·vot·cheek*
You can reach me at the…Hotel.	**Вы можете найти меня в гостинице…** *vih moh·zhih·tee nie·tee mee·nyah v gahs·tee·nee·tseh…*
I'm here until…	**Я буду здесь до…** *yah boo·doo zdyes' dah…*
I need to…	**Мне нужно…** *mnyeh noozh·nah…*
make a call	**позвонить** *pah·zvah·neet'*
make a photocopy	**сделать копию** *zdyeh·laht' koh·pee·yoo*
send an e-mail	**послать электронное сообщение** *pah·slaht' ee·leek·tron·nah·yeh sah·ahp·shcheh·nee·yeh*
send a fax	**послать факс** *pah·slaht' fahks*
send a package (overnight)	**отправить (срочную) посылку** *aht·prah·veet' (sroch·noo·yoo) pah·sihl·koo*
It was a pleasure to meet you.	**Был рад *m* /Была рада *f* встретиться с вами.** *bihl rahd/bih·lah rah·dah fstryeh·tee·tsah s vah·mee*

For Communications, see page 50.

Russian business interactions are generally curt and matter-of-fact, without niceties such as 'at your earliest convenience' or 'please feel free to.' As a result, when translated literally, Russian business conversations can sound rude and demanding. Keep in mind that cultural differences like these may lead to unnecessary misunderstandings.

YOU MAY HEAR...

У Вас назначена встреча? *oo vahs nahz•nah•chee•nah fstreh•chah*	Do you have an appointment?
С кем? *s kyem*	With whom?
Он/Она на встрече. *on/ah•nah nah fstreh•cheh*	He/She is in a meeting.
Одну минуту, пожалуйста. *ahd•noo mee•noo•too pah•zhahl•stah*	One moment, please.
Присаживайтесь. *pree•sah•zhih•vie•tees'*	Have a seat.
Не желаете что-нибудь выпить? *nee zhih•lah•ee•tee shtoh•nee•boot' vih•peet'*	Would you like something to drink?
Спасибо за визит. *spah•see•bah zah vee•zeet*	Thank you for coming.

Traveling with Children

ESSENTIAL

Is there a discount for children?	**Есть скидка для детей?** *yest' skeet•kah dlyah dee•tyey*
Can you recommend a babysitter?	**Вы можете порекомендовать няню?** *vih moh•zhih•tee pah•ree•kah•men•dah•vaht' nyah•nyoo*
Could we have a child's seat/highchair?	**Можно детский/высокий стульчик?** *mozh•nah dyets•keey/vih•soh•keey stool'•cheek*
Where can I change the baby?	**Где можно переодеть ребёнка?** *gdyeh mozh•nah pee•ree•ah•dyet' ree•byon•kah*

Out & About

Can you recommend something for the kids?	**Можете порекомендовать что-нибудь для детей?** _moh_-zhih-tee pah-ree-kah-meen-dah-_vaht'_ _shtoh_-nee-boot' dlyah dee-_tyey_
Where's...?	**Где...?** gdyeh...
the amusement park	**парк с аттракционами** pahrk s aht-rahk-tsih-_oh_-nah-mee
the arcade	**зал аттракционов** zahl aht-rahk-tsih-_oh_-nahf
the kiddie pool	**детский бассейн** _dyets_-keey bah-_seyn_
the park	**парк** pahrk
the playground	**детская площадка** _dyets_-kah-yah plah-_shchaht_-kah
the zoo	**зоопарк** zah-ah-_pahrk_
Are kids allowed?	**Детям можно?** _dyeh_-tyam _mozh_-nah
Is it safe for kids?	**Здесь неопасно для детей?** zdyes' nee-ah-_pahs_-nah dlyah dee-_tyey_
Is it suitable for...year olds?	**Это подходит для...летних?** _eh_-tah paht-_khoh_-deet dlyah..._let_-neekh

For Numbers, see page 157.

Baby Essentials

Do you have...?	**У Вас есть...?** oo vahs yest'...
a baby bottle	**детская бутылочка** _dyets_-kah-yah boo-_tih_-lahch-kah
baby food	**детское питание** _deht_-skoh-ye pee-_tah_- nee-yeh
baby wipes	**гигиенические салфетки** gee-gee-ee-_nee_-chees-kee-yeh sahl-_fyet_-kee
a car seat	**детское сиденье** _dyets_-kah-yeh see-_dyen'_-yeh
a children's menu/portion	**меню/порции для детей** mee-_nyoo_/ _por_-tsih-ee dlyah dee-_tyey_

a child's seat/ highchair	**детский/высокий стульчик** _dyets_•keey/ vih•soh•keey _stool_•cheek
a crib/cot	**колыбель/детская кроватка** kah•lih•_byel'_/ _dyets_•kah•yah krah•_vaht_•kah
diapers [nappies]	**подгузники** pahd•_gooz_•nee•kee
formula	**молочная смесь** mah•_loch_•nah•yah smyes'
a pacifier [dummy]	**соска** _sos_•kah
a playpen	**манеж** mah•_nyesh_
a stroller [pushchair]	**прогулочная коляска** prah•_goo_•lahch•nah•yah kah•_lyas_•kah
Can I breastfeed the baby here?	**Я могу здесь покормить грудью ребёнка?** yah mah•_goo_ zdyes' pah•kahr•_meet'_ _grood'_•yoo ree•_byon_•kah
Where can I breastfeed/ change the baby?	**Где можно покормить/переодеть ребёнка?** gdyeh _mozh_•nah pah•kahr•_meet'_/pee•ree•ah•_dyet'_ ree•_byon_•kah

For Dining with Children, see page 66.

YOU MAY HEAR...

Какой хорошенький! _m_ /**Какая** **хорошенькая** _f_! kah•_koy_ khah•_roh_•shen'•keey/ kah•_kah_•yah khah•_roh_•shihn'•kah•yah	How cute!
Как его/её зовут? kak yee•_voh_/yee•_yoh_ zah•_voot_	What's his/her name?
Сколько ему/ей лет? _skol'_•kah ee•_moo_/ yey lyet	How old is he/she?

Babysitting

Can you recommend a babysitter?	**Вы можете порекомендовать няню?** vih moh·zhih·tee pah·ree·kah·meen·dah·_vaht'_ nyah·nyoo
What's the charge?	**Сколько стоит?** _skol'_·kah _stoh_·eet
We'll be back by...	**Мы вернёмся к...** mih veer·_nyom_·syah k...
I can be reached at...	**Со мной можно связаться...** sah mnoy _mozh_·nah svee·_zah_·tsah...

For Time, see page 159.

Health & Emergency

Can you recommend a pediatrician?	**Можете порекомендовать педиатра?** _moh_·zhih·tee pah·ree·kah·meen·dah·_vaht'_ pee·_dee_·aht·rah
My child is allergic to...	**У моего ребёнка аллергия на...** oo mah·ee·_voh_ ree·_byon_·kah ah·leer·_gee_·yah nah...
My child is missing.	**У меня пропал ребёнок.** oo mee·_nyah_ prah·_pahl_ ree·_byoh_·nahk
Have you seen a boy/girl?	**Вы видели мальчика/девочку?** vih _vee_·dee·lee _mahl'_·chee·kah/_dyeh_·vahch·koo

For Meals & Cooking, see page 68.

For Health, see page 145.

For Police, see page 143.

Disabled Travelers

ESSENTIAL

Is there...?	**Есть...?** yest'...
access for the disabled	**условия для инвалидов** oos·_loh_·vee·yah dlyah een·vah·_lee_·dahf

a wheelchair ramp	**пандус для инвалидного кресла** _pahn_-doos dlyah een-vah-_leed_-nah-vah _kryes_-lah
a disabled-accessible toilet	**туалет с условиями для инвалидов** too-ah-_lyet_ s oos-_loh_-vee-yah-mee dlyaheen-vah-_lee_-dahf
I need assistance.	**Мне нужна помощь.** mnyeh _noozh_-nah poh-mahshch
I need an elevator [lift].	**Мне нужен лифт.** mnyeh _noo_-zhehn left
I need a ground-floor room.	**Мне нужен номер на первом этаже.** mnyeh _noo_-zhehn _noh_-meer nah _pyer_-vahm eh-tah-_zheh_

Asking for Assistance

I'm disabled.	**Я инвалид.** yah een-vah-_leet_
I'm deaf.	**Я глухой m /глухая f.** yah gloo-_khoy_/ gloo-_khah_-yah
I'm visually/hearing impaired.	**У меня плохое зрение/слух.** oo mee-_nyah_ plah-_khoh_-yeh zryeh-nee-yeh/slookh
I'm unable to walk far/use the stairs.	**Я не могу ходить далеко/пользоваться лестницей.** yah nee mah-_goo_ khah-_deet'_ dah-lee-koh/_pol'_zah-vah-tsah _lyes_-nee-tsey
Can I bring my wheelchair?	**Я могу привезти своё инвалидное кресло?** yah mah-_goo_ pree-vees-_tee_ svah-yoh een-vah-_leed_-nah-yeh _kres_-lah
Are guide dogs permitted?	**Сюда допускаются собаки-поводыри?** syoo-_dah_ dah-poos-_kah_-yoo-tsah sah-_bah_-kee pah-vah-dih-_ree_
Help me, please.	**Помогите мне, пожалуйста.** pah-mah-_gee_-tee mnyeh pah-_zhahl_-stah
Please open/hold the door.	**Пожалуйста, откройте/придержите дверь.** pah-_zhahl_-stah aht-_kroy_-tee/pree-deer-_zhih_-tee dvyer'

In an Emergency

Emergencies

ESSENTIAL

Help!	**Помогите!** pah·mah·<u>gee</u>·tee
Go away!	**Идите отсюда!** ee·<u>dee</u>·tee aht·<u>syoo</u>·dah
Stop, thief!	**Держите вора!** deer·<u>zhih</u>·tee <u>voh</u>·rah
Get a doctor!	**Вызовите врача!** <u>vih</u>·zah·vee·tee vrah·<u>chah</u>
Fire!	**Пожар!** pah·<u>zhahr</u>
I'm lost.	**Я заблудился** m /**заблудилась** f. yah zah·bloo·<u>deel</u>·syah/zah·bloo·<u>dee</u>·lahs'
Help me, please.	**Помогите мне, пожалуйста.** pah·mah·<u>gee</u>·tee mnyeh pah·<u>zhahl</u>·stah

In an emergency, dial: **02** for the police
01 for the fire brigade
03 for the ambulance

YOU MAY HEAR...

Заполните бланк. zah·<u>pol</u>·nee·tyeh blahnk	Please fill out this form.
Ваши документы, пожалуйста. <u>vah</u>·shih dah·koo·<u>myen</u>·tih pah·<u>zhahl</u>·stah	Your identification, please.
Где/Когда это произошло? gdyeh/kahg·<u>dah</u> <u>eh</u>·tah prah·ee·zah·<u>shloh</u>	When/Where did it happen?
Как он/она выглядит? kahk on/ah·<u>nah</u> <u>vih</u>·glyah·deet	What does he/she look like?

ESSENTIAL

Call the police!	**Вызовите милицию!** _vih_·zah·vee·tee _mee·lee·tsih·yoo_
Where's the police station?	**Где отделение милиции?** _gdyeh aht·dee·lyeh·nee·yeh mee·lee·tsih·ee_
There has been an accident.	**Произошла авария.** _prah·ee·zah·shlah ah·vah·ree·yah_
My child is missing.	**У меня пропал ребёнок.** _oo mee·nyah prah·pahl ree·byoh·nahk_
I need an interpreter.	**Мне нужен переводчик.** _mnyeh noo·zhehn pee·ree·vot·cheek_
I need to contact my lawyer.	**Мне нужно связаться с моим адвокатом.** _mnyeh noozh·nah svyah·zah·tsah s mah·eem ahd·vah·kah·tahm_
I need to make a phone call.	**Мне нужно позвонить.** _mnyeh noozh·nah pah·zvah·neet'_
I'm innocent.	**Я невиновен.** _yah nee·vee·noh·veen_

Crime & Lost Property

I want to report...	**Я хочу заявить о...** _yah khah·chyoo zah·ee·veet' ah..._
a mugging	**ограблении** _ah·grahb·lyeh·nee·ee_
a rape	**изнасиловании** _eez·nah·see·lah·vah·nee·ee_
a theft	**краже** _krah·zheh_
I've been mugged.	**Меня ограбили.** _Meh·nya oh·grah·bee·lee_
I've been robbed.	**Меня ограбили.** _mee·nyah ah·grah·bee·lee_

I've lost my…	**Я потерял** *m* /**потеряла** *f*… *yah pah•tee•ryahl/pah•tee•ryah•lah…*
My…has been stolen.	**У меня украли…** *oo mee•nyah oo•krah•lee…*
backpack	**рюкзак** *ryoog•zahk*
bicycle	**велосипед** *vee•lah•see•pyet*
camera	**фотоаппарат** *fah•tah•ah•pah•raht*
car	**машину** *mah•shih•noo*
computer	**компьютер** *kahm•pyoo•ter*
credit card	**кредитную карточку** *kree•deet•noo•yoo kahr•tahch•koo*
jewelry	**драгоценности** *drah•gah•tseh•nahs•tee*
money	**деньги** *dyen'•gee*
passport	**паспорт** *pahs•pahrt*
purse [handbag]	**сумочку** *soo•mach•koo*
traveler's cheques	**дорожные чеки** *dah•rozh•nih•ee cheh•kee*
wallet	**бумажник** *boo•mahzh•neek*
I need a police report.	**Мне нужно обратиться в полицию.** *mneh nuzh•noh oh•brah•tee t'•sya v poh•lee•tsih•yoo*
Where is the British/ American/Irish embassy?	**Где находится британское/американское/ ирландское консульство?** *gdyeh nah•khoh•deet•sya bree•tahn•sko•ye/ ah•meh•ree•kahn•sko•ye/eer•lahnd•sko•ye kon•sool'•stvoh*

Health

ESSENTIAL

I'm sick [ill].	**Я заболел** *m* **/заболела** *f.* yah zah·bah·<u>lyel</u>/ zah·bah·<u>lyeh</u>·lah
I need an English-speaking doctor.	**Мне нужен англоговорящий врач.** mnyeh <u>noo</u>·zhen <u>ahn</u>·glah·gah·vah·<u>ryah</u>·shcheey vrahch
It hurts here.	**Мне больно вот здесь.** mnyeh <u>bohl'</u>·nah voht zdyehs'
I have a stomachache.	**У меня болит живот.** oo mee·<u>nyah</u> bah·<u>leet</u> zhih·<u>voht</u>

Finding a Doctor

Can you recommend a doctor/dentist?	**Можете порекомендовать врача/дантиста?** <u>moh</u>·zhih·tee pah·ree·kah·meen·dah·<u>vaht'</u> vrah·<u>chah</u>/dahn·<u>tees</u>·tah
Could the doctor come to see me here?	**Не мог бы врач прийти осмотреть меня здесь?** nee mog bih vrahch pree·<u>tee</u> ah·smah·<u>tryet'</u> mee·<u>nyah</u> zdyes'
I need an English-speaking doctor.	**Мне нужен англоговорящий врач.** mnyeh <u>noo</u>·zhihn <u>ahn</u>·glah·gah·vah·<u>ryah</u>·shcheey vrahch
What are the office hours?	**Какие часы работы?** kah·<u>kee</u>·yeh chah·<u>sih</u> rah·<u>boh</u>·tih
Can I make an appointment...?	**Можно записаться к врачу на прием...?** <u>mozh</u>·nah zah·pee·<u>sah</u>·tsah k vrah·<u>choo</u> nah pree·<u>yom</u>...
for today	**на сегодня** nah see·<u>vod</u>·nyah
for tomorrow	**на завтра** nah <u>zahf</u>·trah

145

as soon as	**как можно скорее** *kahk mozh·nah
possible	skah·ryeh·yeh*
It's urgent.	**Это срочно.** *eh·tah sroch·nah*

Symptoms

I'm...	**У меня...** *oo mee·nyah...*
bleeding	**кровотечение** *krah·vah·tee·cheh·nee·yeh*
constipated	**запор** *zah·por*
dizzy	**кружится голова** *kroo·zhih·tsah gah·lah·vah*
I'm nauseous/	**Меня подташнивает/тошнит.** *mee·nyah
vomiting.	paht·tahsh·nee·vah·eet/tahsh·neet*
It hurts here.	**Мне больно вот здесь.** *mnyeh bohl'·nah vaht zdyes'*
I have...	**У меня...** *oo mee·nyah...*
an allergic	**аллергическая реакция**
reaction	*ah·leer·gee·chees·kah·yah ree·ahk·tsih·yah*
a chest pain	**боли в груди** *boh·lee v groo·dee*
cramps	**спазмы** *spah·zmih*
diarrhea	**понос** *pah·nohs*
an earache	**болит ухо** *bah·leet oo·khah*
a fever	**жар** *zhahr*
pain	**боли** *boh·lee*
a rash	**сыпь** *sihp'*
a sprain	**растяжение** *rahs·tee·zheh·nee·yeh*
some swelling	**опухоль** *oh·poo·khahl'*
a sore throat	**болит горло** *boh·leet gohr·loh*
a stomachache	**болит живот** *bah·leet zhih·voht*
sunstroke	**солнечный удар** *sol·neech·niy oo·dahr*
I've been sick [ill]	**Я болею...дней.** *yah bah·lyeh·yoo...dnyey*
for...days.	

For Numbers, see page 157.

Conditions

I'm...	**У меня...** *oo mee·nyah...*
anemic	**анемия** *ah·nee·mee·yah*
asthmatic	**астма** *ahst·mah*
diabetic	**диабет** *dee·ah·byet*
epileptic	**эпилепсия** *ehpee·lehp·see·ya*
I'm allergic to antibiotics/ penicillin.	**У меня аллергия на антибиотики/ пенициллин.** *oo mee·nyah ah·leer·gee·yah nah ahn·tee·bee·oh·tee·kee/pee·nee·tsih·leen*
I have arthritis/ high/low blood pressure.	**У меня артрит/высокое/низкое давление.** *oo mee·nyah ahrt·reet/ vih·soh·kah·ye/nees·kah·yeh dahv·lyeh·nee·ya*
I have a heart condition.	**У меня больное сердце.** *oo mee·nyah bahl'·noh·yeh ser·tseh*
I'm on...	**Я принимаю...** *yah pree·nee·mah·yoo...*

For Meals & Cooking, see page 68.

YOU MAY HEAR...

Что случилось? *shtoh sloo·chee·lahs'*	What's wrong?
Где болит? *gdyeh bah·leet*	Where does it hurt?
Вы принимаете другое лекарство? *vih pree·nee·mah·ee·tee droo·goh·yeh lee·kahr·stvah*	Are you taking any other medication?
Аллергия на что-нибудь? *ah·leer·gee·yah nah shtoh·nee·boot'*	Are you allergic to anything?
Откройте рот. *aht·kroy·tee rot*	Open your mouth.
Дышите глубоко. *dih·shih·tee gloo·bah·koh*	Breathe deeply.
Покашляйте. *poh·kahsch·lyai·tye*	Cough, please.
Обратитесь в больницу. *obh·rah·tee·tehs' v bohl'·nee·tsoo*	Go to the hospital.

Treatment

Do I need a prescription/medicine?	**У меня нет рецепта/лекарства?** *oo meh·nya neht reh·tsehp·tah/leh·kahr·stvah*
Can you prescribe a generic drug [unbranded medication]?	**Вы можете прописать непатентованный препарат [без марочного названия]?** *vih moh·zheh·teh proh·pee·saht' neh·pah·tehn·toh·vah·niy preh·pah·raht [bez naz vah neeya]*
Where can I get it?	**Где можно его приобрести?** *gdyeh mozh·noh ye·voh pree·ohb·rehs·tee*

For Pharmacy, see page 150.

Hospital

Please notify my family.	**Пожалуйста, сообщите моей семье.** *pah·zhahl·stah sah·ahb·shchee·tee mah·yey seem'·yeh*
I'm in pain.	**У меня боли.** *oo mee·nyah boh·lee*
I need a doctor/ nurse.	**Мне нужен врач/нужна медсестра.** *mnyeh noo·zhihn vrach/noozh·nah myet·sees·trah*
When are visiting hours?	**Когда часы посещений?** *kahg·dah chah·sih pah·see·shcheh·neey*
I'm visiting...	**Я навещаю...** *yah nah·vee·shchah·yoo...*

Dentist

I've broken a tooth/ lost a filling.	**У меня сломался зуб/выпала пломба.** *oo mee·nyah slah·mahl·syah zoop/vih·pah·lah plom·bah*
I have a toothache.	**У меня болит зуб.** *oo mee·nyah bah·leet zoop*
Can you fix this denture?	**Вы можете починить этот протез?** *vih moh·zhih·tee pah·chee·neet' eh·taht prah·tes*

Gynecologist

I have menstrual cramps/a vaginal infection.	**У меня менструальные колики/вагинальная инфекция.** oo mee-*nyah* meen-stroo-*ahl'*-nih-ee *koh*-lee-kee/vah-gee-*nahl'*-nah-yah een-*fyek*-tsih-yah
I missed my period.	**У меня не было менструации.** oo mee-*nyah nyeh*-bih-lah meen-stroo-*ah*-tsih-ee
I'm on the Pill.	**Я принимаю противозачаточные таблетки.** yah pree-nee-*mah*-yoo prah-tee-vah-zah-*chah*-tahch-nih-ee tahb-*lyet*-kee
I'm (...months) pregnant.	**Я беременна (на...месяце).** ya beh-*reh*-meh-nah (nah ... *meh*-sya-tse)
I'm (not) pregnant.	**Я (не) беременна.** yah (nee) bee-*ryeh*-mee-nah
I haven't had my period for...months.	**У меня нет менструации уже...месяца.** oo mee-*nyah* nyet meen-stroo-*ah*-tsih-ee oo-*zheh*...*myeh*-see-tsah

For Numbers, see page 157.

Optician

I've lost...	**Я потерял** *m* /**потеряла** *f*... yah pah-tee-*ryahl*/pah-tee-*ryah*-lah...
a contact lens	**контактную линзу** kahn-*tahkt*-noo-yoo *leen*-zoo
my glasses	**мои очки** mah-*ee* ahch-*kee*
a lens	**линзу** *leen*-zoo

Payment & Insurance

How much?	**Сколько?** *skol'*-kah
Can I pay by credit card?	**Можно платить кредитной карточкой?** *mozh*-nah plah-*teet'* kree-*deet*-nie *kahr*-tahch-kie
I have insurance.	**У меня есть страховка.** oo mee-*nyah* yest' strah-*khof*-kah

| Can I have a receipt for my insurance? | **Можете дать мне квитанцию для моей страховки?** *moh•zhih•tee daht' mnyeh kvee•tahn•tsih•yoo dlyah mah•yey strah•khof•kee* |

Pharmacy

ESSENTIAL

Where's the nearest pharmacy?	**Где ближайшая аптека?** *gdyeh blee•zhie•shah•yah ahp•tyeh•kah*
What time does it open/close?	**Во сколько аптека открывается/ закрывается?** *vah skol'•kah ahp•tyeh•kah aht•krih•vah•ee•tsah/zah•krih•vah•ee•tsah*
What would you recommend for…?	**Что порекомендуете от…?** *shtoh pah•ree•kah•meen•doo•ee•tee aht…*
How much should I take?	**Сколько нужно принимать?** *skol'•kah noozh•nah pree•nee•maht'*
Can you fill [make up] this prescription for me?	**Вы можете приготовить это лекарство?** *vih moh•zhih•tee pree•gah•toh•veet' eh•tah lee•kahr•stvah*
I'm allergic to…	**У меня аллергия на…** *oo mee•nyah ah•leer•gee•yah nah…*

In Russia, a wide range of medication is available without a prescription. **Аптека** ahp•*tyeh*•kah (a pharmacy) in Russia's larger cities is likely to carry many brand-name medications. Drugs are also available from kiosks, but it is best to obtain them from a pharmacy or private clinics and hospitals, such as the American Clinic in Moscow or the American Medical Center in St. Petersburg. As a foreigner, you will have to pay for treatment in state-run hospitals. Russian doctors in these facilities are not well paid, and it is customary to give them something to express your gratitude for their care, a box of chocolates or a bottle of wine, for example. Before leaving home, be sure that your insurance coverage is valid for treatment in Russia.

What to Take

How much do I take?	**Какая дозировка?**	kah•*kah*•ya doh•zee•*rohv*•kah
How often?	**Как часто?**	kahk *chahs*•tah
Is it suitable for children?	**Это можно детям?**	*eh*•tah *mozh*•nah *dyeh*•tyahm
I'm taking...	**Я принимаю...**	yah pree•nee•*mah*•yoo...
Are there side effects?	**Есть побочные эффекты?**	yest' pah•*boch*•nih•ee ee•*fyek*•tih
I'd like some medicine for...	**Мне нужно лекарство от...**	mnyeh *noozh*•nah lee•*kahrs*•tvah aht...
a cold	**простуды**	prah•*stoo*•dih
a cough	**кашля**	*kahsh*•lyah
diarrhea	**поноса**	pah•*noh*•sah
a headache	**головной боли**	goh•lohv•*noi boh*•lee
insect bites	**укусов насекомых**	oo•*koo*•sahf nah•see•*koh*•mihkh
motion [travel] sickness	**морской болезни**	mahr•*skoy* bah•*lyez*•nee

a sore throat	**воспаления горла** vahs·pah·*lyeh*·nee·yah *gor*·lah
sunburn	**солнечного ожёга** *sol*·neech·nah·vah ah·*zhoh*·gah
a toothache	**зубной боли** zoob·*noi* boh·lee
an upset stomach	**расстройства желудка** rahs·*troy*·stvah zhih·*loot*·kah

YOU MAY SEE…

ОДИН/ТРИ РАЗА В ДЕНЬ ah·*deen*/tree *rah*·zah v dyen'	once/three times a day
ТАБЛЕТКИ tahb·*lyet*·kee	tablets
КАПЛИ *kahp*·lee	drops
ДО/ПОСЛЕ/ВО ВРЕМЯ ЕДЫ doh/*pos*·lee/ vah *vryeh*·myah yeh·*dih*	before/after/with meals
НА ПУСТОЙ ЖЕЛУДОК (НАТОЩАК) nah poos·*toy* zhih·*loo*·dahk (nah·tah·*shchahk*)	on an empty stomach
ТОЛЬКО ДЛЯ НАРУЖНОГО ПРИМЕНЕНИЯ *tol'*·kah dlyah nah·*roozh*·nah·vah pree·mee·*nyeh*·nee·yah	for external use only

Basic Supplies

I'd like…	**Я хотел m /хотела f бы…** yah khah·*tyel*/ khah·*tyeh*·lah bih…
acetaminophen [paracetamol]	**парацетамол** pah·rah·tsih·tah·*mol*
antiseptic cream	**антисептическую мазь** ahn·tee·sep·*tee*·chees·koo·yoo mahz'
aspirin	**аспирин** ahs·pee·*reen*
bandages [plasters]	**пластырь** *plahs*·tihr'
a comb	**расчёску** rah·*shchos*·koo

I'd like…	**Я хотел** *m* **/хотела** *f* **бы…** *yah khah•tyel/ khah•tyeh•lah bih…*	
condoms	**презервативы** *pree•zeer•vah•tee•vih*	
contact lens solution	**раствор для контактных линз** *rahst•vor dlyah kahn•tahkt•nihkh leens*	
deodorant	**дезодорант** *dee•zah•dah•rahnt*	
a hairbrush	**щётку для волос** *shchot•koo dlyah vah•los*	
hair spray	**лак для волос** *lahk dlyah vah•los*	
ibuprofen	**ибупрофен** *ee•boo•prah•fyen*	
insect repellent	**репеллент** *ree•pee•lyent*	
lotion	**лосьон** *lohs' yohn*	
a nail file	**пилочку для ногтей** *pee•lahch•koo dlyah nahk•tyey*	
a (disposable) razor	**(одноразовую) бритву** *(ahd•nah•rah•zah•voo•yoo) breet•voo*	
razor blades	**лезвия** *lyez•vee•yah*	
sanitary napkins [towels]	**гигиенические салфетки** *gee•gee•ee•nee•chees•kee•yeh sahl•fyet•kee*	
shampoo/ conditioner	**шампунь/кондиционер** *shahm•poon'/ kahn•dee•tsih•ah•nyer*	
soap	**мыло** *mih•lah*	
sunscreen	**крем для загара** *kryem dlyah zah•gah•rah*	
tampons	**тампоны** *tahm•poh•nih*	
tissues	**бумажные салфетки** *boo•mahzh•nih•ee sahl•fet•kee*	
toilet paper	**туалетную бумагу** *too•ah•lyet•noo•yoo boo•mah•goo*	
a toothbrush	**зубную щетку** *zoob•noo•yoo shchot•koo*	
toothpaste	**зубную пасту** *zoob•noo•yoo pahs•too*	

For Baby Essentials, see page 137.

153

The Basics

Grammar

Verbs

The infinitive of most verbs ends in **–ть**. Russian verbs follow two conjugation patterns in the present and future tenses; following are the patterns for the verbs **жить** *zhiht'* (to live) and **говорить** *gah·vah·reet'* (to speak):

ЖИТЬ (to live)		Present	Future
I	я	живу	буду жить
you (sing.)	ты	живёшь	будешь жить
he/she/it	он/она/оно	живёт	будет жить
we	мы	живём	будем жить
you (pl.)	вы	живёте	будете жить
they	они	живут	будут жить

ГОВОРИТЬ (to speak)		Present	Future
I	я	говорю	буду говорить
you (sing.)	ты	говоришь	будешь говорить
he/she/it	он/она/оно	говорит	будет говорить
we	мы	говорим	будем говорить
you (pl.)	вы	говорите	будете говорить
they	они	говорят	будут говорить

Some verbs have a mixed conjugation, combining the first and second patterns.

The past tense is formed by removing the **–ть** of the infinitive and adding:

–л *(l)*	masculine ending
–ла *(lah)*	feminine ending
–ло *(loh)*	neuter ending
–ли *(lee)*	plural ending

It is the gender and number of the subject that control the ending, for example:

ГОВОРИТЬ (to speak)		Past
I	я	говорил
you (sing.)	ты	говорил
he	он	говорил
she	она	говорила
it	оно	говорило
we	мы	говорили
you (pl.)	вы	говорили
they	они	говорили

There are no irregular verbs in the Russian language.

Word Order

In the Russian language, word order is rather flexible. Though the Russian sentence is generally arranged subject-verb-object, grammar rules allow virtually any combination of subject, verb and object within the sentence. You can form a simple question in Russian by adding an interrogatory intonation (letting the voice rise at the end of the sentence).

Счёт включает обслуживание. *shchot fklyoo·chah·eet ahp·sloo·zhih·vah·nee·yeh*   Service is included.

Счёт включает обслуживание? *shchot fklyoo·chah·eet ahp·sloo·zhih·vah·nee·yeh*   Is service included?

Negation

To form a negative sentence, add **не** *nee* (not) before the verb.
Example:

Мы курим. *mih <u>koo</u>•reem*	We smoke.
Мы не курим. *mih nee <u>koo</u>•reem*	We don't smoke.

Imperatives

Imperative sentences, or sentences that are commands, are formed by adding
the appropriate ending to the stem of the verb (i.e. the verb in the infinitive
without the **–ть**, **–сь**, **–ся** ending). Example: Speak!

you (sing.)	**Говори!** *gah-vah-<u>ree</u>*
you (pl.)	**Говорите!** *gah-vah-<u>ree</u>-tee*

Nouns

There are three genders in Russian: masculine, feminine and neuter. The
endings of nouns vary according to their role in the sentence. There are six
different cases (roles) in both the singular and plural. Adjectives agree in
number and gender with the noun they modify.

There are no articles in Russian.

Adjectives

Adjectives agree in number and gender with the noun they modify.

masculine ending	**–ый**, **–ой**, **–ий**
feminine ending	**–ая**
neuter ending	**–ое**

Example:

красный *m* <u>krahs</u>•niy	red
красная *f* <u>krahs</u>•nah•yah	red
красное *n* <u>krahs</u>•nah•yeh	red

Comparatives & Superlatives

The comparative may be formed by adding **более** _boh·lee·yeh_ (more) or **менее** _myeh·nee·yeh_ (less) before the adjective or adverb. However, more often these are formed with the help of the endings **–e** and **–ee** which are added to the stem.

The superlative is formed by adding **самый** _sah·miy_ (the most) and **наимение** _nah·ee·myeh·nee·yeh_ (the least) before the adjective.

большой _bahl'·shoy_	big
больше _bol'·sheh_	bigger
самый большой _sah·miy bahl'·shoy_	biggest
дорогой _dah·rah·goy_	expensive
менее дорогой _myeh·nee·yeh dah·rah·goy_	more expensive
наименее дорогой _nah·ee·myeh·nee·yeh dah·rah·goy_	most expensive

Adverbs & Adverbial Expressions

Many adverbs are formed by adding **–o** to the stem of an adjective:

хороший _khah·roh·shiy_ good	**хорошо** _khah·rah·shoh_ well
красивый _krah·see·viy_ beautiful	**красиво** _krah·see·vah_ beautifully

Numbers

ESSENTIAL

0	**ноль** _nol'_	
1	**один** _ah·deen_	
2	**два** _dvah_	
3	**три** _tree_	
4	**четыре** _chee·tih·ree_	
5	**пять** _pyaht'_	
6	**шесть** _shest'_	
7	**семь** _syem'_	

8	**восемь** _voh_•seem'
9	**девять** _dyeh_•veet'
10	**десять** _dyeh_•seet'
11	**одиннадцать** ah•_dee_•nah•tsaht'
12	**двенадцать** dvee•_nah_•tsaht'
13	**тринадцать** tree•_nah_•tsaht'
14	**четырнадцать** chee•_tihr_•nah•tsaht'
15	**пятнадцать** peet•_nah_•tsaht'
16	**шестнадцать** shihs•_nah_•tsaht'
17	**семнадцать** seem•_nah_•tsaht'
18	**восемнадцать** vah•seem•_nah_•tsaht'
19	**девятнадцать** dee•veet•_nah_•tsaht'
20	**двадцать** _dvah_•tsaht'
21	**двадцать один** _dvah_•tsaht' ah•_deen_
22	**двадцать два** _dvah_•tsaht' dvah
30	**тридцать** _tree_•tsaht'
31	**тридцать один** _tree_•tsaht' ah•_deen_
40	**сорок** _soh_•rahk
50	**пятьдесят** peet'•dee•_syaht_
60	**шестьдесят** sheez'•dee•_syaht_
70	**семьдесят** _syem_'•dee•seet
80	**восемьдесят** _voh_•seem'•dee•seet
90	**девяносто** dee•vee•_nos_•tah
100	**сто** stoh
101	**сто один** stoh ah•_deen_
200	**двести** _dvyes_•tee
500	**пятьсот** peet•_sot_
1,000	**тысяча** _tih_•see•chah
10,000	**десять тысяч** _dyeh_•seet' _tih_•seech
1,000,000	**миллион** mee•lee•_on_

Ordinal Numbers

first	**первый** _pyer·viy_
second	**второй** _ftah·roy_
third	**третий** _tryeh·teey_
fourth	**четвёртый** _cheet·vyor·tiy_
fifth	**пятый** _pyah·tiy_
once	**один раз** _ah·deen rahs_
twice	**два раза** _dvah rah·zah_
three times	**три раза** _tree rah·zah_

Один _ah·deen_ (one) has three gender forms: **один** _m ah·deen_, **одна** _f ahd·nah_ and **одно** _n ahd·noh_.
Два _dvah_ (two) has two forms: **два** _dvah_ for both masculine and neuter and **две** _dveh_ for feminine.
Ordinal numbers follow the pattern of adjectives.

Time

ESSENTIAL

What time is it?	**Который час?** _kah·toh·riy chahs_
It's noon [midday].	**Сейчас полдень.** _see·chahs pol·deen'_
At midnight.	**В полночь.** _f pol·nahch_
From nine o'clock to five o'clock.	**С девяти до пяти часов.** _s dee·vyah·tee dah pyah·tee chah·sof_
Twenty after [past] four.	**Двадцать минут пятого.** _dvah·tsaht' mee·noot pyah·tah·vah_
A quarter to nine.	**Без четверти девять.** _byes chet·veer·tee dyeh·veet'_
5:30 a.m./p.m.	**Пять тридцать утра/вечера.** _pyaht' tree·tsaht' oot·rah/vyeh·chee·rah_

Russians have a different way of thinking about and expressing time. For them, the hour between 12 and 1 is the 'first hour,' the hour between 1 and 2 is the 'second hour,' etc. Up until half past the hour, time is expressed by stating how many minutes into the given hour it is.

Example: **десять минут третьего** <u>dyeh</u>·seet' mee·noot <u>tryey</u>·tee·vah (ten after two) would be 'ten minutes of (into) the third (hour)'.

After half past the hour, time is expressed by using **без** byez (without) and the number of minutes remaining until the next hour.

Example: **без двадцати восемь** byez dvah·tsah·<u>tee</u> <u>voh</u>·seem' (twenty to eight) would be 'eight without twenty'.

Days

ESSENTIAL

Monday	**понедельник** pah·nee·<u>dyel'</u>·neek
Tuesday	**вторник** <u>ftohr</u>·neek
Wednesday	**среда** sree·<u>dah</u>
Thursday	**четверг** cheet·<u>vyerk</u>
Friday	**пятница** <u>pyaht</u>·nee·tsah
Saturday	**суббота** soo·<u>boh</u>·tah
Sunday	**воскресенье** vahs·kree·<u>syen'</u>·yeh

Dates

yesterday	**вчера** *fchee·rah*
today	**сегодня** *see·vod·nyah*
tomorrow	**завтра** *zahf·trah*
day	**день** *dyen'*
week	**неделя** *nee·dyeh·lyah*
month	**месяц** *myeh·seets*
year	**год** *got*

It is standard practice to write dates with the day of the month first followed by the month and then the year. Periods [full stops] are often used to separate the numbers (forward slashes are less common and hyphens are never used). So June 7, 2008 would be expressed as 07.06.08 or 07/06/08.

Months

January	**январь** *yeen·vahr'*
February	**февраль** *feev·rahl'*
March	**март** *mahrt*
April	**апрель** *ahp·ryel'*
May	**май** *mie*
June	**июнь** *ee·yoon'*
July	**июль** *ee·yool'*
August	**август** *ahf·goost*
September	**сентябрь** *seen·tyahbr'*
October	**октябрь** *ahk·tyahbr'*
November	**ноябрь** *nah·yahbr'*
December	**декабрь** *dee·kahbr'*

Seasons

spring	**весна** _vees_•_nah_
summer	**лето** _lyeh_•tah
fall [autumn]	**осень** _oh_•seen'
winter	**зима** zee•_mah_

Holidays

January 1, New Year's Day	**Новый Год** _noh_•viy got
January 7, Christmas Day	**Рождество** razh•dyes•_tvoh_
March 8, International Women's Day	**Международный Женский День** myezh•doo•nah•_rohd_•nihy zhen•skeey dyen'
May 1, May Day/ Labor Day	**1-е мая** _pyer_•vah•yeh _mah_•yah
May 9, Victory in Europe Day	**День Победы** dyen' pah•_byeh_•dih
June 12, Independence Day	**День Независимости России** dyen' nyeh•zah•_vee_•see•mahs•tee rahs•_see_•ee
November 4, Day of National Unity	**День Национального Единства** dyen' nah•tsih•ah•_nahl_'•nah•vah yeh•_deen_•stvah
December 12, Constitution Day	**День Конституции** dyen' kahn•stee•_too_•tsee•ee
Movable Dates: Easter	**Пасха** _pahs_•khah

Conversion Tables

When you know	Multiply by	To find
ounces	28.3	grams
pounds	0.45	kilograms
inches	2.54	centimeters
feet	0.3	meters
miles	1.61	kilometers
square inches	6.45	sq. centimeters
square feet	0.09	sq. meters
square miles	2.59	sq. kilometers
pints (U.S./Brit)	0.47/0.56	liters
gallons (U.S./Brit)	3.8/4.5	liters
Fahrenheit	5/9, after 32	Centigrade
Centigrade	9/5, then +32	Fahrenheit

Kilometers to Miles Conversions

1 km	0.62 miles	20 km	12.4 miles
5 km	3.10 miles	50 km	31.0 miles
10 km	6.20 miles	100 km	61.0 miles

Measurement

1 gram	**грамм** *grahm*	= 0.035 oz.
1 kilogram (kg)	**килограмм** *kee·lah·grahm*	= 2.2 lb
1 liter (l)	**литр** *leetr*	= 1.06 U.S./ 0.88 Brit. quarts
1 centimeter (cm)	**сантиметр** *sahn·tee·myetr*	= 0.4 inch
1 meter (m)	**метр** *myetr*	= 3.28 feet
1 kilometer (km)	**километр** *kee·lah·myetr*	= 0.62 mile

Temperature

-40°C – -40°F	**-1°C** – 30°F	**20°C** – 68°F
-30°C – -22°F	**0°C** – 32°F	**25°C** – 77°F
-20°C – -4°F	**5°C** – 41°F	**30°C** – 86°F
-10°C – 14°F	**10°C** – 50°F	**35°C** – 95°F
-5°C – 23°F	**15°C** – 59°F	

Oven Temperature

100°C – 212°F	**177°C** – 350°F
121°C – 250°F	**204°C** – 400°F
149°C – 300°F	**260°C** – 500°F

Dictionary

English–Russian

A

a few несколько _nyeh·skahl'·kah_

a little немного _nee·mnoh·gah_

a lot много _mnoh·gah_

a.m. до полудня _dah pah·lood·nyah_

about (approximately) около _oh·kah·lah_

abroad заграницей _zah·grah·nee·tsey_

accept _v_ принимать _pree·nee·maht'_

access _n_ допуск _doh·poosk_

accessories принадлежности _pree·nahd·lyezh·nah·stee_

accident несчастный случай _nee·shchas·niy sloo·chie;_ **(road)** авария _ah·vah·ree·yah_

accompany провожать _prah·vah·zhaht'_

accountant бухгалтер _boo·gahl·teer_

acetaminophen парацетамол _pah·rah·tsih·tah·mol_

acne прыщ _prihshch_

across через _cheh·rees_

adapter адаптер _ah·dahp·ter_

address адрес _ah·drees_

adhesive bandage пластырь _plahs·tihr'_

admission charge входная плата _fkhahd·nah·yah plah·tah_

adult взрослый _vzros·liy_

after после _pos·lee_

aftershave лосьон после бритья _las'·yon pos·lee breet'·yah_

age _n_ возраст _voz·rahst_

agree соглашаться _sah·glah·shah·tsa_

air воздух _voz·dookh_

air conditioning кондиционер _kahn·dee·tsih·ah·nyer_

air mail авиапочта _ah·vee·ah·poch·tah_

air pump воздушный насос _vahz·doosh·niy nah·sos_

air sickness bag гигиенический пакет _gee·gee·ee·nee·chees·keey pah·kyet_

airport аэропорт _ah·eh·rah·port_

aisle seat место у прохода _myes·tah oo prah·khoh·dah_

alarm clock будильник _boo·deel'·neek_

allergy аллергия _ah·leer·gee·yah_

almost почти _pahch·tee_

---

adj	adjective	**BE**	British English	**prep**	preposition
adv	adverb	**n**	noun	**v**	verb

alone один *ah*•*deen*

already уже *oo*•*zheh*

also также *tahg*•*zheh*

alter переделывать
pee•*ree*•*dyeh*•*lih*•*vaht'*

aluminum foil фольга *fahl'*•*gah*

always всегда *fseeg*•*dah*

amazing поразительный
pah•*rah*•*zee*•*teel'*•*niy*

ambassador посол *pah*•*sol*

ambulance скорая помощь
skoh•*rah*•*yah poh*•*mahshch*

American *adj* американский
ah•*mee*•*ee*•*kahn*•*skeey*

amount сумма *soo*•*mah*

anesthetic обезболивающее *ah*•*beez*
•*boh*•*lee*•*vah*•*yoo*•*shchee*•*yeh*

animal животное *zhih*•*vot*•*nah*•*yeh*

another другой *droo*•*goy*

antibiotic *n* антибиотик
ahn•*tee*•*bee*•*oh*•*teek*

antique антикварный
ahn•*tee*•*kvahr*•*niy*

antiques store антикварный
магазин *ahn*•*tee*•*kvahr*•*niy*
mah•*gah*•*zeen*

antiseptic *n* антисептик
ahn•*tee*•*sep*•*teek*

any какой-либо *kah*•*koy*•*lee*•*bah*

anyone кто-нибудь *ktoh*•*nee*•*boot'*

anything что-нибудь *shtoh*•*nee*•*boot'*

apartment квартира *kvahr*•*tee*•*rah*

apologize просить прощения
prah•*seet' prah*•*shcheh*•*nee*•*yah*

appendix аппендикс *ah*•*pyen*•*deeks*

appointment приём *pree*•*yom*

approximately приблизительно
pree•*blee*•*zee*•*teel'*•*nah*

area code код *kot*

arm рука *roo*•*kah*

around (place) по *pah;* **(time)** около
oh•*kah*•*lah*

arrive прибывать *pree*•*bih*•*vaht'*

art gallery картинная галерея
kahr•*teen*•*nah*•*yah gah*•*lee*•*ryeh*•*yah*

ashtray пепельница
pyeh•*peel'*•*nee*•*tsah*

ask просить *prah*•*seet'*

aspirin аспирин *ah*•*spee*•*reen*

asthmatic *n* астматик *ahst*•*mah*•*teek*

at в *v*

ATM банкомат *bahn*•*kah*•*maht*

attack *n* нападение
nah•*pah*•*dyeh*•*nee*•*yeh*

attractive привлекательный
pree•*vlee*•*kah*•*teel'*•*niy*

authentic настоящий
nah•*stah*•*yah*•*shcheey*

authenticity подлинность
pod•*leen*•*nahst'*

available (unoccupied) свободный
svah•*bod*•*niy*

B

baby ребёнок *ree·byoh·nahk*

babysitter няня *nyah·nyah*

back спина *spee·nah*

backache боль в спине *bol' f spee·nyeh*

backpack рюкзак *ryoog·zahk*

bad плохой *plah·khoy*

baggage [BE] багаж *bah·gahzh*

baggage check багажная квитанция *bah·gahzh·nah·yah kvee·tahn·tsih·yah*

bakery булочная *boo·lahch·nah·yah*

balcony балкон *bahl·kon*

ball мяч *myahch*

ballet балет *bah·lyet*

band (musical group) группа *groo·pah*

bank банк *bahnk*

bar бар *bahr*

barber парикмахер *pah·reekh·mah·kheer*

basement подвал *pahd·vahl*

basket корзина *kahr·zee·nah*

basketball баскетбол *bahs·keet·bol*

battery (car) аккумулятор *ah·kah·moo·lyah·tahr;* **(camera, etc.)** батарея *bah·tah·ryeh·yah*

be быть *biht'*

beach пляж *plyahsh*

beautiful красивый *krah·see·viy*

because потому что *pah·tah·moo·shtah*

bed кровать *krah·vaht'*

bedding постельное бельё *pahs·tel'·nah·yeh beel'·yoh*

bedroom спальня *spahl'·nyah*

before (time) до *dah*

begin начинать *nah·chee·naht'*

belong принадлежать *pree·nahd·lee·zhaht'*

belt ремень *ree·myen'*

bicycle велосипед *vee·lah·see·pyet*

big большой *bahl'·shoy*

bikini бикини *bee·kee·nee*

bill счёт *shchot*

binoculars бинокль *bee·noh·kahl'*

bird птица *ptee·tsah*

birthday день рождения *dyen' rahzh·dyeh·nee·yah*

bite *n* укус *oo·koos;* *v* кусать *koo·saht'*

bizarre причудливый *pree·chood·lee·viy*

bladder мочевой пузырь *mah·chee·voy poo·zihr'*

blanket одеяло *ah·dee·yah·lah*

bleach отбеливатель *aht·byeh·lee·vah·teel'*

bleeding *n* кровотечение *krah·vah·tee·cheh·nee·yeh*

blister волдырь *vahl·dihr'*

blood кровь *krof'*

blood pressure кровяное давление
krah•vee•noh•yeh dahv•lyeh•nee•yeh

blouse блузка *bloos•kah*

blow-dry фен *fyen*

boarding card посадочный талон
pah•sah•dahch•niy tah•lon

boat лодка *lot•kah*

boat trip водная экскурсия
vod•nah•yah ehks•koor•see•yah

bone кость *kost'*

book *n* книга *knee•gah;* *v* заказывать
zah•kah•zih•vaht'

bookstore книжный магазин
kneezh•niy mah•gah•zeen

boots сапоги *sa•pah•gee*

borrow одолжить *ah•dahl•zhit'*

botanical garden ботанический сад
bah•tah•nee•chees•keey saht

bottle opener открывалка
aht•krih•vahl•kah

boy мальчик *mahl'•cheek*

boyfriend друг *drook*

bra бюстгальтер *byoost•gahl•tyer*

bracelet браслет *brahs•lyet*

break *v* сломать *slah•maht'*

break down *v* сломаться
slah•mah•tsah

break-in *n* взлом *vzlom*

breast грудь *groot'*

breathe дышать *dih•shaht'*

breathtaking захватывающий

zah•khvah•tih•vah•yoo•shcheey

bridge мост *most*

British *adj* британский
bree•tahn•skeey

brochure брошюра *brah•shoo•rah*

brooch брошь *brosh*

browse *v* просматривать
prah•smah•tree•vaht'

bruise *n* синяк *see•nyahk*

bucket ведро *veed•roh*

build строить *stroh•eet'*

building здание *zdah•nee•yeh*

burn *n* ожог *ah•zhok*

bus автобус *ahf•toh•boos*

bus route автобусный маршрут
ahf•toh•boos•niy mahrsh•root

bus station автобусная станция
ahf•toh•boos•nah•yah stahn•tsih•yah

bus stop автобусная остановка
ahf•toh•boos•nah•yah ahs•tah•nof•kah

business бизнес *beez•nees*

business trip командировка
kah•mahn•dee•rof•kah

busy *adj* **(occupied)** занятый
zah•nyah•tiy

but но *noh*

butane gas газовый баллон
gah•zah•viy bah•lon

button кнопка *knop•kah*

buy покупать *pah•koo•paht'*

by (time) к *k*

C

cabin каюта *kah·yoo·tah*

calendar календарь *kah·leen·dahr'*

call v звать *zvaht';* **(for someone)** заходить за *zah·khah·deet' zah;* **(phone)** звонить *zvah·neet'*

camera фотоаппарат *foh·tah·ah·pah·raht*

camera case футляр *foot·lyahr*

campbed раскладушка *rahs·klah·doosh·kah*

camping кемпинг *kyem·peenk*

camping equipment снаряжение *snah·ree·zheh·nee·yeh*

campsite палаточный лагерь *pah·lah·tahch·niy lah·geer'*

can n банка *bahn·kahn;* v мочь *moch*

can opener консервный нож *kahn·syerv·niy nosh*

cancel отменять *aht·mee·nyaht'*

candle свеча *svee·chah*

cap (dental) коронка *kah·ron·kah*

car машина *mah·shih·nah;* **(train compartment)** вагон *vahh·gon*

car hire [BE] прокат автомобилей *prah·kaht ahf·tah·mah·bee·leey*

car park [BE] автостоянка *ahf·tah·stah·yahn·kah*

carafe графин *grah·feen*

careful осторожный *ahs·tah·rozh·niy*

carpet (rug) ковер *kah·vyor*

cart тележка *tee·lyesh·kah*

carton пакет *pah·kyet*

cash наличные *nah·leech·nih·yeh*

cash desk касса *kah·sah*

cashier кассир *kah·seer*

casino казино *kah·zee·noh*

castle замок *zah·mahk*

cathedral собор *sah·bor*

cave пещера *pee·shcheh·rah*

CD компакт-диск *kahm·pahkt deesk*

CD player лазерный проигрыватель *lah·zeer·niy prah·eeg·rih·vah·teel'*

cell phone мобильный телефон *mah·beel'·niy tee·lee·fon*

center центр *tsentr*

ceramics керамика *kee·rah·mee·kah*

certificate свидетельство *svee·dyeh·teel'·stvah*

chain цепочка *tsih·poch·kah*

change n сдача *zdah·chah;* v **(alter)** поменять *pah·mee·nyaht';* **(buses, etc.)** делать пересадку *dyeh·laht' pee·ree·saht·koo;* **(baby)** перепеленать *pee·ree·pee·lee·naht';* **(money)** обменять *ahb·mee·nyaht'*

charge n плата *plah·tah*

charter flight чартерный рейс *chahr·ter·niy reys*

cheap дешёвый *dee·shoh·viy*

check n чек *chek;* v проверять *prah·veh·ryaht'*

check in v регистрироваться
ree·gees·tree·rah·vah·tsah

check-in desk регистрационная
стойка *ree·gee·strah·tsih·on·nah·yah
stoy·kah*

check out v **(hotel)** выезжать
vih·eezh·zhaht'

chemist [BE] аптека *ahp·tyeh·kah*

cheque [BE] чек *chek*

chess шахматы *shahkh·mah·tih*

chest (body part) грудная клетка
grood·nah·yah klyet·kah

child *adj* детский *dyets·keey;* n
ребёнок *ree·byoh·nahk*

child seat (in car) детское сиденье
dyets·kah·yeh see·dyen'·yeh

children дети *dyeh·teeh*

church церковь *tser·kahf'*

cigarette сигарета *see·gah·ryeh·tah*

cigar сигара *see·gah·rah*

cinema [BE] кинотеатр
kee·nah·tee·ahtr

class (type of seat, etc.) класс *klahs*

clean *adj* чистый *chees·tiy;* v чистить
chees·teet'

cliff скала *skah·lah*

cling film [BE] продуктовая плёнка
prah·dook·toh·vah·yah plyon·kah

clock часы *chah·sih*

close v **(store, etc.)** закрываться
zah·krih·vah·tsah

clothes одежда *ah·dyezh·dah*

cloudy облачный *ob·lahch·niy*

clubs (golf) клюшки *klyoosh·kee*

coach (long-distance bus)
междугородний автобус
meezh·doo·gah·rod·niy ahf·toh·boos

coast побережье *pah·bee·ryezh·yeh*

coat пальто *pahl'·toh*

coatcheck гардероб *gahr·dee·rop*

code (area, dialing) код *kot*

coin монета *mah·nyeh·tah*

cold *adj* холодный *khah·lod·niy;* n
(flu) простуда *prah·stoo·dah*

colleague коллега *kah·lyeh·gah*

collect v забирать *zah·bee·raht'*

color цвет *tsvyet*

comb расчёска *rah·shchos·kah*

come приходить *pree·khah·deet'*

commission комиссионный сбор
kah·mee·see·oh·niy zbor

compact компактный
kahm·pahk·tniy

company (business) предприятие
preet·pree·yah·tee·yeh;
(companionship) компания
kahm·pah·nee·yah

compartment (train) купе *koo·peh*

complaint жалоба *zhah·lah·bah*

concert концерт *kahn·tsert*

concert hall концертный зал
kahn·tsert·niy zahl

concussion сотрясение мозга
 sah·tree·syeh·nee·yeh moz·gah

conditioner кондиционер
 kahn·dee·tsih·ah·nyer

condom презерватив
 pree·zeer·vah·teev

conductor дирижёр *dee·ree·zhor*

confirm (reservation) подтвердить
 paht·tveer·deet'

consulate консульство
 kon·sool'·stvah

consult v консультироваться
 kahn·sool'·tee·rah·vah·tsah

contact v связаться *svyah·zah·tsah*

contagious инфекционный
 een·feek·tsih·oh·niy

contain v содержать *sah·deer·zhaht'*

cook n повар *poh·vahr;* v готовить
 gah·toh·veet'

cooker [BE] плита *plee·tah*

copper медь *myet'*

copy n копия *koh·pee·yah*

corkscrew штопор *shtoh·pahr*

corner угол *oo·gahl*

correct adv правильно *prah·veel'·nah*

cosmetics косметика
 kahs·myeh·tee·kah

cottage дача *dah·chah*

cotton вата *vah·tah*

cough n кашель *kah·shihl';* v кашлять
 kahsh·lyaht'

country (nation) страна *strah·nah*

cramps судороги *soo·dah·rah·gee*

credit card кредитная карточка
 kree·deet·nah·yah kahr·tahch·kah

crib детская кроватка *dets·kah·yah
 krah·vaht·kah*

crossroad перекрёсток
 pee·ree·kryos·tahk

cruise n круиз *kroo·eez*

crutches костыли *kahs·tih·lee*

crystal хрусталь *khroos·tal'*

cup чашка *chahsh·kah*

cupboard шкаф *shkahf*

currency валюта *vah·lyoo·tah*

currency exchange office обмен
 валюты *ahb·myen vah·lyoo·tih*

curtains занавеси *zah·nah·vee·see*

customs таможня *tah·mozh·nyah*

customs declaration таможенная
 декларация *tah·moh·zhih·nah·yah
 deek·lah·rah·tsih·yah*

cut порез *pah·ryes*

cycle route велосипедный маршрут
 vee·lah·see·pyed·niy mahrsh·root

cycling велоспорт *vyeh·lah·sport*

D

daily ежедневно *ee·zhee·dnyev·nah*

damage v повредить *pah·vree·deet'*

damp adv сыро *sih·rah;* n сырость
 sih·rahst'

dance *n* танец _tah_·neets

dangerous *adj* опасный ah·_pahs_·niy

dark тёмный _tyom_·niy

dawn рассвет rahs·_vyet_

day день dyen'

deaf глухой gloo·_khoy_

deck chair шезлонг shez·_lonk_

declare предъявлять
    preed·yahv·_lyaht'_

deep глубокий gloo·_boh_·keey

degree (temperature) градус
    grah·doos

delay задержка zah·_dyersh_·kah

deliver доставлять dah·stahv·_lyat'_

denim джинсовый dzhihn·_soh_·viy

dentist зубной врач zoob·_noy_ vrahch

dentures протез prah·_tes_

deodorant дезодорант
    dee·zah·dah·_rahnt_

depart (train, bus) отправляться
    aht·prahv·_lyah_·tsah

department отдел aht·_dyel_

departure lounge зал вылета zahl
    vih·lee·tah

deposit аванс ah·_vahns_

describe описывать ah·_pee_·sih·vaht'

destination место назначения
    myes·tah nahz·nah·_cheh_·nee·yah

details подробности
    pahd·_rob_·nahs·tee

detergent моющее средство
    moh·yoo·shchee·yeh _sryet_·stvah

diabetes диабет dee·ah·_byet_

diabetic *n* диабетик dee·ah·_byeh_·teek

diagnosis диагноз dee·_ahg_·nahs

diamond брильянт breel'·_yahnt_

diaper пелёнка pee·_lyon_·kah

diarrhea понос pah·_nos_

dice кости _kos_·tee

dictionary словарь slah·_vahr'_

diesel дизельное топливо
    dee·zeel'·_nah_·yeh _top_·lee·vah

diet *n* диета dee·_yeh_·tah

difficult трудный _trood_·niy

dining car вагон-ресторан vah·_gon_
    rees·tah·_rahn_

dining room столовая
    stah·_loh_·vah·yah

dinner ужин _oo_·zhihn

direct *adj* **(train)** прямой pryah·_moy_;
    v направлять nah·prahv·_lyaht'_

direction направление
    nah·prahv·_lyeh_·nee·yeh

director директор dee·_ryek_·tahr

directory (telephone) телефонный
    справочник tee·lee·_foh_·niy
    sprah·vahch·neek

dirty грязный _gryahz_·niy

disabled инвалид een·vah·_leet_

discount скидка _skeet_·kah

dish (meal) блюдо _blyoo_·dah

dishcloth тряпка _tryahp_·kah

dishwasher посудомоечная машина
*pah•soo•dah•moh•eech•nah•yah
mah•shih•nah*

dishwashing liquid средство для
мытья посуды *sryet•stvah dlyah
miht'•yah pah•soo•dih*

disturb беспокоить *bees•pah•koh•eet'*

dive нырять *nih•ryaht'*

diving equipment снаряжение для
дайвинга *snah•ree•zheh•nee•yeh
dlyah die•veen•gah*

divorce развод *rahz•vod*

doctor врач *vrahch*

doll кукла *kook•lah*

door дверь *dvyer'*

double bed двуспальная кровать
dvoo•spahl'•nah•yah krah•vaht'

double room двухместный номер
dvookh•myes•niy noh•meer

downtown area центр города *tsentr
goh•rah•dah*

dozen дюжина *dyoo•zhih•nah*

dress платье *plaht'•yeh*

drink *v* пить *peet'*

drive *v* ехать *yeh•khaht'*

driver водитель *vah•dee•teel'*

driver's licence водительские права
vah•dee•teel'•skee•ye prah•vah

drugstore аптека *ahp•tyeh•kah*

drunk *adj* пьяный *pyah•niy*

dry clean *v* отдавать в химчистку

aht•dah•vaht' f kheem•cheest•koo

dry cleaner химчистка
kheem•cheest•kah

during во время *vah vrye•myah*

dustbin [BE] мусорный бак
moo•sahr•niy bahk

duty пошлина *posh•lee•nah*

E

ear ухо *oo•khah*

earache боль в ухе *bol' v oo•khee*

early ранний *rahn•neey*

earrings серьги *syer'•gee*

easy лёгкий *lyokh•keey*

eat есть *yest'*

economy class пассажирский класс
pah•sah•zhihr•skeey klahs

electric outlet розетка *rah•zyet•kah*

electric shaver электробритва
eh•lyek•trah•breet•vah

electricity электричество
eh•leek•tree•cheest•vah

elevator лифт *leeft*

else еще *ee•shchoh*

e-mail электронная почта
ee•leek•troh•nah•yah poch•tah

e-mail address адрес электронной
почты *ah•drees ee•leek•tron•nie
poch•tih*

e-ticket электронный билет
ee•leek•tron•niy bee•lyet

embassy посольство *pah·sol'·stvah*

emerald изумруд *ee·zoom·root*

emergency крайний случай *krie·neey sloo·chie*

emergency exit аварийный выход *ah·vah·reey·niy vih·khaht*

empty *adj* пустой *poos·toy*

enamel эмаль *ee·mahl'*

end *v* кончаться *kahn·chah·tsah*

England Англия *ahn·glee·yah*

English *adj* английский *ahn·gleey·skeey*

enjoy нравиться *nrah·vee·tsah*

enough достаточно *dah·stah·tahch·nah*

entrance fee входная плата *fkhahd·nah·yah plah·tah*

entry visa въездная виза *vyezd·nah·yah vee·zah*

envelope конверт *kahn·vyert*

epileptic *n* эпилептик *ee·pee·lyep·teek*

equipment оборудование *ah·bah·roo·dah·vah·nee·yeh;*
(sports) снаряжение *snah·ryah·zheh·nee·yeh*

error ошибка *ah·shihp·kah*

escalator эскалатор *ees·kah·lah·tahr*

essential основной *ahs·nahv·noy*

European Union (EU) Европейский союз *yev·rah·pey·skeey sah·yoos*

event событие *sah·bih·tee·yeh*

every каждый *kahzh·diy*

example пример *pree·myer*

except кроме *kroh·mee*

excess luggage перевес багажа *pee·ree·vyes bah·gah·zhah*

exchange *v* обменивать *ahb·myeh·nee·vaht'*

exchange rate курс обмена *koors ahb·myeh·nah*

excursion экскурсия *eks·koor·see·yah*

exit *n* выход *vih·khaht*

expensive дорогой *dah·rah·goy*

express экспресс *eks·pres*

extension добавочный номер *dah·bah·vahch·niy noh·meer*

extra *adv* ещё *ee·shchoh*

extract *v* удалять *oo·dah·lyaht'*

eye глаз *glahs*

F

fabric (material) ткань *tkahn'*

face лицо *lee·tsoh*

facial чистка лица *cheest·kah lee·tsah*

facilities удобства *oo·dops·tvah*

family семья *seem'·yah*

fan (air) вентилятор *veen·tee·lyah·tahr*

far далеко *dah·lee·koh*

far-sighted дальнозоркий *dahl'·nah·zor·keey'*

fare плата *plah·tah*

farm ферма _fyer_•mah

fast adv быстро _bihst_•rah

faucet кран krahn

favorite любимый lyoo•_bee_•miy

fax факс faks

feed кормить kar•_meet'_

ferry паром pah•_rom_

fever жар zhahr

few мало _mah_•lah

filling (dental) пломба _plom_•bah

film [BE] **(movie)** фильм _feel'm;_
(camera) плёнка _plyon_•kah

filter фильтр _feel'_•tr

finger палец _pah_•leets

fire n пожар pah•_zhahr_

fire alarm пожарная тревога
pah•zhahr•nah•yah tree•_voh_•gah

fire escape пожарная лестница
pah•zhahr•nah•yah _lyes_•nee•tsah

fire extinguisher огнетушитель
ahg•nee•too•_shih_•teel'

firewood дрова drah•_vah_

first class первый класс _pyer_•viy klahs

fit v **(clothes)** подходить
paht•khah•_deet'_

fitting room примерочная
pree•_myeh_•rahch•nah•yah

fix v чинить chee•_neet'_

flashlight фонарь fah•_nahr'_

flight рейс reys

floor этаж eh•_tahsh_

florist цветочный магазин
tsvyeh•toch•_niy_ mah•gah•_zeen_

flower цветок tsvee•_tok_

flu грипп greep

fog туман too•_mahn_

folk народный nah•_rod_•niy

follow v **(pursue)** преследовать
pree•_slyeh_•dah•vaht'

food n еда yee•_dah_

foot (body) нога nah•_gah_

football [BE] футбол food•_bol_

footpath тропинка trah•_peen_•kah

for на nah

foreign currency иностранная
валюта ee•nah•_strah_•nah•yah
vah•_lyoo_•tah

forest лес lyes

forget забывать zah•bih•_vaht'_

fork вилка _veel_•kah

form n бланк blahnk

fountain фонтан fahn•_tahn_

foyer (hotel, theater) фойе fie•_yeh_

fracture (a bone) перелом
pee•ree•_lom_

frame n **(glasses)** оправа ah•_prah_•vah

free adj **(not busy/available)**
свободный svah•_bod_•niy

freezer морозильная камера
mah•rah•_zeel'_•nah•yah _kah_•mee•rah

frequently часто _chahs_•tah

fresh свежий _svyeh_•zhiy

friend друг *drook*

friendly *adj* дружеский
droo·zhees·keey

from (place) из *eez;* **(time)** с *s*

frost мороз *mah·roz*

frying pan сковорода
skah·vah·rah·dah

full *adj* полный *pol·niy*

fun веселье *vee·syel'·yeh*

furniture мебель *myeh·beel'*

G

game игра *eeg·rah*

garage гараж *gah·rash*

garbage bag мусорный мешок
moo·sahr·niy mee·shok

garden сад *saht*

gas (fuel) бензин *been·zeen*

gas station заправочная
станция *zah·prah·vahch·nah·yah
stahn·tsih·yah*

gate (airport) выход *vih·khaht*

gauze бинт *beent*

genuine настоящий
nah·stah·yah·shcheey

get (receive) получать
pah·loo·chaht'; **(to destination)**
добираться до *dah·bee·rah·tsah doh*

gift подарок *pah·dah·rahk*

gift store магазин подарков
mah·gah·zeen pah·dahr·kahf

girl девочка *dyeh·vahch·kah*

girlfriend подруга *pah·droo·gah*

give давать *dah·vaht'*

glass стакан *stah·kahn*

glasses (optical) очки *ahch·kee*

glove перчатка *peer·chaht·kah*

go ходить *khah·deet'*

go away уходить *oo·khah·deet'*

gold золото *zoh·lah·tah*

golf гольф *gol'f*

golf course поле для гольфа *poh·lyeh
dlyah gol'·fah*

good хороший *khah·roh·shiy*

gram грамм *grahm*

grass трава *trah·vah*

gray серый *syeh·riy*

Great Britain Великобритания
vee·lee·kah·bree·tah·nee·yah

group группа *groo·pah*

guarantee гарантия
gah·rahn·tee·yah

guide (tour) гид *geet*

guidebook путеводитель
poo·tee·vah·dee·teel'

guided tour экскурсия
eks·koor·see·yah

guitar гитара *gee·tah·rah*

gum десна *dees·nah*

gym спортзал *sport·zahl*

gynecologist гинеколог
gee·nee·koh·lahk

H

hair волосы <u>voh</u>·lah·sih

hairbrush щётка для волос
<u>shchot</u>·kah dlyah vah·<u>los</u>

haircut стрижка <u>streesh</u>·kah

hairdresser парикмахер
pah·reek·<u>mah</u>·kheer

hairspray лак для волос lahk dlyah
vah·<u>los</u>

half половина pah·lah·<u>vee</u>·nah

hand рука roo·<u>kah</u>

hand luggage ручная кладь
rooch·<u>nah</u>·yah klahd'

handbag [BE] сумка <u>soom</u>·kah

handicapped инвалид een·vah·<u>leet</u>

handicraft ремесло ree·mees·<u>loh</u>

handkerchief платок plah·<u>tok</u>

hanger вешалка <u>vyeh</u>·shahl·kah

hangover похмелье pahkh·<u>myel'</u>·yeh

harbor гавань <u>gah</u>·vahn'

hat шапка <u>shahp</u>·kah

hay fever сенная лихорадка
see·<u>nah</u>·yah lee·khah·<u>raht</u>·kah

head голова gah·lah·<u>vah</u>

headache головная боль
gah·lahv·<u>nah</u>·yah bol'

health insurance медицинское
страхование mee·dee·<u>tsihn</u>·skah·yah
strah·<u>khof</u>·kah

hear слышать <u>slih</u>·shaht'

hearing aid слуховой аппарат

sloo·khah·<u>voy</u> ah·pah·<u>raht</u>

heart сердце <u>syer</u>·tseh

heart attack сердечный приступ
seer·<u>dyech</u>·niy <u>prees</u>·toop

heart condition заболевание сердца
zah·bah·lee·<u>vah</u>·nee·yeh <u>syer</u>·tsah

heater обогреватель
ah·bah·gree·<u>vah</u>·teel'

heating n отопление
ah·tahp·<u>lyeh</u>·nee·yeh

heavy тяжёлый tee·<u>zhoh</u>·liy

height рост rost

helmet шлем shlyem

help v помогать pah·mah·<u>gaht'</u>

here здесь zdyes'

high высокий vih·<u>soh</u>·keey

high blood pressure высокое
давление vih·<u>soh</u>·kha·yeh
dahv·<u>lyeh</u>·nee·yeh

highlight v (**hair**) мелировать
mee·<u>lee</u>·rah·vaht'

highway шоссе shah·<u>seh</u>

hiking n поход pah·<u>khot</u>

hill холм kholm

hire [BE] v взять напрокат vzyaht'
nah·prah·<u>kaht</u>

hobby хобби <u>khoh</u>·bee

hold on v подождать pah·dah·<u>zhdaht'</u>

hole (in clothes) дырка <u>dihr</u>·kah

holiday [BE] отпуск <u>ot</u>·poosk

home дом dom

honeymoon медовый месяц
mee-doh-viy myeh-syahts
horse лошадь *loh-shahd'*
horseracing бега *bee-gah*
hospital больница *bahl'-nee-tsah*
hot *adj* горячий *gah-ryah-cheey*
hotel гостиница *gahs-tee-nee-tsah*
hotel room номер *noh-meer*
hour час *chahs*
house дом *dom*
hungry голодный *gah-lod-niy*
hurt *v* болеть *bah-lyet'*
husband муж *moosh*

I

icy гололёд *gah-lah-lyot*
identification документ
dah-koo-myent
ill [BE] больной *bahl'-noy*
illegal незаконный *nee-zah-koh-niy*
immediately немедленно
nee-myeh-dlee-nah
in (place) в *v;* **(time)** через *cheh-rees*
incredible невероятный
nee-vee-rah-yaht-niy
indigestion изжога *eezh-zhoh-gah*
indoor закрытый *zah-krih-tiy*
inexpensive недорогой
nee-dah-rah-goy
infect заразить *zah-rah-zeet'*
infection инфекция *een-fyek-tsih-yah*

inflammation воспаление
vahs-pah-lyeh-nee-yeh
information информация
een-fahr-mah-tsih-yah
injection укол *oo-kol*
injury травма *trahv-mah*
innocent невиновен
nee-vee-noh-veen
insect насекомое
nah-see-koh-mah-yeh
insert *v* вставлять *fstahv-lyat'*
inside внутри *vnoo-tree*
insist настаивать *nah-stah-ee-vaht'*
insomnia бессоница
bees-soh-nee-tsah
instructions инструкция
een-strook-tsih-yah
insulin инсулин *een-soo-leen*
insurance страховка *strah-khof-kahh*
insurance claim страховой иск
strah-khah-voy eesk
insurance company страховая
компания *strah-khah-vah-yah
kahm-pah-nee-yah*
interesting интересный
een-tee-ryes-niy
internet интернет *een-ter-net*
internet cafe интернет-кафе
een-ter-net kah-feh
interpreter переводчик
pee-ree-vot-cheek

intersection перекресток
pee·ree·kryos·tahk
invitation приглашение
pree·glah·sheh·nee·yeh
invite приглашать *pree·glah·shaht'*
iron утюг *oo·tyook*
itemized bill детальный счёт
dee·tahl'·niy shchot

J

jacket куртка *koort·kah*
jar банка *bahn·kah*
jaw челюсть *cheh·lyoost'*
jazz джаз *dzhahs*
jeans джинсы *dzhihn·sih*
jeweler ювелирный магазин
yoo·vee·leer·niy mah·gah·zeen
job работа *rah·boh·tah*
joke шутка *shoot·kah*
journalist журналист *zhoor·nah·leest*
journey поездка *pah·yest·kah*

K

kettle чайник *chie·neek*
key ключ *klyooch*
key card электронный ключ
eh·leek·tron·niy klyooch
key ring брелок *bree·lok*
kiddie pool детский бассейн
dyets·keey bah·seyn
kidney почка *poch·kah*

kind (pleasant) любезный
lyoo·byez·niy
kiss v целовать *tsih·lah·vaht'*
kitchen кухня *kookh·nyah*
knee колено *kah·lyeh·nah*
knife нож *nosh*
kosher кошерный *kah·sher·niy*

L

label n ярлык *yahr·lihk*
lace кружево *kroo·zhih·vah*
ladder стремянка *stree·myahn·kah*
lake озеро *oh·zee·rah*
lamp лампа *lahm·pah*
land v приземляться
pree·zeem·lyah·tsah
language course языковые курсы
yah·zih·kah·vih·yeh koor·sih
large большой *bahl'·shoy*
last adj последний *pahs·lyed·neey*
late adj поздний *poz·neey*
laugh v смеяться *smee·yah·tsah*
launderette [BE] прачечная
prah·cheech·nah·yah
laundromat прачечная
prah·cheech·nah·yah
lawyer адвокат *ahd·vah·kaht*
leader (of group) руководитель
roo·kah·vah·dee·teel
leaflet брошюра *brah·shoo·rah*
leak v (roof, pipe) течь *tyech*

learn (language) изучать
ee·zoo·chaht'

leather кожа *koh·zhah*

leave *v* уезжать *oo·eezh·zhaht'*

left *adj* левый *leh·viy*

left-luggage office [BE]
камера хранения *kah·mee·rah
khrah·nyeh·nee·yah*

leg нога *nah·gah*

legal законный *zah·koh·niy*

lend дать взаймы *daht' vzie·mih*

length длина *dlee·nah*

less меньше *myen'·sheh*

lesson урок *oo·rok*

letter письмо *pees'·moh*

library библиотека
bee·blee·ah·tyeh·kah

lifeboat спасательная лодка
spah·sah·teel'·nah·yah lot·kah

lifeguard спасатель *spah·sah·teel'*

lifejacket спасательный жилет
spah·sah·teel'·niy zhih·lyet

lift [BE] *n* лифт *leeft*

lift pass пропуск на подъёмник
proh·poosk nah pahd·yom·neek

light *adj* **(weight)** лёгкий *lyokh·keey;*
(color) светлый *svyet·liy;* **(electric)**
свет *svyet*

light bulb лампочка *lahm·pahch·kah*

lighter (cigarette) зажигалка
zah·zhih·gahl·kah

like *v* нравиться *nrah·vee·tsah*

line (subway) линия *lee·nee·yah*

linen лён *lyon*

lip губа *goo·bah*

lipstick губная памада *goob·nah·yah
pah·mah·dah*

liquor store винный магазин *vee·niy
mah·gah·zeen*

little (small) маленький
mah·leen'·keey

liver печень *pyeh·cheen'*

living room гостиная
gahs·tee·nah·yah

lobby (theater, hotel) фойе *fah·yeh*

local местный *mes·niy*

lock *n* замок *zah·mok*

login вход в систему *fhot f
sees·tyeh·moo*

long длинный *dlee·niy*

long-distance bus междугородний
автобус *myezh·doo·gah·rod·niy
ahf·toh·boos*

long-sighted [BE] дальнозоркий
dahl'·nah·zor·keey

loose (clothing) свободный
svah·bod·niy

lose потерять *pah·tee·ryaht'*

lost-and-found бюро находок
byoo·roh nah·khoh·dahk

loud громкий *grom·keey*

love *v* любить *lyoo·beet'*

luggage багаж *bah·gahsh*

lunch обед *ah·byet*

lung лёгкое *lyokh·kah·yeh*

M

magazine журнал *zhoor·nahl*

magnificent великолепный
vee·lee·kah·lyep·niy

mail *n* почта *poch·tah*; *v* отправлять
aht·prahv·lyaht'

mailbox почтовый ящик
pahch·toh·viy yah·shcheek

main главный *glahv·niy*

main course второе *ftah·roh·yeh*

make-up макияж *mah·kee·yahsh*

male мужской *moosh·skoy*

mall (shopping) торговый центр
tahr·goh·viy tsentr

man (male) мужчина
moo·shchee·nah

manicure маникюр *mah·nee·kyoor*

manual *n* **(for smth)** руководство
roo·kah·vod·stvah

many много *mnoh·gah*

map карта *kahr·tah*

market рынок *rih·nahk*

married (man) женат *zhih·naht*;
(woman) замужем *zah·moo·zhem*

mascara тушь *toosh*

mask (diving) маска *mahs·kah*

massage массаж *mah·sahsh*

match (sport) матч *mahch*

matches спички *speech·kee*

mattress матрас *maht·rahs*

meal блюдо *blyoo·dah*

mean *v* значить *znah·cheet'*

measure *v* измерить *eez·myeh·reet'*

measurement измерение
eez·mee·ryeh·nee·yeh

medication лекарство *lee·kahr·stvah*

meet *v* встречаться *fstree·chah·tsah*

message сообщение
sah·ahp·shcheh·nee·yeh

metal металл *mee·tahl*

microwave микроволновая печь
meek·rah·vahl·noh·vah·yah pyech

migraine мигрень *meeg·ryen'*

mileage километраж
kee·lah·mee·trahsh

mine мой *moy*

minute минута *mee·noo·tah*

mirror зеркало *zyer·kah·lah*

miss *v* **(pass)** пропустить
prah·poos·teet'; **(get lost)** пропасть
prah·pahst'

mistake ошибка *ah·shihp·kah*

misunderstanding недоразумение
nee·dah·rah·zoo·myeh·nee·yeh

mobile phone [BE] мобильный
телефон *mah·beel'·niy tee·lee·fon*

modern современный
sah·vree·myen·niy

money деньги <u>dyen'</u>·gee

month месяц <u>myeh</u>·syahts

mop швабра <u>shvahb</u>·rah

more больше <u>bol'</u>·sheh

mosque мечеть mee·<u>chet'</u>

mosquito bite комариный укус
  kah·mah·<u>ree</u>·niy oo·<u>koos</u>

motion sickness морская болезнь
  mahr·<u>skah</u>·yah bah·<u>lyezn'</u>

motorboat моторка mah·<u>tor</u>·kah

motorway [BE] шоссе shah·<u>seh</u>

mountain гора gah·<u>rah</u>

mouth рот rot

movie фильм feel'm

movie theater кинотеатр
  kee·nah·tee·<u>ahtr</u>

Mr. господин gahs·pah·<u>deen</u>

Mrs. госпожа gahs·pah·<u>zhah</u>

much много <u>mnoh</u>·gah

mug n кружка <u>kroosh</u>·kah; v ограбить
  ah·<u>grah</u>·beet'

mugging n ограбление
  ah·grahb·<u>lyeh</u>·nee·yeh

museum музей moo·<u>zyey</u>

music музыка <u>moo</u>·zih·kah

my мой moy

myself сам <u>sahm</u>

N

name (first name) имя <u>ee</u>·myah;
  (family name) фамилия

  fah·<u>mee</u>·lee·yah

napkin салфетка sahl·<u>fyet</u>·kah

nappy [BE] пелёнка pee·<u>lyon</u>·kah

narrow узкий <u>oos</u>·keey

national национальный
  nah·tsih·ah·<u>nahl'</u>·niy

nationality национальность
  nah·tsih·ah·<u>nahl'</u>·nahst'

nature reserve заповедник
  zah·pah·<u>vyed</u>·neek

near около <u>oh</u>·kah·lah

nearby рядом <u>ryah</u>·dahm

near-sighted близорукий
  blee·za·<u>roo</u>·keey

neck шея <u>sheh</u>·yah

necklace ожерелье ah·zhih·<u>ryel'</u>·yeh

nerve нерв nyerf

nesting doll матрёшка
  maht·<u>ryosh</u>·kah

never никогда nee·kahg·<u>dah</u>

new новый <u>noh</u>·viy

newspaper газета gah·<u>zyeh</u>·tah

newsstand газетный киоск
  gah·<u>zyet</u>·niy kee·<u>osk</u>

next следующий
  <u>slyeh</u>·doo·yoo·shcheey

nice хороший khah·<u>roh</u>·shiy

niece племянница
  plee·<u>myah</u>·nee·tsah

no нет nyet

no one никто nee·<u>ktoh</u>

noisy шумный _shoom•niy_

non-alcoholic безалкогольный
beez•ahl•kah•gol'•niy

non-smoking некурящий
nee•koo•ryah•shcheey

nonsense ерунда _ee•roon•dah_

normal нормальный _nahr•mahl'•niy_

nose нос _nos_

nothing ничего _nee•chee•voh_

notify сообщать _sah•aph•shchaht'_

number (phone) номер _noh•meer_

nurse сестра _sees•trah_

O

occupied занятый _zah•nee•tiy_

odds (betting) шансы _shahn•sih_

off-license [BE] винный магазин
vee•niy mah•gah•zeen

office офис _oh•fees_

often часто _chahs•tah_

old старый _sta•riy_

on (day, date) в _v;_ **(place)** на _nah_

once один раз _ah•deen rahs_

one-way ticket билет в один конец
bee•lyet v ah•deen kah•nyets

open _adj_ открытый _aht•krih•tiy; v_
открывать _aht•krih•vaht'_

opening hours часы работы _chah•sih_
rah•boh•tih

opera опера _oh•pee•rah_

operation операция
ah•pee•rah•tsih•yah

opposite напротив _nah•proh•teef_

optician оптика _op•tee•kah_

or или _ee•lee_

orchestra оркестр _ahr•kyestr_

order _v_ заказывать _zah•ka•zih•vaht'_

ordering заказ _zah•kahs_

Orthodox православный
prah•vah•slahv•niy

other другой _droo•goy_

outdoor на открытом воздухе _nah_
aht•krih•tahm voz•doo•khee

outside на улице _nah oo•lee•tseh_

oven духовка _doo•khof•kah_

overheat перегреться
pee•ree•gryeh•tsah

overlook _n_ смотровая площадка
smah•trah•vah•yah plah•shchaht•kah

owner владелец _vlah•dyeh•leets_

P

pacifier соска _sos•kah_

pack _v_ упаковывать
oo•pah•koh•vih•vaht'

package посылка _pah•sihl•kah_

packet пакет _pah•kyet_

paddling pool [BE] детский бассейн
dyets•keey bah•seyn

pain боль _bol'_

painkiller болеутоляющее _boh•lee•oo_
•tah•lyah•yoo•shchee•yeh

painting картина *kahr·tee·nah*

pair пара *pah·rah*

palace дворец *dvah·ryets*

panorama панорама
pah·nah·rah·mah

pants брюки *bryoo·kee*

paper бумага *boo·mah·gah*

paracetamol [BE] парацетамол
pah·rah·tsih·tah·mol

parents родители *rah·dee·tee·lee*

park парк *pahrk*

parking lot автостоянка
ahf·tah·stah·yahn·kah

party (social) вечеринка
vee·chee·reen·kah

pass v проезжать *prah·eezh·zhaht'*

passport паспорт *pahs·pahrt*

pastry store кондитерская
kahn·dee·teer·skah·yah

patch v заштопать *zah·shtoh·paht'*

path тропинка *trah·peen·kah*

patient n пациент *pah·tsih·yent*

pay v платить *plah·teet'*

pay phone телефон-автомат
tee·lee·fon ahf·tah·maht

payment оплата *ah·plah·tah*

peak пик *peek*

pearl жемчуг *zhem·chook*

pedestrian crossing переход
pee·ree·khot

pedestrian zone пешеходная зона
pee·shih·khod·nah·yah zoh·nah

pedicure педикюр *pee·dee·kyoor*

pen ручка *rooch·kah*

pencil карандаш *kah·rahn·dahsh*

people люди *lyoo·dee*

perhaps может быть *moh·zhiht biht'*

period n (historical) период
pee·ree·aht; (menstrual)
менструация *meen·stroo·ah·tsih·yah*

petrol [BE] бензин *been·zeen*

pharmacy аптека *ahp·tyeh·kah*

phone v звонить *zvah·neet'*

phone card телефонная карточка
tee·lee·foh·nah·yah kahr·tahch·kah

phone call звонок *zvah·nok*

photo фотография
fah·tah·grah·fee·yah

photocopier ксерокс *ksyeh·rahks*

photography фотография
fah·tah·grah·fee·yah

phrase фраза *frah·zah*

phrase book разговорник
rahz·gah·vor·neek

pick up v (get) взять *vzyaht'*; (collect)
забирать *zah·bee·raht'*

picnic пикник *peek·neek*

piece n кусочек *koo·soh·cheek*

pill таблетка *tahb·lyet·kah*

pillow подушка *pah·doosh·kah*

pipe (smoking) трубка *troop·kah*

piste [BE] трасса *trah·sah*

pizzeria пиццерия *pee·tsih·<u>ree</u>·yah*

place (space) место *<u>myes</u>·tah*

plane самолёт *sah·mah·<u>lyot</u>*

plan план *plahn*

plant *n* растение *rahs·<u>tyeh</u>·nee·yeh*

plastic bag пакет *pah·<u>kyet</u>*

plastic wrap продуктовая плёнка
prah·dook·<u>toh</u>·vah·yah plyon·kah

plate тарелка *tah·<u>rel</u>·kah*

platform [BE] платформа
plaht·<u>for</u>·mah

platinum платина *<u>plah</u>·tee·nah*

play *n* игра *eeg·<u>rah</u>; v* **(games,
etc.)** играть *eeg·<u>raht'</u>;* **(perform)**
исполнять *ees·pahl·<u>nyaht'</u>*

playground детская площадка
<u>dyets</u>·kah·yah plah·<u>shchaht</u>·kah

playpen манеж *mah·<u>nyesh</u>*

pleasant приятный *pree·<u>yaht</u>·niy*

please пожалуйста *pah·<u>zhahl</u>·stah*

plug штепсель *<u>shtep</u>·seel'*

plunger вантуз *<u>vahn</u>·toos*

point *v* **(at)** показывать (на)
pah·<u>kah</u>·zih·vaht' (nah)

poison *n* яд *yaht*

poles палки *<u>pahl</u>·kee*

police милиция *mee·<u>lee</u>·tsih·yah*

police station отделение милиции
aht·dee·<u>lyeh</u>·nee·yeh mee·<u>lee</u>·tsih·ee

popular популярный
pah·poo·<u>lyahr</u>·niy

port (harbor) порт *port*

porter носильщик *nah·<u>seel</u>·'shcheek*

portion порция *<u>por</u>·tsih·yah*

possible возможно *vahz·<u>mozh</u>·nah*

post *n* почта *<u>poch</u>·tah; v* отправлять
aht·prahv·<u>lyaht'</u>

postbox [BE] почтовый ящик
pahch·<u>toh</u>·viy <u>yah</u>·shcheek

postcard открытка *aht·<u>kriht</u>·kah*

pottery керамика *kee·<u>rah</u>·mee·kah*

pound (sterling) фунт *foont*

pregnant беременная
bee·<u>reh</u>·mee·nah·yah

prescribe выписывать
vih·<u>pee</u>·sih·vaht'

prescription рецепт *ree·<u>tsept</u>*

present *n* **(gift)** подарок
pah·<u>dah</u>·rahk

press *v* гладить *<u>glah</u>·deet'*

pretty красивый *krah·<u>see</u>·viy*

print *v* печатать *pee·<u>chah</u>·taht'*

program *n* программа
prah·<u>grah</u>·mah

pronounce *v* произносить
prah·eez·nah·<u>seet'</u>

pump насос *nah·<u>sos</u>*

puncture прокол *prah·<u>kol</u>*

puppet show кукольный театр
<u>koo</u>·kahl'·niy tee·<u>ahtr</u>

pure (material) чистый *<u>chees</u>·tiy*

purpose цель *tsel'*

purse сумка _soom_•kah

pushchair [BE] прогулочная коляска
prah•_goo_•lahch•nah•yah kah•_lyas_•kah

put _v_ поставить pah•_stah_•veet'

Q

quality качество _kah_•chees•tvah

queue [BE] _v_ стоять в очереди
stah•_yaht_' _v_ _oh_•chee•ree•dee

quick быстрый _bihs_•triy

quiet тихий _tee_•kheey

R

racetrack ипподром ee•pah•_drom_

racket (tennis) ракетка rah•_kyet_•kah

railroad железная дорога
zhee•_lyez_•nah•yah dah•_roh_•gah

railway [BE] железная дорога
zhee•_lyez_•nah•yah dah•_roh_•gah

rain _v_ идёт дождь ee•_dyot_ doshch

raincoat плащ plahshch

rape _n_ изнасилование
eez•nah•_see_•lah•vah•nee•yeh

rapids пороги pah•_roh_•gee

rash сыпь sihp'

razor бритва _breet_•vah

read _v_ читать chee•_taht_'

ready готовый gah•_toh_•viy

real (genuine) настоящий
nah•stah•_yah_•shcheey

receipt квитанция kvee•_tahn_•tsih•yah

reception (desk) регистрация
ree•gee•_strah_•tsih•yah

receptionist портье pahrt'•_yeh_

recommend рекомендовать
ree•kah•meen•dah•_vaht_'

reduction (in price) скидка _skeet_•kah

refrigerator холодильник
khah•lah•_deel_'•neek

refund вернуть деньги veer•_noot_'
dyen'•gee

region район rah•_yon_

regular _adj_ **(size)** средний _sryed_•neey

religion религия ree•lee•gee•yah

remember помнить _pom_•neet'

rent _v_ взять напрокат vzyat'
nah•prah•_kaht_

repair _v_ чинить chee•_neet_'

repeat _v_ повторять pahf•tah•_ryaht_'

report _v_ заявить zah•yah•_veet_'

reservation заказ zah•_kahs_

reserve _v_ заказать zah•kah•_zaht_'

rest _v_ отдыхать aht•dih•_khaht_'

restaurant ресторан rees•tah•_rahn_

restroom туалет too•ah•_lyet_

retail торговля tahr•_gov_•lyah

retired на пенсии nah _pyen_•see•ee

return _v_ **(surrender)** возвратить
vahz•vrah•_teet_'

return ticket [BE] билет туда
и обратно bee•_lyet_ too•_dah_ ee
ahb•_raht_•nah

revolting отвратительный
aht·vrah·<u>tee</u>·teel'·niy

rib ребро *reeb·<u>roh</u>*

right *adj* **(correct)** правильный
<u>prah</u>·veel·'niy

ring кольцо *kahl'·<u>tsoh</u>*

river река *ree·<u>kah</u>*

road дорога *dah·<u>roh</u>·gah*

road map карта дорог *<u>kahr</u>·tah
dah·<u>rok</u>*

robbery грабеж *grah·<u>byosh</u>*

romantic романтичный
rah·mahn·<u>teech</u>·niy

roof (house, car) крыша *<u>krih</u>·shah*

room комната *<u>kom</u>·nah·tah*

room service
обслуживание номеров
*ahp·<u>sloo</u>·zhih·vah·nee·yeh
nah·mee·<u>rof</u>*

rope веревка *vee·<u>ryof</u>·kah*

round *adj* круглый *<u>kroog</u>·liy;* *n* **(of
game)** раунд *<u>rah</u>·oond*

round-trip ticket билет туда
и обратно *bee·<u>lyet</u> too·<u>dah</u> ee
ahb·<u>raht</u>·nah*

rubbish [BE] мусор *<u>moo</u>·sahr*

ruble [rouble] рубль *roobl'*

Russia Россия *rahs·<u>see</u>·yah*

Russian *adj* русский *<u>roos</u>·keey*

Russian language русский язык
<u>roos</u>·kee yah·<u>zihk</u>

S

safe *adj* безопасный *bee·zah·<u>pahs</u>·niy;*
n сейф *seyf*

safety безопасность
bee·zah·<u>pahs</u>·nahst'

safety pin булавка *boo·<u>lahf</u>·kah*

sailboat яхта *<u>yahkh</u>·tah*

sales tax НДС *en deh es*

same тот же самый *tot zheh <u>sah</u>·miy*

sand песок *pee·<u>sok</u>*

sandals сандалии *sahn·<u>dah</u>·lee*

sandy beach песчаный пляж
pee·<u>shchah</u>·niy plyahsh

sanitary napkins
гигиенические салфетки
*gee·gee·ee·<u>nee</u>·chees·kee·yeh
sahl·<u>fyet</u>·kee*

saucepan кастрюля *kahs·<u>tryoo</u>·lyah*

sauna сауна *<u>sah</u>·oo·nah*

say *v* говорить *gah·vah·<u>reet'</u>*

scarf шарф *shahrf*

scenic route живописный маршрут
zhi·vah·<u>pees</u>·niy mahrsh·<u>root</u>

schedule *n* расписание
rahs·pee·<u>sah</u>·nee·yeh

scissors ножницы *<u>nozh</u>·nee·tsih*

screwdriver отвёртка *aht·<u>vyort</u>·kah*

sea море *<u>moh</u>·ryeh*

seat место *<u>myes</u>·tah*

second class (train) купейный вагон
koo·<u>pey</u>·niy vah·<u>gon</u>

second-hand подержанный
pah·dyer·zhah·niy

secretary секретарь *seek·ree·tahr'*

sedative успокаивающее *oos·pah·ka h·ee·vah·yoo·shchee·yeh*

see видеть *vee·deet'*

self-service самообслуживание *sah· mah·ahp·sloo·zhih·vah·nee·yeh*

sell продавать *prah·dah·vaht'*

send посылать *pah·sih·laht'*

senior citizen пенсионер
pyen·see·ah·nyer

separately отдельно *ahd·del'·nah*

serious серьёзный *see·ryoz·niy*

service (religious)
служба *sloozh·bah;* **(in restaurant)** обслуживание *ahp·sloo·zhih·vah·nee·yeh*

shade тень *tyen'*

shallow мелкий *myel·keey*

shampoo шампунь *shahm·poon'*

shape *n* форма *for·mah*

share *v* **(a room)** делить *dee·leet'*

sheet (bedding) простыня
prahs·tih·nyah

ship корабль *kah·rahbl'*

shirt рубашка *roo·bahsh·kah*

shoe repair ремонт обуви *ree·mont oh·boo·vee*

shoe store обувной магазин
ah·boov·noy mah·gah·zeen

shoes туфли *toof·lee*

shop магазин *mah·gah·zeen*

shop assistant продавец
prah·dah·vyets

shopping basket корзинка
kahr·zeen·kah

shopping centre [BE] торговый центр *tahr·goh·viy tsentr*

short *adj* **(height)** низкий *nees·keey*

short-sighted [BE] близорукий
blee·zah·roo·keey

shorts шорты *shor·tih*

shoulder плечо *plee·choh*

shovel совок *sah·vok*

show *v* показывать *pah·kah·zih·vaht'*

shower душ *doosh*

shut *adj* закрытый *zah·krih·tiy; v* закрываться *zah·krih·vah·tsah*

sick больной *bahl'·noy;*

side *n* **(of road)** сторона *stah·rah·nah*

sightseeing tour обзорная экскурсия *ahb·zor·nah·yah eeks·koor·see·yah*

sign (road) знак *znahk*

silk шёлк *sholk*

silver серебро *see·ree·broh*

single (unmarried) холостой
khah·lash·toy

single room одноместный номер
ahd·nah·myes·niy noh·meer

single ticket [BE] билет в один конец

bee•lyet v _ah•deen kah•nyets_

sink раковина _rah•kah•vee•nah_

sit v сесть _syest'_

size размер _rahz•myer_

skates коньки _kahn'•kee_

ski boots лыжные ботинки
lihzh•nih•yeh bah•teen•kee

skin кожа _koh•zhah_

skirt юбка _yoop•kah_

skis лыжи _lih•zhih_

sleep v спать _spaht'_

sleeping bag спальный мешок
spahl'•niy mee•shok

sleeping pill снотворное
snaht•vor•nah•yeh

sleeve рукав _roo•kahf_

slippers тапочки _tah•pach•kee_

slow adj медленный _myed•lee•niy_

small (in size) маленький
mah•leen'•keey

smell n запах _zah•pahkh_

smoke v курить _koo•reet'_

smoking adj курящий
koo•ryah•shcheey

snack bar буфет _boo•fyet_

sneakers теннисные туфли
teh•nees•nih•ee toof•lee

snorkel n трубка _troop•kah_

snow снег _snyek_

soap мыло _mih•lah_

soccer футбол _food•bol_

socket розетка _rah•zyet•kah_

socks носки _nahs•kee_

sole (shoes) подошва _pah•dosh•vah_

some какой-то _kah•koy tah_

someone кто-то _ktoh•tah_

something что-то _shtoh•tah_

sometimes иногда _ee•nahg•dah_

soon скоро _skoh•rah_

soother [BE] соска _sos•kah_

sore throat ангина _ahn•gee•nah_

souvenir сувенир _soo•vee•neer_

souvenir store магазин сувениров
mah•gah•zeen soo•vee•nee•rahf

spa спа _spah_

space место _myes•tah_

spare (extra) лишний _leesh•neey_

speak v говорить _gah•vah•reet'_

specialist специалист
spee•tsih•ah•leest

spell v называть по буквам
nah•zih•vaht' pah book•vahm

spend v тратить _trah•teet'_

spine позвоночник
pahz•vah•noch•neek

spoon ложка _losh•kah_

sport спорт _sport_

sports club спортклуб _sport•kloop_

sporting goods store спорттовары
spor•tah•vah•rih

sprain n растяжение
rahs•tee•zheh•nee•yeh

square *adj* квадратный
kvahd•*raht*•niy; *n* площадь
ploh•shchaht'

stadium стадион stah•dee•*on*

staff персонал peer•sah•*nahl*

stainless steel нержавеющая сталь
nee•rzhah•*vye*•yoo•shchah•yah stahl'

stamp марка *mahr*•kah

stand *v* стоять stah•*yaht'*

start *v* (**commence**) начинать
nah•chee•*naht'*; (**car**) заводить
zah•vah•*deet'*

station вокзал vahg•*zahl*

stationery канцелярские товары
kahn•tsih•*lyahr*•skee•yeh tah•*vah*•rih

statue статуя *stah*•too•yah

stay *v* остаться ah•*stah*•tsah

sting укус oo•*koos*

stockings чулки chool•*kee*

stomach живот zhih•*vot*

stomachache болит живот bah•*leet*
zhih•*vot*

stop *n* (**bus, etc.**) остановка
ah•stah•*nof*•kah; *v* останавливаться
ah•stah•*nahv*•lee•vah•tsah

store магазин mah•gah•*zeen*

store guide перечень отделов
pyeh•ree•cheen' ahd•*dyeh*•lahf

storm буря *boo*•ryah

stove плита plee•*tah*

strange странный *strah*•niy

stream ручей roo•*chey*

stroller прогулочная коляска
prah•*goo*•lahch•nah•yah
kah•*lyas*•kah

strong (**potent**) сильный *seel'*•niy

student студент stoo•*dyent*

study *v* учиться oo•*chee*•tsah

stunning ошеломляющий
ah•shih•lahm•*lyah*•yoo•shchey

style стиль steel'

subtitled с субтитрами s
soop•*teet*•rah•mee

subway метро meet•*roh*

subway station станция метро
stahn•tsih•yah meet•*roh*

suggest предлагать preed•lah•*gaht'*

suit костюм kahs•*tyoom*

sunbathe *v* загорать zah•gah•*raht'*

sunburn солнечный ожёг
sol•neech•niy ah•*zhok*

sunglasses солнечные очки
sol•neech•nih•ee ahch•*kee*

sunny солнечно *sol*•nyech•nah

sunstroke солнечный удар
sol•neech•niy oo•*dahr*

superb превосходный
pree•vahs•*khod*•niy

supermarket универсам
oo•nee•veer•*sahm*

supervision присмотр pree•*smotr*

supplement доплата dah•*plah*•tah

surfboard доска для серфинга
dahs·kah dlyah ser·feen·gah

surname фамилия _fah·mee·lee·yah_

suspicious подозрительный
pah·dah·zree·teel'·niy

sweater пуловер _poo·loh·veer_

sweatshirt байка _bie·kah_

swelling опухоль _oh·poo·khahl'_

swim v плавать _plah·vaht'_

swimming плавание
plah·vah·nee·yeh

swimming pool бассейн _bah·seyn_

swimming trunks плавки _plahf·kee_

swimsuit купальник _koo·pahl'·neek_

symptoms симптомы _seemp·toh·mih_

synagogue синагога _see·nah·goh·gah_

synthetic синтетический
seen·teh·tee·chees·keey

T

T-shirt майка _mie·kah_

table столик _stoh·leek_

take (carry) нести _nyes·tee;_
(medication) принимать
pree·nee·maht'; **(time)** занимать
zah·nee·maht'

talk v разговаривать
rahz·gah·vah·ree·vaht'

tall высокий _vih·soh·keey_

tampon тампон _tahm·pon_

tan загар _zah·gahr_

taxi такси _tahk·see_

taxi rank [BE] стоянка такси
stah·yahn·kah tahk·see

taxi stand стоянка такси
stah·yahn·kah tahk·see

team команда _kah·mahn·dah_

teaspoon чайная ложка _chie·nah·yah
losh·kah_

teddy bear мишка _meesh·kah_

telephone n телефон _tee·lee·fon_

telephone bill счёт за телефон
shchot zah tee·lee·fon

telephone booth телефон-автомат
tee·lee·fon·ahf·tah·maht

telephone call телефонный звонок
tee·lee·foh·niy zvah·nok

telephone directory телефонный
справочник _tee·lee·foh·niy
sprah·vahch·neek_

telephone number номер телефона
noh·meer tee·lee·foh·nah

tell v рассказывать
rahs·kah·zih·vaht'

temperature (body) температура
teem·pee·rah·too·rah

tennis теннис _teh·nees_

tennis court теннисный корт
teh·nees·niy kort

tent палатка _pah·laht·kah_

tent pegs колышки _koh·lihsh·kee_

tent pole шест _shest_

terminal (bus) (авто) вокзал (*ahf·tah*) vahg·*zahl*

terrible ужасный ooh·*zhahs*·niy

theater театр tee·*ahtr*

theft кража *krah*·zhah

then (time) затем zah·*tyem*

there там tahm

thermometer термометр teer·*moh*·meetr

thermos термос *ter*·mahs

thick толстый *tols*·tiy

thief вор vor

thigh бедро beed·*roh*

thin тонкий *ton*·keey

think думать *doo*·maht'

throat горло *gor*·lah

through через *chyeh*·rees

thumb большой палец *bahl'·shoy pah·leets*

ticket билет bee·*lyet*

ticket office билетные кассы bee·*lyet*·nih·yeh *kah*·sih

tie галстук *gahls*·took

tight (loose) тесно *tyehs*·niy

tights колготки kahl·*got*·kee

time время *vryeh*·myah

timetable [BE] расписание rahs·pee·*sah*·nee·yeh

tin [BE] банка *bahn*·kah

tin opener [BE] консервный нож kahn·*serv*·niy nosh

tire n шина *shih*·nah

tired усталый oos·*tah*·liy

tissue бумажная салфетка boo·*mahzh*·nah·yah salh·*fyet*·kah

to (place) в v

tobacco табак tah·*bahk*

toe палец ноги *pah*·leets nah·*gee*

together вместе *vmyes*·tee

toilet [BE] туалет too·ah·*lyet*

toilet paper туалетная бумага too·ah·*lyet*·nah·yah boo·*mah*·gah

tongue язык yah·*zihk*

too слишком *sleesh*·kahm

tooth зуб zoop

toothache зубная боль zoob·*nah*·yah bol'

toothbrush зубная щётка zoob·*nah*·yah *shchot*·kah

toothpaste зубная паста zoob·*nah*·yah *pahs*·tah

top крышка *krihsh*·kah

tour экскурсия eeks·*koor*·see·yah

tour guide экскурсовод eeks·koor·sah·*vot*

tourist турист too·*reest*

tourist office туристическое бюро too·rees·tee·*chees*·kah·yeh byoo·*roh*

tow truck буксир book·*seer*

tow v отбуксировать aht·book·*see*·rah·vaht'

towel полотенце pah·lah·*tyen*·tseh

tower башня _bahsh_·nyah

town город _goh_·raht

town hall горсовет _gor_·sah·_vyet_

toy игрушка _eeg_·_roosh_·kah

track платформа _plaht_·_for_·mah

traditional традиционный
trah·dee·tsih·_oh_·niy

traffic дорожное движение
dah·_rozh_·nah·yeh dvee·_zheh_·nee·yeh

traffic jam пробка _prop_·kah

traffic lights светофор _svee_·tah·_for_

trail трасса _trah_·sah

trailer трейлер _trey_·leer

train поезд _poh_·eest

train station вокзал _vahg_·_zahl_

tram трамвай _trahm_·_vie_

transit n проездом _prah_·_yez_·dahm

translate v переводить
pee·ree·vah·_deet'_

translation перевод _pee_·ree·_vot_

translator переводчик
pee·ree·_vot_·cheek

trash мусор _moo_·sahr

trash can мусорный бак _moo_·sahr·niy
bahk

travel agency бюро путешествий
byoo·_roh_ poo·tee·_shest_·veey

travel sickness [BE] морская болезнь
mahr·_skah_·yah bah·_lyezn'_

traveler's check дорожный чек
dah·_rozh_·niy chehk

tray поднос _pahd_·_nos_

tree дерево _dyeh_·ree·vah

trim (hair) постричь _pah_·_streech_

trip (journey) поездка _pah_·_yest_·kah

trolley [BE] тележка _tee_·_lyesh_·kah

trousers [BE] брюки _bryoo_·kee

true правда _prahv_·dah

tunnel тунель _too_·_nel'_

turn down (volume, heat)
уменьшать _oo_·meen'·_shaht'_

turn off выключать _vih_·klyoo·_chaht'_

turn on включать _fklyoo_·_chaht'_

turn up (volume, heat) увеличивать
_oo_·vee·_lee_·chee·vaht'

turning поворот _pah_·vah·_rot_

TV телевизор _teh_·leh·_vee_·zahr

typical типичный _tee_·_peech_·niy

U

ugly некрасивый _nee_·krah·_see_·viy

ulcer язва _yahz_·vah

umbrella зонт zont

uncle дядя _dyah_·dyah

unconscious без сознания byes
sahz·_nah_·nee·yah

under под paht

underground [BE] метро _meet_·_roh_

underground station [BE] станция
метро _stahn_·tsih·yah meet·_roh_

understand понимать
pah·nee·_maht'_

uneven (ground) неровный
nee•rov•niy

unfortunately к сожалению *k
sah•zhih•lyeh•nee•yoo*

uniform форма *for•mah*

unit (for phonecard, etc.) единица
ee•dee•nee•tsah

unleaded (gas) без свинца *bees
sveen•tsah*

unlock отпирать *aht•pee•raht'*

unpleasant неприятный
nee•pree•yaht•niy

upper (berth) верхний *vyerkh•neey*

urgent срочно *sroch•nah*

urine моча *mah•chah*

use *v* пользоваться *pol'•zah•vah•tsah*

V

vacant свободный *svah•bod•niy*

vacation отпуск *oht•poosk*

vacuum cleaner пылесос *pih•lee•sos*

vaginal infection вагинальная
инфекция *vah•gee•nahl'•nah•yah
een•fyek•tsih•yah*

valid действителен *deey•stvee•tee•len*

valley долина *dah•lee•nah*

valuable ценный *tseh•niy*

value стоимость *stoh•ee•mahst'*

VAT [ВЕ] НДС *en deh es*

vegetarian вегетарианец
vee•gee•tah•ree•ah•neets

vein вена *vyeh•nah*

very очень *oh•cheen'*

village деревня *dee•ryev•nyah*

visa виза *vee•zah*

visit *n* визит *vee•zeet;* *v* посещать
pah•see•shchaht'

visiting hours часы посещений
chee•sih pah•see•shcheh•neey

vitamins витамины
vee•tah•mee•nih

volleyball волейбол *vah•leey•bol*

voltage напряжение
nah•pree•zheh•nee•yeh

vomit тошнить *tahsh•neet'*

W

wait ждать *zhdaht'*

waiter официант *ah•fee•tsih•ahnt*

waiting room зал ожидания *zahl
ah•zhih•dah•nee•yah*

wake (someone) разбудить
rahz•boo•deet'

walk *v* идти *eet•tee*

walking route пешеходный
маршрут *pee•shih•khod•niy
mahrsh•root*

wallet кошелёк *kah•shih•lyohk*

want хотеть *khah•tet'*

war memorial мемориал
mee•mah•ree•ahl

ward (hospital) палата *pah•lah•tah*

warm тёплый _tyop·liy_

washing machine стиральная машина _stee·rahl'·nah·yah mah·shih·nah_

watch часы _chah·sih_

water вода _vah·dah_

water skis водные лыжи _vod·nih·yeh lih·zhee_

waterfall водопад _vah·dah·paht_

waterproof водонепроницаемый _vo h·dah·nee·prah·nee·tsah·ee·miy_

wave волна _vahl·nah_

wear v одевать _ah·dee·vaht'_

weather погода _pah·goh·dah_

weather forecast прогноз погоды _prahg·nos pah·goh·dih_

wedding свадьба _svahd'·bah_

week неделя _nee·deh·lyah_

weekend выходные _vih·khahd·nih·yeh_

weigh вес _vyes_

wheelchair инвалидное кресло _een·vah·leed·nah·yeh kryes·lah_

wide широкий _shih·roh·keey_

wife жена _zhih·nah_

windbreaker ветровка _veet·rof·kah_

window окно _ahk·noh_

window seat место у окна _myes·tah oo ahk·nah_

windscreen ветровое стекло _vee·trah·voh·yeh steek·loh_

windsurfer виндсерфер _veend·syer·fyer_

windy ветер _vyeh·teer_

wireless internet беспроводной интернет _bees·prah·vahd·noy een·ter·net_

with c _s_

withdraw снимать _snee·maht'_

without без _bes_

wood лес _lyes_

wool шерсть _sherst'_

work v работать _rah·boh·taht'_

wound n рана _rah·nah_

wrong неправильный _nee·prah·veel'·niy_

X

X-ray рентген _reen·gyen_

Y

yacht яхта _yahkh·tah_

yellow жёлтый _zhol·tiy_

young молодой _mah·lah·doy_

youth hostel общежитие _ahp·shchee·zhih·tee·yeh_

Z

zebra crossing переход _pee·ree·khot_

zipper молния _mol·nee·yah_

zoo зоопарк _zah·ah·pahrk_

А

аванс *ah·vahns* deposit

аварийный выход *ah·vah·reey·niy vih·khaht* emergency exit

автобус *ahf·toh·boos* bus

автобусная остановка *ahf·toh·boos·nah·yah ahs·tah·nof·kah* bus stop

автобусная станция *ahf·toh·boos·nah·yah stahn·tsih·yah* bus station

автовокзал *ahf·tah·vahg·zahl* terminal (bus)

автостоянка *ahf·tah·stah·yahn·kah* parking lot [car park BE]

адаптер *ah·dahp·ter* adapter

адвокат *ahd·vah·kaht* lawyer

адрес *ah·drees* address

адрес электронной почты *ah·drees ee·leek·tron·nie poch·tih* e-mail address

аккумулятор *ah·kah·moo·lyah·tahr* battery

аллергия *ah·leer·gee·yah* allergy

американский *ah·mee·ree·kahn·skeey adj* American

ангина *ahn·gee·nah* sore throat

английский *ahn·gleey·skeey* English

антибиотики *ahn·tee·bee·oh·tee·kee* antibiotics

антикварный *ahn·tee·kvahr·niy* antique

антисептик *ahn·tee·sep·teek* antiseptic

аппендикс *ah·pyen·deeks* appendix

аптека *ahp·tyeh·kah* pharmacy [chemist BE]

аспирин *ah·spee·reen* aspirin

астматик *ahst·mah·teek n* asthmatic

аэропорт *ah·eh·rah·port* airport

Б

багаж *bah·gahsh* luggage [baggage BE]

багажная квитанция *bah·gahzh·nah·yah kvee·tahn·tsih·yah* baggage check

багажная тележка *bah·gahzh·nah·yah tee·lyesh·kah* luggage cart [trolley BE]

байка *bie·kah* sweatshirt

балет *bah·lyet* ballet

балкон *bahl·kon* balcony

банк *bahnk* bank

банка *bahn·kah* jar; can [tin BE]

банкомат *bahn·kah·maht* ATM

бар *bahr* bar (hotel, etc.)

баскетбол *bahs·keet·bol* basketball

бассейн _bah·seyn_ swimming pool

башня _bahsh·nyah_ tower

бега _bee·gah_ horse racing

бедро _beed·roh_ thigh

без _byez_ without

без сознания _byes sah·znah·nee·yah_ unconscious

безопасность _bee·zah·pahs·nahst'_ safety

безопасный _bee·zah·pahs·niy adj_ safe

бензин _been·zeen_ gas [petrol BE]

беременна _bee·ryeh·mee·nah_ pregnant

беспокоить _bees·pah·koh·eet'_ disturb

беспроводной интернет _bees·prah·vahd·noy een·ter·net_ wireless internet

бессоница _bees·soh·nee·tsah_ insomnia

библиотека _bee·blee·ah·tyeh·kah_ library

бизнес _beez·nees_ business

бикини _bee·kee·nee_ bikini

билет _bee·lyet_ ticket

билет в один конец _bee·lyet v ah·deen kah·nyets_ one-way [single BE] ticket

билет туда и обратно _bee·lyet too·dah ee ahb·raht·nah_ round-trip [return BE] ticket

билетная касса _bee·lyet·nah·yah kah·sah_ ticket office

бинокль _bee·noh·kahl'_ binoculars

близорукий _blee·zah·roo·keey_ near-sighted [short-sighted BE]

блузка _bloos·kah_ blouse

болеть _bah·lyet' v_ hurt

болеутоляющее _boh·lee·oo·tah·lya h·yoo·shchee·yeh_ painkiller

боль _bol'_ pain

больница _bahl'·nee·tsah_ hospital

большой _bahl'·shoy_ big

большой палец _bahl'·shoy pah·leets_ thumb

ботанический сад _bah·tah·nee·chees·keey saht_ botanical garden

бояться _bah·yah·tsah_ frightened

браслет _brahs·lyet_ bracelet

брат _braht_ brother

брильянт _breel'·yahnt_ diamond

британский _bree·tahn·skeey_ British

бритва _breet·vah_ razor

бронхит _brahn·kheet_ bronchitis

брошь _brosh_ brooch

брошюра _brah·shoo·rah_ brochure

брюки _bryoo·kee_ pants [trousers BE]

будильник _boo·deel'·neek_ alarm clock

буксир _book·seer_ tow truck

буксировать _book·see·rah·vaht'_ tow

булавка *boo·lahf·kah* safety pin

булочная *boo·lahch·nah·yah* bakery

бумага *boo·mah·gah* paper

бумажная салфетка *boo·mahzh·nah·yah sahl·fyet·kah* tissue

буря *boo·ryah* storm

буфет *boo·fyet* snack bar

бухгалтер *boo·gahl·teer* accountant

быстрый *bihs·triy* quick

быть *biht'* be

бюро находок *byoo·roh nah·khoh·dahk* lost-and-found [lost property office BE]

бюстгальтер *byoost·gahl·ter* bra

В

вагинальная инфекция *vah·gee·nahl'·nah·yah een·fyek·tsih·yah* vaginal infection

вагон *vah·gon* car [coach BE] (train) *вагон-ресторан vah·gon rees·tah·rahn* dining car

валюта *vah·lyoo·tah* currency

вантуз *vahn·toos* plunger

вата *vah·tah* cotton

вегетарианец *vee·gee·tah·ree·ah·neets* vegetarian

ведро *veed·roh* bucket

Великобритания *vee·lee·kah·bree·tah·nee·yah* Great Britain

великолепный *vee·lee·kah·lyep·niy* magnificent

велосипед *vee·lah·see·pyet* bicycle

велосипедный маршрут *vee·lah·see·pyed·niy mahrsh·root* cycle route

велоспорт *vyeh·lah·sport* cycling

вена *vyeh·nah* vein

вентилятор *veen·tee·lyah·tuhr* fan (air)

веревка *vee·ryof·kah* rope

верхний *vyerkh·neey* upper

вес *vyes* weight

веселье *vee·syel'·yeh* fun

ветер *vyeh·teer* wind

ветровка *veet·rof·kah* windbreaker

ветровое стекло *vee·trah·voh·yeh steek·loh* windscreen

вечеринка *vee·chee·reen·kah* party (social)

вешалка *vye·shahl·kah* peg

взлом *vzlom* break-in

взрослый *vzros·liy* adult

взять напрокат *vzyat' nah·prah·kaht* v rent [hire BE]

видеть *vee·deet'* see

виза *vee·zah* visa

визит *vee·zeet* n visit

вилка *veel·kah* fork

виндсерфер *veend·syer·fyer* windsurfer

винный магазин _vee·niy mah·gah·zeen_ liquor store [off-license BE]

витамины _vee·tah·mee·nih_ vitamins

витрина _vee·tree·nah_ window (in store)

владелец _vlah·dyeh·leets_ owner

вместе _vmyes·tee_ together

внутри _vnoo·tree_ inside

вовремя _voh·vryeh·myah_ on time

вода _vah·dah_ n water

водитель _vah·dee·teel'_ driver

водительские права _vah·dee·teel'·skee·yeh prah·vah_ driver's license

водная экскурсия _vod·nah·yah eks·koor·see·yah_ boat trip

водные лыжи _vod·nih·yeh lih·zhih_ water skis

водонепроницаемый _voh·dah·nee·prah·nee·tsah·ee·miy_ waterproof

водопад _vah·dah·paht_ water fall

воздух _voz·dookh_ air

возраст _voz·rahst_ n age

вокзал _vahg·zahl_ train [railway BE] station

волдырь _vahl·dihr'_ blister

волейбол _vah·leey·bol_ volleyball

волна _vahl·nah_ n wave

волосы _voh·lah·sih_ hair

вор _vor_ thief

воспаление _vahs·pah·lyeh·nee·yeh_ inflammation

врач _vrahch_ doctor

время _vryeh·myah_ time

все _fsyoh_ all

все еще _vsyoh ee·shchoh_ still

всегда _fseeg·dah_ always

вставлять _fstahv·lyat'_ v insert

встречаться _fstree·chah·tsah_ meet

второй _ftah·roy_ second

вход в систему _fkhot f sees·tyeh·moo_ n login

входная плата _fkhahd·nah·yah plah·tah_ entrance fee

въездная виза _vyezd·nah·yah vee·zah_ entry visa

вывихнуть _vih·veekh·noot'_ v twist

выезжать _vih·eezh·zhaht'_ check-out (hotel)

вызывать _vih·zih·vaht'_ v call (the police)

выписывать _vih·pee·sih·vaht'_ prescribe

высокий _vih·soh·keey_ high

высокий _vih·soh·keey_ tall

высокое давление _vih·soh·kah·yeh dahv·lyeh·nee·yeh_ high blood pressure

выход _vih·khaht_ n exit

выходные _vih·khahd·nih·yeh_ weekend

г

гавань _gah_·vahn' harbor

газета gah·_zyeh_·tah newspaper

газетный киоск gah·_zyet_·niy kee·_osk_
newsstand

галлон gah·_lon_ gallon

галстук _gahls_·took tie

гандикап gahn·dee·_kahp_ handicap
(golf)

гараж gah·_rahsh_ garage

гарантия gah·_rahn_·tee·yah guarantee

гардероб gahr·dee·_rop_ coatcheck

гигиенические салфетки
gee·gee·ee·_nee_·chees·kee·yeh
sahl·_fyet_·kee sanitary napkins [pads
BE]

гид geet guide (tour)

гинеколог gee·nee·_koh_·lahk
gynecologist

гитара gee·_tah_·rah guitar

главный _glahv_·niy main

глаз glahs eye

глубокий gloo·_boh_·keey deep

глухой gloo·_khoy_ deaf

говорить gah·vah·_reet_' speak

голова gah·lah·_vah_ head

головная боль gah·lahv·_nah_·yah
bol' headache

голодный gah·_lod_·niy hungry

гололёд gah·lah·_lyot_ icy

гольф gol'f golf

гора gah·_rah_ mountain

горло _gor_·lah throat

город _goh_·raht town

горсовет gor·sah·_vyet_ town hall

горячий gah·_rya_·cheey hot

гостиная gahs·tee·_nah_·yah living
room

гостиница gahs·_tee_·nee·tsah hotel

готовить gah·_toh_·veet' prepare

готовый gah·_toh_·viy ready

грабеж grah·_byosh_ robbery

градус _grah_·doos degree
(temperature)

грамм grahm gram

графин grah·_feen_ carafe

грипп greep flu

громче _grom_·chee louder

грудная клетка grood·_nah_·yah
klyet·kah chest (body)

грудь groot' breast

группа _groo_·pah group

группа крови _groo_·pah _kroh_·vee
blood group

грязный _gryahz_·niy dirty

губа goo·bah lip

губная памада goob·_nah_·yah
pah·_mah_·dah lipstick

д

давать dah·_vaht_' give

далеко dah·lee·_koh_ far

дальнозоркий *dahl'•nah•zor•keey* far-sighted [long-sighted BE]

дать взаймы *daht' vzie•mih* lend

дача *dah•chah* summer cottage

дверь *dvyer'* door

движение *dah•rozh•nah•yeh dvee•zheh•nee•yeh* traffic

дворец *dvah•ryets* palace

двухместный *dvookh•myes•niy* double

девочка *dyeh•vahch•kah* girl

дезодорант *dee•zah•dah•rahnt* deodorant

действителен *deey•stvee•tee•lyen* valid

делать *ставку dyeh•laht' stahf•koo* place a bet

день *dyen'* day

день рождения *dyen' rahzh•dyeh•nee•yah* birthday

деньги *dyen'•gee* money

деревня *dee•ryev•nyah* village

дерево *dyeh•ree•vah* tree

десна *dees•nah* gum

детальный счёт *dee•tahl'•niy shchot* itemized bill

дети *dyeh•tee* children

детская площадка *dyets•kah•yah plah•shchaht•kah* playground

детское сиденье *dyets•kah•yeh see•dyen'•yeh* child seat (in car)

дешевле *dee•shev•lee* cheaper

дешёвый *dee•shoh•viy* cheap

джаз *dzhahs* jazz

джинсовый *dzhihn•soh•viy adj* denim

джинсы *dzhihn•sih* jeans

диабет *dee•ah•byet* diabetes

диабетик *dee•ah•byeh•teek* diabetic (person)

диагноз *dee•ahg•nahs* diagnosis

диета *dee•yeh•tah n* diet

дизельное топливо *dee•zeel'•nah•yeh top•lee•vah* diesel

директор *dee•ryek•tahr* director (of company)

дирижёр *dee•ree•zhor* conductor (orchestra)

длина *dlee•nah* length

длинный *dlee•niy* long

дневное представление *dneev•noh•yeh preet•stahv•lyeh•nee•yeh* matinée

до *dah* until

добавочный номер *dah•bah•vahch•niy noh•meer* extension

добираться *dah•bee•rah•tsah* get (to destination)

дождь *dosch n* rain

долина *dah•lee•nah* valley

дом *dom* house

допуск *doh•poosk n* access

дорога _dah·<u>roh</u>·gah_ road

дорогой _dah·rah·<u>goy</u>_ expensive

дорожная пробка _dah·<u>rozh</u>·nah·yah <u>prop</u>·kah_ traffic jam

дорожный чек _dah·<u>rozh</u>·niy chehk_ traveler's check [cheques BE]

доска для серфинга _dahs·kah dlyah <u>ser</u>·feen·gah_ surfboard

доставлять _dah·stahv·<u>lyat'</u>_ deliver

достаточно _dah·<u>stah</u>·tahch·nah_ enough

дрова _drah·<u>vah</u>_ firewood

друг _drook_ friend

другие _droo·<u>gee</u>·yeh_ others

другой _droo·<u>goy</u>_ other

дружеский _<u>droo</u>·zhees·keey_ friendly

дублирован _doob·<u>lee</u>·rah·vahn_ dubbed

думать _<u>doo</u>·maht'_ think

духовка _doo·<u>khof</u>·kah_ oven

душ _doosh_ shower

дырка _<u>dihr</u>·kah_ hole (in clothes)

дышать _dih·<u>shaht'</u>_ breathe

дюжина _<u>dyoo</u>·zhih·nah_ dozen

дядя _<u>dyah</u>·dyah_ uncle

Е

Европейский союз _yev·rah·<u>pey</u>·skeey sah·<u>yoos</u>_ European Union (EU)

ежедневно _ee·zhee·<u>dnyev</u>·nah_ daily

ерунда _ee·roon·<u>dah</u>_ nonsense

есть _yest'_ eat

ехать _<u>yeh</u>·khaht'_ drive

ещё _ee·<u>shchoh</u>_ extra (additional)

Ж

жалоба _<u>zhah</u>·lah·bah_ complaint

жар _zhahr_ fever

ждать _zhdaht'_ wait

жёлтый _<u>zhol</u>·tiy_ yellow

жемчуг _<u>zhem</u>·chook_ pearl

жена _zhih·<u>nah</u>_ wife

женат _zhih·<u>naht</u>_ married (man)

живописный маршрут _zhih·vah·<u>pees</u>·niy mahrsh·root_ scenic route

живот _zhih·<u>vot</u>_ stomach

животное _zhi·<u>vot</u>·nah·yeh_ animal

журнал _zhoor·<u>nahl</u>_ magazine

З

забирать _zah·bee·<u>raht'</u>_ collect

заблокирован _zah·blah·<u>kee</u>·rah·vahn_ blocked

заболевание сердца _zah·bah·lee·<u>vah</u>·nee·yeh <u>syer</u>·tsah_ heart condition

заболеть _zah·bah·<u>lyet'</u>_ get sick [ill BE]

забывать _zah·bih·<u>vaht'</u>_ forget

загар _zah·<u>gahr</u>_ tan

загорать _zah·gah·<u>raht'</u>_ sunbathe

заграницей *zah·grah·nee·tsey* abroad

задержка *zah·dyersh·kah n* delay

зажигалка *zah·zhih·gahl·kah* lighter (cigarette)

заказывать *zah·kah·zih·vaht' v* order

законный *zah·kon·niy* legal

закрываться *zah·krih·vah·tsah v* close (store, etc.)

закрытый *zah·krih·tiy adj* shut

закрытый бассейн *zah·krih·tiy bah·seyn* indoor pool

зал вылета *zahl vih·lee·tah* departure lounge

зал ожидания *zahl ah·zhih·dah·nee·yah* waiting room

замок *zah·mahk* castle

замок *zah·mok n* lock

замужем *zah·moo·zhihm* married (woman)

занят *zah·nyaht* busy

занятый *zah·nee·tiy* occupied

запах *zah·pahkh* smell

заповедник *zah·pah·vyed·neek* nature reserve

заправочная станция *zah·prah·vahch·nah·yah stahn·tsih·yah* gas station

затем *zah·tyem* then (time)

захватывающий *zah·khvah·tih·vah·yoo·shchey* breathtaking

заштопать *zah·shtoh·paht'* patch

звонить *zvah·neet' v* call (phone)

здание *zdah·nee·yeh* building

здесь *zdyes'* here

зелёный *zee·lyoh·niy* green

зеркало *zyer·kah·lah* mirror

знак *znahk* sign (road)

значить *znah·cheet' v* mean

золото *zoh·lah·tah* gold

зонт *zont* umbrella

зоопарк *zah·ah·pahrk n* zoo

зуб *zoop* tooth

зубная боль *zoob·nah·yah bol'* tooth-ache

зубная паста *zoob·nah·yah pahs·tah* toothpaste

зубная щётка *zoob·nah·yah shchot·kah* toothbrush

зубной врач *zoob·noy vrahch* dentist

И

игра *eeg·rah* game

играть *eeg·raht' v* play (games, etc.)

игрушка *eeg·roosh·kah n* toy

идти за покупками *eet·tee zah pah·koop·kah·mee* go shopping

идти пешком *eet·tee peesh·kom v* walk

из-за *eez·zah* because of

измерение *eez·mee·ryeh·nee·yeh*
measurement

измерить *eez·myeh·reet'* v measure

изнасилование
eez·nah·see·lah·vah·nee·yeh n rape

изумруд *ee·zoom·root* emerald

изучать *ee·zoo·chaht'* learn
(language)

имя *ee·myah* name (first name)

инвалид *een·vah·leet* n handicapped
[disabled BE]

инвалидное кресло
een·vah·leed·nah·yeh kryes·lah
wheelchair

иногда *ee·nahg·dah* sometimes

иностранная валюта
ee·nah·strah·nah·yah vah·lyoo·tah
foreign currency

инструкция *een·strook·tsih·yah*
instructions

инсулин *een·soo·leen* insulin

интересный *een·tee·ryes·niy*
interesting

интернет *een·ter·net* internet

интернет-кафе *een·ter·net kah·feh*
internet cafe

инфекция *een·fyek·tsih·yah* infection

информация *een·fahr·mah·tsih·yah*
information

ипподром *ee·pah·drom* racetrack

исполнять *ees·pahl·nyaht'* perform

К

к сожалению *k sah·zhih·lyeh·nee·yoo*
unfortunately

к счастью *k shchahst'·yoo*
fortunately

каждый *kahzh·diy* every

казино *kah·zee·noh* casino

какой-либо *kah·koy·lee·bah* any

какой-то kah·koy tah some

календарь *kah·leen·dahr'* calendar

камера хранения *kah·mee·rah
khrah·nyeh·nee·yah* luggage locker

канцелярские товары
kahn·tsih·lyahr·skee·yeh tah·vah·rih
stationery

карандаш *kah·rahn·dahsh* pencil

карта *kahr·tah* map

карта дорог *kahr·tah dah·rok* road
map

картина *kahr·tee·nah* painting

картинная галерея
kahr·teen·nah·yah gah·lee·ryeh·yah
art gallery

карты *kahr·tih* cards

кассета *kah·syeh·tah* cassette

кассир *kah·seer* cashier

кастрюля *kahs·tryoo·lyah* saucepan

качество *kah·chees·tvah* quality

кашель *kah·shihl'* n cough

кашлять *kahsh·lyaht'* v cough

каюта *kah·yoo·tah* cabin

квадратный kvahd·raht·niy adj
square

квартира kvahr·tee·rah apartment
[flat BE]

кемпинг kyem·peenk camping

керамика kee·rah·mee·kah pottery

километраж kee·lah·mee·trahsh
mileage

кинотеатр kee·nah·tee·ahtr movie
theater [cinema BE]

кишечник kee·shech·neek bowel

класс klahs class (type of seat, etc.)

ключ klyooch key

клюшка klyoosh·kah club (golf)

книга knee·gah book

книжный магазин kneezh·niy
mah·gah·zeen bookstore

кнопка knop·kah button

ковер kah·vyor carpet (rug)

код kot area code

кожа koh·zhah leather (material); skin
(body)

колготки kahl·got·kee tights

колено kah·lyeh·nah knee

кольцо kahl'·tsoh n ring

команда kah·mahn·dah team

командировка
kah·mahn·dee·rof·kah business
trip

комариный укус kah·mah·ree·niy
oo·koos mosquito bite

комиссионный сбор
kah·mee·see·oh·niy zbor n
commission

комната kom·nah·tah room (house)
компакт-диск kahm·pahkt deesk CD

компания kahm·pah·nee·yah
company (companionship)

конверт kahn·vyert envelope

кондитерская
kahn·dee·teer·skah·yah pastry store

кондиционер kahn·dee·tsih·ah·nyer
conditioner

консервный нож kahn·syerv·niy
nosh can [tin BE] opener

консульство kon·sool'·stvah
consulate

консультироваться
kahn·sool'·tee·rah·vah·tsah consult

контактные линзы
kahn·tahkt·nih·yeh leen·zih contact
lenses

концерт kahn·tsert concert

концертный зал kahn·tsert·niy zahl
concert hall

кончаться kahn·chah·tsah v end

коньки kahn'·kee skates

копия koh·pee·yah copy

корабль kah·rahbl' ship

корзина kahr·zee·nah basket

кормить kahr·meet' feed

коронка kah·ron·kah cap (dental)

косметика *kahs•myeh•tee•kah* cosmetics

костыли *kahs•tih•lee* crutches

кость *kost'* bone

костюм *kahs•tyoom* n suit

кошелёк *kah•shih•lyok* wallet

кошерный *kah•sher•niy* kosher

кража *krah•zhah* theft

крайний случай *krie•neey sloo•chie* emergency

кран *krahn* faucet [tap BE]

красивый *krah•see•viy* beautiful

кредитная карточка *kree•deet•nah•yah kahr•tahch•kah* credit card

крем для загара *kryem dlyah zah•gah•rah* sun-tan cream

кровать *krah•vaht'* bed

кровотечение *krah•vah•tee•cheh•nee•yeh* bleeding

кровь *krof'* blood

кровяное давление *krah•vee•noh•yeh dahv•lyeh•nee•yeh* blood pressure

кроме *kroh•mee* except

круглый *kroog•liy* round

кружево *kroo•zhih•vah* lace

кружка *kroosh•kah* n mug

круиз *kroo•ees* cruise

крыша *krih•shah* roof (house, car)

ксерокс *ksyeh•rahks* photocopier

кто-нибудь *ktoh•nee•boot'* anyone

кто-то *ktoh•tah* someone

кукла *kook•lah* doll

кукольный театр *koo•kahl'•niy tee•ahtr* puppet show

купальник *koo•pahl'•neek* swimsuit

купе *koo•peh* compartment (train)

курить *koo•reet'* v smoke

курс обмена *koors ahb•myeh•nah* exchange rate

курящий *koo•ryah•shcheey* adj smoking

кусочек *koo•soh•cheek* piece

Л

лавина *lah•vee•nah* avalanche

лазерный проигрыватель *lah•zeer•niy prah•eeg•rih•vah•teel'* CD-player

лак для волос *lahk dlyah vah•los* hair spray

лампа *lahm•pah* lamp

лампочка *lahm•pahch•kah* light bulb

лёгкий *lyokh•keey* light (opp. heavy); easy

лёгкое *lyokh•kah•yeh* lung

лезвие *lyez•vee•yeh* razor blade

лекарство *lee•kahr•stvah* medication

лес *lyes* forest

линия *lee•nee•yah* line (metro)

лифт *leeft* elevator [lift BE]

лицо *lee·tsoh* face

лишний *leesh·neey* spare (extra)

лодка *lot·kah* boat

ложка *losh·kah* spoon

лосьон после бритья *lahs'·yon pos·lee breet'·yah* after-shave

лошадь *loh·shahd'* horse

лучше *looch·sheh* better

лыжи *lih·zhih* skis

лыжные ботинки *lizh·nih·yeh bah·teen·kee* ski boots

любезный *lyoo·byez·niy* kind (pleasant)

любимый *lyoo·bee·miy* favorite

любить *lyoo·beet'* v love

люди *lyoo·dee* people

М

магазин *mah·gah·zeen* store

майка *mie·kah* T-shirt

макияж *mah·kee·yash* n make-up

маленький *mah·leen'·keey* little (small)

мало *mah·lah* few; little

мальчик *mahl'·cheek* boy

манеж *mah·nyesh* playpen

маникюр *mah·nee·kyoor* manicure

марка *mahr·kah* stamp

маска *mahs·kah* mask (diving)

массаж *mah·sahsh* n massage

матрас *maht·rahs* mattress

матрёшка *maht·ryosh·kah* nesting doll

матч *mahch* match (sport)

машина *mah·shih·nah* car

мебель *myeh·beel* furniture

медленный *myed·lee·niy* slow

медовый месяц *mee·doh·viy myeh·syats* honeymoon

медсестра *myet·sees·trah* nurse

медь *myet'* copper

междугородний автобус *meezh·doo·gah·rod·niy ahf·toh·boos* coach (long-distance bus)

мелировать *mee·lee·rah·vaht'* v highlight (hair)

мелкий *mel·keey* shallow

мемориал *mee·mah·ree·ahl* war memorial

менять *mee·nyaht'* v change

местный *myes·niy* local

местный наркоз *myes·niy nahr·kos* local anesthetic

место *myes·tah* place (space)

место багажа *myes·tah bah·gah·zhah* piece of luggage

место назначения *myes·tah nahz·nah·cheh·nee·yah* destination

место у окна *myes·tah oo ahk·nah* window seat

место у прохода *myes·tah oo prah·khoh·dah* aisle seat

месяц _myeh·syahts_ month

металл _mee·tahl_ metal

метро _meet·roh_ subway [underground BE]

мечеть _mee·chet'_ mosque

мигрень _meeg·ryen'_ migraine

микроволновая печь
meek·rah·vahl·noh·vah·yah pyech
microwave

милиция _mee·lee·tsih·yah_ police

минута _mee·noo·tah_ minute

мобильный телефон _mah·beel'·niy
tee·lee·fon_ cell [mobile BE] phone

мой _moy_ my

молния _mol·nee·yah_ zipper

молодой _mah·lah·doy_ young

монета _mah·nyeh·tah_ coin

море _moh·ryeh_ sea

мороз _mah·ros_ frost

морозильная камера
mah·rah·zeel'·nah·yah kah·mee·rah
freezer

морская болезнь _mahr·skah·yah
bah·lyezn'_ motion [travel BE]
sickness

мост _most_ bridge

моторка _mah·tor·kah_ motorboat

мотоцикл _mah·tah·tsihkl_ motorbike

моча _mah·chah_ urine

мочевой пузырь _mah·chee·voy
poo·zihr'_ bladder

моющее средство
moh·yoo·shchee·yeh sryet·stvah
detergent

муж _moosh_ husband

мужчина _moo·shchee·nah_ man
(male)

музей _moo·zyey_ museum

музыка _moo·zih·kah_ music

мусор _moo·sahr_ trash [rubbish BE]

мусорный бак _moo·sahr·niy bahk_
trash can [dustbin BE]

мы _mih_ we

мыло _mih·lah_ soap

мышца _mihsh·tsah_ muscle

мяч _myahch_ ball

Н

на открытом воздухе _nah
aht·krih·tahm voz·doo·khee_ outdoor

на пенсии _nah pyen·see·ee_ retired

на улице _nah oo·lee·tseh_ outside

называть по буквам _nah·zih·vaht'
pah book·vahm v_ spell

наконец _nah·kah·nyets_ at last

наличные _nah·leech·nih·yeh n_ cash

нападение _nah·pah·dyeh·nee·yeh
n_ attack

направление
nah·prahv·lyeh·nee·yeh direction

направлять _nah·prahv·lyaht' v_ direct

например _nah·pree·myer_ for example

напротив nah·*proh*·teef opposite

напряжение nah·pree·*zheh*·nee·yeh voltage

народная музыка nah·*rod*·nah·yah *moo*·zih·kah folk music

народное искусство nah·*rod*·nah·yeh ees·*koos*·tvah folk art

насекомое nah·see·*koh*·mah·yeh insect

насос nah·*sos* n pump

настаивать nah·*stah*·ee·vaht′ insist

настоящий nah·stah·*yah*·shcheey real (genuine)

национальность nah·tsih·ah·*nahl*′·nahst′ nationality

национальный nah·tsih·ah·*nahl*′·niy national

начинать nah·chee·*naht*′ begin

начинаться nah·chee·*nah*·tsah v start

НДС en deh es sales tax [VAT BE]

невероятный nee·vee·rah·*yaht*·niy incredible

невиновен nee·vee·*noh*·veen innocent

неделя nee·*deh*·lyah week

недоразумение nee·dah·rah·zoo·*myeh*·nee·yeh misunderstanding

недорогой nee·dah·rah·*goy* inexpensive

незаконный nee·zah·*kon*·niy illegal

некрасивый nee·krah·*see*·viy ugly

некурящий nee·koo·*ryah*·shcheey adj non-smoking

немедленно nee·*myeh*·dlee·nah immediately

неплохо nee·*ploh*·khah not bad

неправильный nee·*prah*·veel′·niy wrong

неприятный nee·pree·*yaht*·niy unpleasant

нерв nyerf nerve

нержавеющая сталь nee·rzhah·*vyeh*·yoo·shchah·yah stahl stainless steel

неровный nee·*rov*·niy uneven (ground)

несложный nyeh·*slozh*·niy easy

несчастный случай nee·*shchahs*·niy *sloo*·chie accident

низкий *nees*·keey short (height)

никогда nee·kahg·*dah* never

никто nee·*ktoh* no one

ничего nee·chee·*voh* nothing

новый *noh*·viy new

нога nah·*gah* foot; leg

нож nosh knife

ножницы *nozh*·nee·tsih scissors

номер *noh*·meer number (telephone)

нормальный nahr·*mahl*′·niy normal

нос nos nose

носильщик *nah-seel'-shcheek* porter

носки *nahs-kee* socks

ночной *nahch-noy* all-night

ночью *noh-chyoo* at night

нравиться *nrah-vee-tsah* v enjoy

нырять *nih-ryat'* v dive

O

обед *ah-byet* lunch

обезболивающее *ah-beez-boh-lee-v ah-yoo-shchee-yeh* anaesthetic

обзорная экскурсия *ahb-zor-nah-yah eeks-koor-see-yah* sightseeing tour

облачно *ob-lahch-nah* cloudy

обмен валюты *ahb-myen vah-lyoo-tih* currency exchange office

обменивать *ahb-myeh-nee-vaht'* exchange

обогреватель *ah-bah-gree-vah-teel'* heater

обслуживание номеров *ahp-sloo-zhih-vah-nee-yeh nah-mee-rof* room service

обувной магазин *ah-boov-noy mah-gah-zeen* shoe store

общежитие *ahp-shchee-zhih-tee-yeh* youth hostel

обязательный *ah-bee-zah-teel'-niy* necessary

огнетушитель *ahg-nee-too-shih-teel'* fire extinguisher

ограбление *ah-grahb-lyeh-nee-yeh* mugging; robbery

одевать *ah-dee-vat'* put on; wear

одежда *ah-dyezh-dah* clothes

одеяло *ah-dee-yah-lah* blanket

один *ah-deen* alone

один раз *ah-deen rahs* once

одноместный номер *ahd-nah-myes-niy noh-meer* single room

одолжить *ah-dahl-zhit'* borrow

ожерелье *ah-zhih-ryel'-yeh* necklace

ожог *ah-zhok* n burn

озеро *oh-zee-rah* lake

окно *ahk-noh* window

около *oh-kah-lah* about (approximately); near

опаздывать *ah-pahz-dih-vaht'* be delayed

опасный *ah-pahs-niy* dangerous

опера *oh-pee-rah* opera

операция *ah-pee-rah-tsih-yah* operation

описывать *ah-pee-sih-vaht'* describe

оплата *ah-plah-tah* payment

оправа *ah-prah-vah* n frame (glasses)

оптика *op-tee-kah* optician

оркестр *ahr-kyestr* orchestra

осмотр *ahs·motr* examination (medical)

основной *ahs·nahv·noy* essential

останавливаться *as·stah·nahv·lee·vah·tsah* v stop

остановка *ah·stah·nof·kah* n stop (bus, etc.)

остаться *ah·stah·tsah* v stay

осторожный *ahs·tah·rozh·niy* careful

отбеливатель *aht·byeh·lee·vah·teel'* bleach

отвёртка *aht·vyort·kah* screwdriver

отвратительный *aht·vrah·tee·teel'·niy* revolting

отдавать в химчистку *aht·dah·vaht' f kheem·cheest·koo* v dry clean

отдел *aht·dyel* department (in store)

отделение милиции *aht·dee·lyeh·nee·yeh mee·lee·tsih·ee* police station

отдельно *ahd·del'·nah* separately

отдыхать *aht·dih·khat'* v rest

открывать *aht·krih·vaht'* v open

открытка *aht·kriht·kah* postcard

открытый *aht·krih·tiy* adj open

отменять *aht·mee·nyaht'* cancel (reservation)

отопление *ah·tahp·lyeh·nee·yeh* heating

отпирать *aht·pee·raht'* v unlock

отправляться *aht·prahv·lyah·tsah* depart (train, bus)

отпуск *ot·poosk* vocation [holiday BE]

официант *ah·fee·tsih·ahnt* waiter

очень *oh·cheen'* very

очередь *oh·chee·reet'* n queue

очки *ahch·kee* glasses (optical)

ошеломляющий *ah·shih·lahm·lyah·yoo·shcheey* stunning

ошибка *ah·shihp·kah* n mistake

П

пакет *pah·kyet* carton; packet

палата *pah·lah·tah* ward (hospital)

палатка *pah·laht·kah* tent

палаточный лагерь *pah·lah·tahch·niy lah·geer'* campsite

палец *pah·leets* finger

палец ноги *pah·leets nah·gee* toe

пальто *pahl'·toh* coat

панорама *pah·nah·rah·mah* panorama

пара *pah·rah* pair

парацетамол *pah·rah·tsih·tah·mol* acetaminophen [paracetamol BE]

парикмахер *pah·reek·mah·kheer* hairdresser

парк *pahrk* park

паром *pah·rom* ferry

паспорт *pahs·pahrt* passport

пассажирский класс *pah·sah·zhihr·skeey klahs* economy class

пациент *pah·tsih·yent* n patient

пачка сигарет *pahch·kah see·gah·ryet* packet of cigarettes

педикюр *pee·dee·kyoor* pedicure

пелёнка *pee·lyon·kah* diaper [nappy BE]

пепельница *pyeh·peel'·nee·tsah* ashtray

перевес багажа *pee·ree·vyes bah·gah·zhah* excess luggage

перевод *pee·ree·vot* translation

переводить *pee·ree·vah·deet'* translate

переводчик *pee·ree·vot·cheek* translator (text); interpreter (speech)

перегреться *pee·ree·gryeh·tsah* overheat

перед *pyeh·reet* before

переделывать *pee·ree·dyeh·lih·vaht'* alter

перекрёсток *pee·ree·kryos·tahk* crossroad

перелом *pee·ree·lom* fracture (of a bone)

переход *pee·ree·khot* pedestrian crossing

период *pee·ree·aht* period (historical)

персонал *peer·sah·nahl* n staff

перчатка *peer·chaht·kah* glove

песок *pee·sok* sand

песчаный пляж *pee·shchah·niy plyahsh* sandy beach

печатать *pee·chah·taht'* v print

печень *pyeh·cheen'* liver

пешеходная зона *pee·shih·khod·nah·yah zoh·nah* pedestrian zone [precinct BE]

пешеходный маршрут *pee·shih·khod·niy mahrsh·root* walking route

пешком *peesh·kom* on foot

пещера *pee·shcheh·rah* cave

пикник *peek·neek* picnic

письмо *pees'·moh* letter

пить *peet'* v drink

пиццерия *pee·tsih·ree·yah* pizzeria

плавание *plah·vah·neeh·yeh* swimming

плавать *plah·vaht'* swim

плавки *plahf·kee* swimming trunks

план *plahn* n plan

пластырь *plahs·tihr'* adhesive bandage

плата *plah·tah* n charge

платина *plah·tee·nah* platinum

платить *plah·teet'* v pay

платок *plah·tok* handkerchief

платформа *plaht·for·mah* n track [platform BE]

платье _plaht'·yeh_ dress

плащ _plahshch_ raincoat

плёнка _plyon·kah_ n film (camera)

плечо _plee·choh_ shoulder

плита _plee·tah_ stove [cooker BE]

пломба _plom·bah_ filling (dental)

плохой _plah·khoy_ bad

пляж _plyahsh_ beach

по делу _pah dyeh·loo_ on business

по крайней мере _pah kray·neey myeh·ryeh_ at least

по почте _pah poch·tyeh_ by mail

побережье _pah·bee·ryezh·yeh_ coast

повар _poh·vahr_ n cook

поворот _pah·vah·rot_ n turning

повредить _pah·vree·deet'_ v damage

повторять _pahf·tah·ryaht'_ v repeat

погода _pah·goh·dah_ weather

под _pahd_ under

подарок _pah·dah·rahk_ n present (gift)

подвал _pahd·vahl_ basement

подвозить _pahd·vah·zeet'_ give a lift

подержанный _pah·dyer·zhah·niy_ second-hand

поднос _pahd·nos_ tray

пододеяльник _pah·dah·dee·yahl'·neek_ duvet

подозрительный _pah·dah·zree·teel'·niy_ suspicious

подошва _pah·dosh·vah_ sole (shoes)

подробности _pahd·rob·nahs·tee_ details

подруга _pahd·roo·gah_ girlfriend

подтвердить _paht·tveer·deet'_ confirm (reservation)

подушка _pah·doosh·kah_ pillow

поезд _poh·eest_ train

поездка _pah·yest·kah_ trip (journey)

пожар _pah·zhahr_ fire

пожарная лестница _pah·zhahr·nah·yah lyes·nee·tsah_ fire escape

позвоночник _pahz·vah·noch·neek_ spine

поздний _poz·neey_ adj late

пойти по магазинам _pie·tee pah mah·gah·zee·nahm_ go shopping

пойти потанцевать _pie·tee pah·tahn·tsih·vaht'_ go dancing

показывать _pah·kah·zih·vaht'_ v show

покупать _pah·koo·paht'_ buy

полный _pol·niy_ full

половина _pah·lah·vee·nah_ half

полотенце _pah·lah·tyen·tseh_ towel

получать _pah·loo·chaht'_ get (receive)

пользоваться _pol'·zah·vah·tsah_ v use

помедленнее _pah·myed·lee·nee·yeh_ slow down

поменьше _pah·myen'·sheh_ smaller

помнить _pom·neet'_ remember

помогать _pah·mah·gaht'_ v help

понимать _pah·nee·maht'_ understand

популярный _pah·poo·lyahr·niy_ popular

поразительный _pah·rah·zee·teel'·niy_ amazing

порез _pah·ryes_ n cut (finger)

пороги _pah·roh·gee_ rapids

порт _port_ port (harbor)

портье _pahrt'·yeh_ receptionist

посадочный талон _pah·sah·dahch·niy tah·lon_ boarding card

посещать _pah·see·shchaht'_ v visit

после _pos·lee_ after (time/place)

последний _pahs·lyed·neey_ last

посол _pah·sol_ ambassador

посольство _pah·sol'·stvah_ embassy

постельное бельё _pahs·tel'·nah·yeh beel'·yoh_ n bedding

постричь _pah·streech_ v trim (hair)

построенный _pah·stroh·yeh·niy_ built

посуда _pah·soo·dah_ crockery

посудомоечная машина _pah·soo·dah·moh·eech·nah·yah mah·shih·nah_ dishwasher

посылать _pah·sih·laht'_ send

посылка _pah·sihl·kah_ package (mail)

потерять _pah·tee·ryaht'_ v lose

потерять сознание _pah·tee·ryaht' sah·znah·nee·yeh_ v collapse

потише _pah·tee·sheh_ quieter

потому что _pah·tah·moo·shtah_ because

похмелье _pahkh·myel'·yeh_ n hangover

починить _pah·chee·neet'_ v repair

почка _poch·kah_ kidney

почта _poch·tah_ post office

почта _poch·tah_ mail (letters)

почти _pahch·tee_ almost

почтовый ящик _pahch·toh·viy yah·shcheek_ mailbox [postbox BE]

пошлина _posh·lee·nah_ duty

правда _prahv·dah_ true

правильный _prah·veel'·niy_ right (correct)

православный _prah·vah·slahv·niy_ Orthodox

прачечная _prah·cheech·nah·yah_ laundromat (launderette BE]

превосходный _pree·vahs·khod·niy_ superb

предлагать _preed·lah·gaht'_ suggest

предприятие _preet·pree·yah·tee·yeh_ company (business)

предъявлять _preed·yahv·lyaht'_ declare

презерватив _pree·zeer·vah·teef_ condom

преследовать pree-_slyeh_-dah-vaht'
follow (pursue)

приблизительно
pree-blee-_zee_-teel'-nah
approximately

прибывать pree-bih-_vaht'_ arrive

привлекательный
pree-vlee-_kah_-teel'-niy attractive

приглашать pree-glah-_shaht'_ invite

приглашение
pree-glah-_sheh_-nee-yeh invitation

приземляться pree-zeem-_lyah_-tsah
v land

примерочная
pree-_myeh_-rahch-nah-yah fitting
room

принадлежать pree-nahd-lee-_zhaht'_
belong

принадлежности
pree-nahd-_lyezh_-nah-stee accessories

принимать лекарство
pree-nee-_maht'_ lee-_kahr_-stvah take
medication

присмотр pree-_smotr_ supervision

приходить pree-khah-_deet'_ come

причудливый pree-_chood_-lee-viy
bizarre

приятный pree-_yaht_-niy pleasant

пробор prah-_bor_ parting (hair)

проверить prah-_vyeh_-reet' v check
[cheque BE]

провожать prah-vah-_zhaht'_
accompany

прогноз погоды prahg-_nos_
pah-_goh_-dih weather forecast

программа prah-_grah_-mah program

продавать prah-dah-_vaht'_ sell

продавец prah-dah-_vyets_ shop
assistant

проездом prah-_yez_-dahm in transit

проезжать prah-eezh-_zhaht'_ v pass

произносить prah-eez-nah-_seet'_
pronounce

прокол prah-_kol_ puncture

просить prah-_seet'_ ask for

просматривать
prah-_smah_-tree-vaht' v browse

простуда prah-_stoo_-dah cold; flu

простыня prahs-tih-_nyah_ sheet
(bedding)

протез prah-_tes_ denture

противозачаточное средство pr
oh-tee-vah-zah-_chah_-tahch-nah-yeh
sryet-stvah n contraceptive

профессия prah-_fyeh_-see-yah line
(profession)

прыщ prihshch acne

прямой pryah-_moy_ adj direct (train)

птица _ptee_-tsah bird

пустой poos-_toy_ adj empty

путеводитель poo-tee-vah-_dee_-teel'
guide book

пылесос *pih·lee·sos* vacuum cleaner

пьяный *pyah·niy adj* drunk

Р

работа *rah·boh·tah* job

работать *rah·boh·taht'* v work

разбудить *rahz·boo·deet'* wake someone

разговаривать *rahz·gah·vah·ree·vaht'* v talk

разговорник *rahz·gah·vor·neek* phrasebook

размер *rahz·myer* size

район *rah·yon* region

ракетка *rah·kyet·kah* racket (tennis)

раковина *rah·kah·vee·nah* sink

рана *rah·nah n* wound

ранний *rahn·neey* early

раскладушка *rahs·klah·doosh·kah* camp bed

расписание *rahs·pee·sah·nee·yeh n* schedule [timetable BE]

рассвет *rahs·vyet* dawn

рассказывать *rahs·kah·zih·vaht'* tell

растение *rahs·tyeh·nee·yeh n* plant

растяжение *rahs·tee·zheh·nee·yeh n* sprain

расчёска *rah·shchos·kah n* comb

раунд *rah·oond* round (of golf)

ребёнок *ree·byoh·nahk* baby; child

ребро *reeb·roh* rib

регистрационная стойка *ree·gee·strah·tsih·on·nah·yah stoy·kah* check-in desk

регистрация *ree·gee·strah·tsih·yah* reception (desk)

регистрироваться *ree·gees·tree·rah·vah·tsah v* check-in

рейс *reys* flight

река *ree·kah* river

рекомендовать *ree·kah·meen·dah·vaht'* recommend

религия *ree·lee·gee·yah* religion

ремень *ree·myen'* belt

ремесла *ree·myos·lah* handicrafts

ремонт обуви *ree·mont oh·boo·vee* shoe repair

рентген *reen·gyen* X-ray

ресторан *rees·tah·rahn* restaurant

рецепт *ree·tsept* prescription

родители *rah·dee·tee·lee* parents

розетка *rah·zyet·kah* electric outlet

романтичный *rah·mahn·teech·niy* romantic

Россия *rah·see·yah* Russia

рост *rost* height

рот *rot* mouth

рубашка *roo·bahsh·kah* shirt

рубль *roobl'* ruble [rouble]

рука *roo·kah* arm; hand

рукав *roo·kahf* sleeve

руководитель roo·kah·vah·_dee_·teel′ leader (of group)

руководство roo·kah·_vod_·stvah manual (car)

русский _roos_·keey adj Russian

русский язык _roos_·keey yah·_zihk_ Russian language

ручей roo·_chey_ n stream

ручка _rooch_·kah pen

ручная кладь rooch·_nah_·yah klaht′ hand luggage

рыба _rih_·bah fish

рынок _rih_·nahk market

рюкзак ryoog·_zahk_ rucksack

рядом _ryah_·dahm nearby

рядом с _ryah_·dahm s next to

С

с s with

с субтитрами s soop·_teet_·rah·mee subtitled

сад saht garden

салфетка sahl·_fyet_·kah napkin

самолёт sah·mah·_lyot_ plane

самообслуживание sah·mah·ahp·s _loo_·zhih·vah·nee·yeh self-service

сандалии sahn·_dah_·lee sandals

сапоги sah·pah·_gee_ boots

сауна _sah_·oo·nah sauna

сахар _sah_·khahr sugar

свадьба _svahd_′·bah wedding

свежий _svye_·zhiy fresh

свет svyet n light (electic)

светлый _svyet_·liy adj light (opp. dark)

светофор svee·tah·_for_ traffic lights

свеча svee·_chah_ candle

свидетельство svee·_dyeh_·teel′·stvah certificate

свитер _svee_·teer sweater

свободное время svah·_bod_·nah·yeh _vryeh_·myah free time

свободный svah·_bod_·niy available (unoccupied, free)

связаться svyah·_zah_·tsah v contact

сдача _zdah_·chah change (coins)

сейф seyf n safe (lock up)

секретарь seek·ree·_tahr_′ secretary

семья seem′·_yah_ n family

сенная лихорадка see·_nah_·yah lee·khah·_raht_·kah hay fever

сердечный приступ seer·_dyech_·niy _prees_·toop heart attack

сердце _syer_·tseh heart

серебро see·ree·_broh_ n silver

серый _syeh_·riy gray

серьги _syer_′·gee earrings

серьёзный seer′·_yoz_·niy serious

сесть syest′ sit

сигара see·_gah_·rah cigar

сигарета see·gah·_ryeh_·tah cigarette

сильный _seel_′·niy strong (potent)

симптомы seemp·_toh_·mih symptoms

синагога *see·nah·goh·gah* synagogue

синтетический
seen·teh·tee·chees·keey synthetic

синяк *see·nyahk* bruise

скала *skah·lah* cliff

скидка *skeet·kah* discount

сковорода *skah·vah·rah·dah* frying pan

скорая помощь *skoh·rah·yah poh·mahshch* ambulance

скоро *skoh·rah* soon

слева *slyeh·vah* on the left

следующий *slyeh·doo·yoo·shcheey* next

словарь *slah·vahr'* dictionary

сломан *sloh·mahn* broken

сломать *slah·maht'* v break

сломаться *slah·mah·tsah* v break down (car)

служба *sloozh·bah* n service (religious)

слуховой аппарат *sloo·khah·voy ah·pah·raht* hearing aid

слышать *slih·shaht'* hear

смеяться *smee·yah·tsah* v laugh

смотровая площадка *smah·trah·vah·yah plah·shchaht·kah* overlook

снаряжение *snah·ree·zheh·nee·yeh* equipment (sports)

снаряжение для дайвинга *snah·ree·zheh·nee·yeh dlyah*

die·veen·gah diving equipment

снег *snyek* n snow

снотворное *snah·tvor·nah·yeh* sleeping pill

собор *sah·bor* cathedral

событие *sah·bih·tee·yeh* event

совок *sah·vok* shovel

современный *sah·vree·myen·niy* modern

современный танец *sah·vree·myen·niy tah·neets* contemporary dance

содержать *sah·deer·zhaht'* contain

Соединенные Штаты *sah·ee·dee·nyoh·nih·ee shtah·tih* United States

соленый *sah·lyoh·niy* salty

солнечно *sol·neech·nah* sunny

солнечные очки *sol·neech·nih·ee ahch·kee* sunglasses

солнечный ожёг *sol·neech·niy ah·zhok* sunburn

солнечный удар *sol·neech·niy oo·dahr* sunstroke

сообщение *sah·ahp·shcheh·nee·yeh* message

соска *sos·kah* pacifier [soother BE]

сотрясение мозга *sah·tree·syeh·nee·yeh moz·gah* concussion

спа *spah* spa

спальный мешок _spahl'·niy mee·<u>shok</u>_ sleeping bag

спальня _spahl'·nyah_ bedroom

спасатель _spah·<u>sah</u>·teel'_ lifeguard

спасательная лодка _spah·<u>sah</u>·teel'·nah·yah lot·kah_ lifeboat

спасательный жилет _spah·<u>sah</u>·teel'·niy zhih·<u>lyet</u>_ lifejacket

спать _spaht'_ v sleep

специалист _spee·tsih·ah·<u>leest</u>_ specialist

спина _spee·<u>nah</u>_ back

спички _<u>speech</u>·kee_ matches

спорт _sport_ sport

спортзал _sport·<u>zahl</u>_ gym

спортклуб _sport·<u>kloop</u>_ sports club

спорттовары _spor·tah·<u>vah</u>·rih_ sporting goods store

справа _<u>sprah</u>·vah_ on the right

срочно _<u>sroch</u>·nah_ urgent

стадион _stah·dee·<u>on</u>_ stadium

стакан _stah·<u>kahn</u>_ glass

станция метро _<u>stahn</u>·tsih·yah meet·<u>roh</u>_ subway [underground BE] station

старый _<u>stah</u>·riy_ old

старый город _<u>stah</u>·riy <u>goh</u>·raht_ old town

статуя _<u>stah</u>·too·yah_ statue

стиль _steel'_ style

стиральная машина _stee·<u>rahl</u>'·nah·yah mah·<u>shih</u>·nah_ washing machine

стоимость _<u>stoh</u>·ee·mahst'_ value

столик _<u>stoh</u>·leek_ table

сторона _stah·rah·<u>nah</u>_ side (of road)

стоянка _stah·<u>yahn</u>·kah_ pitch (for camping)

стоянка такси _stah·<u>yahn</u>·kah tahk·<u>see</u>_ taxi stand [rank BE]

стоять в очереди _stah·<u>yaht</u>' v oh·chee·ree·dee_ stand in line

страна _strah·<u>nah</u>_ country (nation)

странный _<u>strah</u>·niy_ strange

страховка _strah·<u>khof</u>·kah_ insurance

стремянка _stree·<u>myahn</u>·kah_ ladder

стрижка _<u>streesh</u>·kah_ haircut

строить _<u>stroh</u>·eet'_ build

студент _stoo·<u>dyent</u>_ student

сувенир _soo·vee·<u>neer</u>_ souvenir

судороги _<u>soo</u>·dah·rah·gee_ cramps

сумка _<u>soom</u>·kah_ purse [handbag BE]

сумма _<u>soo</u>·mah_ amount

сухая стрижка _soo·<u>khah</u>·yah <u>streesh</u>·kah_ dry cut

счёт _shcot_ n bill

счёт за телефон _shcot zah tee·lee·<u>fon</u>_ telephone bill

США _seh sheh ah_ U.S.A.

сыпь _sihp'_ rash

сыро _<u>sih</u>·rah_ adj damp

T

табак *tah·bahk* tobacco

таблетка *tahb·lyet·kah* pill (tablet)

также *tahk·zheh* also

такси *tahk·see* taxi

там *tahm* there

таможенная декларация
*tah·moh·zhih·nah·yah
deek·lah·rah·tsih·yah* customs
declaration

таможня *tah·mozh·nyah* customs

тампон *tahm·pon* tampon

танец *tah·neets* n dance
(performance)

тапочки *tah·pahch·kee* slippers

тарелка *tah·ryel·kah* plate

театр *tee·ahtr* theater

телевизор *tee·lee·vee·zahr* TV-set

тележка *tee·lyesh·kah* cart [trolley BE]

телефон *tee·lee·fon* n phone

телефон-автомат *tee·lee·fon
ahf·tah·maht* pay phone

телефонный *справочник
tee·lee·foh·niy sprah·vahch·neek*
directory (telephone)

тёмный *tyom·niy* dark

температура *teem·pee·rah·too·rah*
temperature

теннис *teh·nees* tennis

теннисные туфли *teh·nees·nih·ee
toof·lee* sneakers

теннисный корт *teh·nees·niy kort*
tennis court

тень *tyen'* shade

тёплый *tyop·liy* warm

термометр *teer·moh·meetr*
thermometer

термос *ter·mahs* thermos flask

тесно *tyes·nah* crowded

тесный *tyes·niy* tight (loose)

течь *tyech v* leak (roof, pipe)

типичный *tee·peech·niy* typical

тихий *tee·kheey* quiet

ткань *tkahn'* fabric (material)

толстый *tols·tiy* thick

тонкий *ton·keey* thin

тонуть *tah·noot'* drown

торговый центр *tahr·goh·viy tsentr*
mall [shopping centre]

тот же самый *tot zheh sah·miy* same

трава *trah·vah* grass

традиционный *trah·dee·tsih·oh·niy*
traditional

трамвай *trahm·vie* tram

трасса *trah·sah* trail [piste BE]

тратить *trah·teet'* spend

трейлер *trey·leer* caravan

тропинка *trah·peen·kah* path

трубка *troop·kah* pipe (smoking)

трудный *trood·niy* difficult

тряпка *tryahp·kah* dish cloth

туалет *too·ah·lyet* restroom [toilet BE]

туалетная бумага
too•ah•lyet•nah•yah boo•mah•gah
toilet paper

туман *too•mahn* fog

туннель *too•nel'* tunnel

турист *too•reest* tourist

туфли *toof•lee* shoes

тушь *toosh* mascara

ты *tih* you (informal)

тяжёлый *tee•zhoh•liy* heavy

У

угол *oo•gahl* corner

уголь *oo•gahl'* charcoal

удалять *oo•dah•lyaht'* extract (tooth)

удобства *oo•dops•tvah* facilities

удостоверение
oo•dah•stah•vee•ryeh•nee•yeh
identification

уезжать *oo•eezh•zhaht'* v leave

ужасный *oo•zhahs•niy* terrible

уже *oo•zheh* already

ужин *oo•zhih* dinner

узкий *oos•keey* narrow

укол *oo•kol* injection

Украина *oo•krah•ee•nah* Ukraine

укус *oo•koos* sting (wasp); bite (dog)

универсам *oo•nee•veer•sahm*
supermarket

упаковочная пленка

oo•pah•koh•vahch•nah•yah plyon•kah
plastic wrap [cling film BE]

упаковывать *oo•pah•koh•vih•vaht'*
v pack

урок *oo•rok* lesson

успокаивающее *oos•pah•kah•ee•va h•yoo•shchee•yeh* sedative

усталый *oos•tah•liy* tired

утюг *oo•tyook* n iron

ухо *oo•khah* ear

уходить *oo•khah•deet'* go away

учитель *oo•chee•teel'* teacher

Ф

факс *fahks* n fax

фамилия *fah•mee•lee•yah* surname

фен *fyen* blow-dry

ферма *fyer•mah* farm

фильм *feel'm* movie [film BE]

фильтр *feel'tr* filter

фойе *fei•yeh* foyer (hotel, theater)

фольга *fahl'•gah* aluminium foil

фонтан *fahn•tahn* fountain

форма *for•mah* uniform

фотоаппарат *foh•tah•ah•pah•raht*
camera

фотография *fah•tah•grah•fee•yah*
photograph

фраза *frah•zah* phrase

фунт *foont* pound (sterling)

футбол *food•bol* soccer [football BE]

Х

химчистка kheem·cheest·kah dry cleaner

хобби khoh·bee hobby (pastime)

холм kholm hill

холодильник khah·lah·deel′·neek refrigerator

холодный khah·lod·niy adj cold

холост khoh·lahst single (unmarried)

хороший khah·roh·shiy good

хотеть khah·tet′ want

хрусталь khroos·tahl′ n crystal

хрустальная посуда
khroos·tahl′·nah·yah pah·soo·dah
cut glass

художественный салон
khoo·doh·zhes·tvee·niy sah·lon craft shop

Ц

цвет tsvyet color

цветок tsvee·tok flower

цветочный магазин tsvye·toch·niy mah·gah·zeen florist

целовать tsih·lah·vaht′ v kiss

цель tsel′ purpose

ценный tseh·niy valuable

центр (города) tsentr (goh·rah·dah) center (of town)

центральное отопление
tsihn·trahl′·nah·yeh

ah·tahp·lyeh·nee·yeh central heating

цепочка tsih·poch·kah chain

церковь tser·kahf′ church

Ч

чайная ложка chie·nah·yah losh·kah teaspoon

чайник chie·neek kettle

чартерный рейс chahr·ter·niy reys charter flight

час chahs hour

час пик chahs peek rush hour

часто chahs·tah often

часы chah·sih clock (watch)

часы посещений chah·sih pah·see·shcheh·neey
visiting hours

часы работы chah·sih rah·boh·tih opening hours

чашка chahsh·kah cup

чек chek receipt

челюсть cheh·lyoost′ jaw

через cheh·rees across

чистить chees·teet′ v clean

чистка лица cheest·kah lee·tsah facial

чистый chees·tiy adj clean

читать chee·taht′ read

что-то shtoh·tah something

чулки chool·kee stockings

Ш

шампунь *shahm-poon'* shampoo

шапка *shahp-kah* hat

шарф *shahrf* scarf

шахматы *shahkh-mah-tih* chess

швабра *shvahb-rah* mop

шезлонг *shez-lonk* deck chair

шёлк *sholk* silk

шерсть *sherst'* wool

шея *sheh-yah* neck

широкий *shih-roh-keey* wide

шкаф *shkahf* cupboard

шлем *shlyem* helmet

шорты *shor-tih* shorts

шоссе *shah-seh* highway [motorway BE]

штепсель *shtep-seel' n* plug

штопор *shtoh-pahr* corkscrew

шторы *shtoh-rih* blinds

шумный *shoom-niy* noisy

шутка *shoot-kah n* joke

щётка для волос *shchot-kah dlyah vah-los* hair brush

Э

экскурсия *eks-koor-see-yah* guided tour

экскурсовод *eeks-koor-sah-vot* tour guide

экспресс *eks-pres* express

электричество *eh-leek-tree-cheest-vah* electricity

электронная почта *ee-leek-troh-nah-yah poch-tah* e-mail

электронный билет *ee-leek-tron-niy bee-lyet* e-ticket

электронный ключ *eh-leek-tron-niy klyooch* key card

эмаль *ee-mahl'* enamel

эпилептик *ee-pee-lyep-teek n* epileptic

эскалатор *ees-kah-lah-tahr* escalator

этаж *eh-tahsh* floor (level)

Ю

юбка *yoop-kah* skirt

ювелирный магазин *yoo-vee-leer-niy mah-gah-zeen* jeweler

Я

я *yah* I

яд *yaht* poison

язва *yahz-vah* ulcer

язык *yah-zihk* tongue

языковые курсы *yah-zih-kah-vih-yeh koor-sih* language course

ярлык *yahr-lihk n* label

ясли *yahs-lee* nursery

яхта *yahkh-tah* yacht